The Contemporary American Monologue

Methuen Drama Engage offers original reflections about key practitioners, movements and genres in the fields of modern theatre and performance. Each volume in the series seeks to challenge mainstream critical thought through original and interdisciplinary perspectives on the body of work under examination. By questioning existing critical paradigms, it is hoped that each volume will open up fresh approaches and suggest avenues for further exploration.

Series Editors

Mark Taylor-Batty
Senior Lecturer in Theatre Studies, Workshop Theatre, University of Leeds, UK

Enoch Brater
Kenneth T. Rowe Collegiate Professor of Dramatic Literature &
Professor of English and Theater University of Michigan, USA

In the same series

Brecht in Practice: Theatre, Theory and Performance
by David Barnett
ISBN 978-1-4081-8503-2

Howard Barker's Theatre: Wrestling with Catastrophe
edited by James Reynolds and Andrew Smith
ISBN 978-1-4081-8439-4

Ibsen in Practice
Relational Readings of Performance, Cultural Encounters and Power
By Frode Helland
ISBN 978-1-4725-1369-4

Postdramatic Theatre and the Political
International Perspectives on Contemporary Performance
edited by Karen Jürs-Munby, Jerome Carroll and Steve Giles
ISBN 978-1-4081-8486-8

Rethinking the Theatre of the Absurd
Ecology, the Environment and the Greening of the Modern Stage
edited by Clare Finburgh and Carl Lavery
ISBN 978-1-4725-0667-2

Ruth Maleczech at Mabou Mines: Woman's Work
by Jessica Silsby Brater
ISBN 978-1-4725-7882-2

Theatre in the Expanded Field: Seven Approaches to Performance
by Alan Read
ISBN 978-1-4081-8495-0

The Contemporary American Monologue

Performance and Politics

Eddie Paterson

Series Editors
Enoch Brater and Mark Taylor-Batty

Bloomsbury Methuen Drama
An imprint of Bloomsbury Publishing Plc

B L O O M S B U R Y
LONDON • OXFORD • NEW YORK • NEW DELHI • SYDNEY

Bloomsbury Methuen Drama
An imprint of Bloomsbury Publishing Plc

Imprint previously known as Methuen Drama

50 Bedford Square	1385 Broadway
London	New York
WC1B 3DP	NY 10018
UK	USA

www.bloomsbury.com

BLOOMSBURY, METHUEN DRAMA and the Diana logo are trademarks of Bloomsbury Publishing Plc

First published 2015

© Eddie Paterson, 2015

Eddie Paterson has asserted his right under the Copyright, Designs and Patents Act, 1988, to be identified as author of this work.

All rights reserved. No part of this publication may be reproduced or transmitted in any form or by any means, electronic or mechanical, including photocopying, recording, or any information storage or retrieval system, without prior permission in writing from the publishers.

No responsibility for loss caused to any individual or organization acting on or refraining from action as a result of the material in this publication can be accepted by Bloomsbury or the author.

British Library Cataloguing-in-Publication Data
A catalogue record for this book is available from the British Library.

ISBN: HB: 978-1-4725-8502-8
PB: 978-1-4725-8501-1
ePDF: 978-1-4725-8504-2
ePub: 978-1-4725-8503-5

Library of Congress Cataloging-in-Publication Data
A catalog record for this book is available from the Library of Congress.

Typeset by Deanta Global Publishing Services, Chennai, India
Printed and bound in India

In memory of my Nan, Dorothy Bunting, 1916-2013

Contents

List of Illustrations	viii
Acknowledgements	ix
Foreword	xi
Introduction	1
1 Monologue in Western Drama	13
2 Monologue in American Performance	39
3 Confessional Monologue and the Legacy of Spalding Gray	53
4 Post-punk Monologue and the Performances of Laurie Anderson	79
5 Rights Monologue and the Work of Anna Deavere Smith	103
6 Radical Monologue and the Performances of Karen Finley	127
7 Future Monologue	155
Notes	173
Bibliography	197
About the Author	209
Index	211

List of Illustrations

Figure 3.1	Spalding Gray (*Photo:* Ken Regan, Camera 5)	57
Figure 3.2	Spalding Gray with Laurie Anderson and Jonathan Demme (*Photo:* Ken Regan, Camera 5)	61
Figure 4.1	Laurie Anderson, in *Empty Places* 1989 (*Photo*: Linda Alaniz-Hornsby)	81
Figure 4.2	Laurie Anderson, in *Empty Places* 1989 (with Globe) (*Photo*: Linda Alaniz-Hornsby)	94
Figure 5.1	Anna Deavere Smith as Katie Miller in *Twilight: Los Angeles, 1992* (*Photo*: Adger W. Cowans)	106
Figure 5.2	Anna Deavere Smith as Cornel West in *Twilight: Los Angeles, 1992* (*Photo*: Adger W. Cowans)	117
Figure 6.1	Karen Finley in *Shut Up and Love Me* (*Photo*: Dona Ann McAdams)	132
Figure 6.2	Karen Finley as Liza Minnelli in *Make Love* (*Photo*: Dona Ann McAdams)	135

Acknowledgements

I would like to thank the artists whose work is the focus of this book: Anna Deavere Smith, Laurie Anderson, and particularly Karen Finley and the late Spalding Gray, whose work was the original inspiration for this project.

The images used in this volume were kindly granted permission by Linda Alaniz-Hornsby and the Martha Swope Collection, the New York Public Library, Adger W. Cowans, Dona Ann McAdams, Ken Regan/Camera 5. Excerpts from *Twilight: Los Angeles, 1992* by Anna Deavere Smith, copyright © 1994 by Anna Deavere Smith. Used by permission of Doubleday, an imprint of Knopf Doubleday Publishing Group, a division of Penguin Random House LLC. Excerpts from *Swimming to Cambodia* by Spalding Gray, copyright © 1984. Used by permission of Theatre Communications Group. Excerpts from *Morning, Noon and Night* by Spalding Gray. Copyright © 1999 by Spalding Gray, Ltd Reprinted by permission of Farrar, Straus and Giroux, LLC., and ICM Partners. Excerpts from *A Different Kind of Intimacy* by Karen Finley, copyright © 2000. Used by permission of Perseus Books Group. Excerpts from *Empty Places* by Laurie Anderson, copyright © 1991. Used by permission of Laurie Anderson, Pomegranate Arts. Excerpts from *The Reality Shows* by Karen Finley, copyright © 2011. All rights reserved. Every effort has been made to contact rights holders prior to publication. The publishers would be happy to rectify any omissions at reprint.

John Boland at www.spaldinggray.com, and staff at The New York Public Library for the Performing Arts and The Brooklyn Academy of Music were always helpful in tracking down archived material and performances. Thanks also to the Davidsons and the Halberstams for making research trips to New York such a pleasure.

This project would likely not have been possible without the support of The University of Melbourne, including a period of extended research leave, travel grants and a publication subsidy. I am also indebted to my friends and colleagues in the School of Culture and Communication and the Creative Writing programme for their ongoing support.

Mark Dudgeon navigated the completion of this, my first book, with a great deal of generosity and precision, and Series Editors Enoch Brater and Mark Taylor-Batty provided critical insights to help refine its final shape. The stylish front cover and design is by Louise Dugdale, and the index by Emma Koch. I am delighted that Deborah R. Geis was able to write the Foreword for this volume and it is a privilege to have this work situated in relation to her own influential treatment of American monologue. At various stages, readings and editorial advice by Georgie Boucher, Paul Rae, Peter Stevens, Hallam Stevens and Sarah Toohey have also greatly enhanced this work.

I remain ever grateful to the two mentors, Denise Varney and Peter Eckersall, who have supported my work for over a decade. They have improved this book in immeasurable ways.

My love to my family and to Lara – the one person for who thanks doesn't even begin to come close. Finally, I have dedicated this work to the memory of my dear Nan, a great reader and as much a reason as any for why I am surrounded and delighted by books today.

Foreword

Eddie Paterson shares my fascination with talkers in plays who talk too much, with those mad crazy moments like we get in Sam Shepard's works (such as *Curse of the Starving Class*) where a character will break free momentarily from the dialogue, sometimes for no apparent reason, and launch into a narrative that seems to be partly for the other character(s), partly for the audience, and partly for him/herself. It was immediately apparent to me that there was something uniquely 'postmodern' about such moments, something that made them different from Shakespearean soliloquies or even from Brechtian proclamations. And then came the solo artists like Spalding Gray and Karen Finley, artists who cracked my world wide open as I realized that there was even more exciting potential in these monologists who had abandoned other characters present on stage, 'plot', and even so-called author/narrator/character separations in order to create dramatic pieces that were unlike anything I had ever seen before.

It was not only these sea changes in the theatrical monologic voice, but also both the traditions and the countercultural movements from which they arose, that compelled me to write *Postmodern Theatric(k)s*, which I began drafting in the late 1980s and which was published by the University of Michigan Press in 1993. During the early 1990s and continuing up to the present, we've had the great fortune of seeing such artists as Anna Deavere Smith, Lisa Kron, and many others bring us forms of documentary monologue that we hadn't seen before, and which I wished could have been part of my own discussion. We saw the immense popularity of 'slam' and performance poetry (a genre in which I still write and perform) and the way that its fusions with hip hop (in the works of Tracie Morris and many others) brought the confessional and the multicultural, the narration of self and the politics of identity differences, into the forefront. And we've also seen the increasing use of mixed-media and intertextuality in solo performance, fuelled in the theatre world by the 'viewpoints' work of Moises Kaufman and others, and in the world at large by a technoculture that simply didn't exist in the same form when I was writing my own study of monologue.

And this is why Eddie Paterson's present work is so important and compelling. There's so much he does in this volume that extends upon and amplifies the theorization of theatrical monologue as we move through the second decade of the twenty-first century. And so much to admire about the way he goes about discussing it. The three major characteristics of contemporary US monologue that he designates – parody, mediatization and performance – strike me as perfect ways to begin articulating a theory of how monologic theatrical speech has developed in the past two decades since my own work appeared. As he himself admits, he comes to US cultural history not through personal experience, but through the 'products' of US media and other cultural artefacts. This means that at times, his perspective on some of these solo artists' works (such as Spalding Gray or Anna Deavere Smith) is a bit different from my own, but I find his insight fascinating in that in the post-9/11 world, monologic theatrical discourse shows its legacy and its continuation/revision as a manifestation of 'political antagonism'. And his deft movement in the final chapter to the term 'post-monologue', with the myriad and layered meanings of the prefix 'post-' that we see in, for example, 'postmodernism', is an apt way to describe how recent solo performance inherits (and is indebted to), revises, and ultimately perhaps breaks from its earlier histories and aesthetic choices.

But enough of my own monologue. Read Eddie Paterson's study. You'll be glad you did.

Deborah R. Geis
January 2015

Introduction

The ideas behind *The Contemporary American Monologue* originate in my discovering a CD of the late Spalding Gray performing *It's a Slippery Slope* (1997) during my first visit to New York as a twenty-year-old. It was an idiosyncratic introduction to the city through Gray's compelling style. At the very same time as I visited Soho and the East Village, looking for traces of the Wooster Group, Gray introduced me to Washington Square Park and walked me down Broadway. While it is difficult to pinpoint exactly what interested me about *It's a Slippery Slope* – a story about an affair, a new relationship, the birth of a son and a skiing obsession – I can still clearly remember hearing Gray's voice at the beginning of that monologue as he describes a New England winter and way the elm trees crack with cold. In hindsight it seems no surprise that a young man with a healthy streak of narcissism and neurosis (I trust you are not unfamiliar with the sort) would engage so enthusiastically with this confessional solo performance. Then, it was my first winter with snow on the ground and sidewalks to slip on. Then, I was falling for cities and lovers and theatre. Then, I listened with that rare intensity that only comes with the electricity of the new.

It was not new of course. Since the late 1970s, the fields of theatre and performance have seen the reinvention and resurgence of monologue as a mode of contemporary solo performance. This book focuses on the connections between two trajectories – solo performance as an integral part of US culture, politics and media, and monologue as it appears in Western dramatic traditions – that come into dynamic interrelationship in the work of several now canonical American artists whose work is emblematic of the trends influencing monologue performance from the 1980s to the early 2000s. I am interested in the development of monologue as a kind of exemplary American form of contemporary performance and I look at this phenomenon through an extended analysis of four of its pioneering practitioners: Spalding Gray, Laurie Anderson, Anna Deavere Smith and Karen Finley. I argue that the monologue genre is reinterpreted by these artists as an innovative form of performance and sophisticated mode of cultural and political critique.

This argument connects with how the notion of the 'contemporary' is deployed in this book. First, the contemporary is occasionally used as a kind of routine synonym for 'recent' and work produced approximately in the last decade. However, in response to philosopher Giorgio Agamben's essay 'What Is the Contemporary?', *The Contemporary American Monologue* is also an attempt to position the artists in this book as being contemporary because of the ways in which their work both 'belongs' to their time and is also simultaneously set at a distance from it.[1] As a student of theatre and performance studies living in Australia on the cusp of the new millennium, my primary contact with American solo performers such as Gray, Anderson, Smith and Finley was through the writings, documentation, mediatization and extensive critical reception of their work. These artists were, for me, already part of a canon of American experimental performance from the 1980s and 1990s that included the work of Robert Wilson, the Wooster Group, Richard Foreman and a host of others. As such, my approach to these artists' performances is one that is historically, geographically and temporally distanced. Rather than a memory of seeing Spalding Gray live, I encounter his work as an already mediatized, anthologized and archived product. And rather than growing up with intimate knowledge of the everyday world of the United States during the 1980s and 1990s, I (along with many others) have primarily experienced the recent historical movements of American society and politics through a flow of media, cultural and artistic product.

However, while these works belong to the past they are also fundamentally contemporary because of the ways in which, in Agamben's terms, they 'hold their gaze' on their own time and, in doing so, 'read history in unforeseen ways'. That is, these artists are contemporary because their work cannot be reduced to their moment.

As Agamben puts it, 'To be contemporary means ... to return to a present where we have never been.'² Put simply, I am interested in revisiting the work of Gray, Anderson, Smith and Finley not only for the way they, in a relatively short space of time, shaped and even redefined the notion of American solo performance and monologue, but because in doing so their work also began to shape and redefine my own understandings of American culture, politics and art. I return, then, to the question of what contemporary American monologuists – through the distinctiveness and durability of their innovations – might teach us about the present where we may have never been, the layers of late-twentieth-century American cultural history and how their work may also be seen as on ongoing response to the current moment, what Agamben calls 'the darkness of the now'.³

In this book I will rethink the work of these canonical *and* contemporary monologue artists. I wish to explore their legacy by suggesting that the critical contribution of these works is a rejuvenated form of monologue solo performance. From the vantage point of Australia, I will begin to historicize how their aesthetic and formal innovations intersect with the observation that solo performance and virtuoso speech appears to hold a privileged historical position in US politics, culture and performance traditions. I do this with the almost obscene benefit of hindsight and with a vision of American culture and performance that comes from afar and, like my initial encounters with many of the works included in this book, is already mediated and filtered. For some readers, of my own and younger generations, this may be their first experience of Karen Finley or Laurie Anderson. For others this book will revisit, after twenty years, the topic of American monologue last explored in detail by Deborah R. Geis in 1993.⁴

I shall argue that the legacy of these artists continues to contribute to more recent developments in American monologue performance and the ways in which aesthetic experimentation can provide significant avenues for reflection and critical contemplation of political and cultural issues. Indeed, I will finally contend that the term 'monologue' is now inadequate when describing the legacy of 1990s American solo performance and I suggest that the term 'post-monologue' may be a better fit. While the addition of any type of 'post' may seem to be another confirmation I am revisiting the 1990s, I mobilize the prefix for two reasons. The first is to suggest that this study of American monologues, in the period from the 1980s to the early 2000s, reveals an *aesthetic* expansion on earlier forms of the monologue in US and Western dramatic history. As Shannon Jackson notes, the addition of the 'post' 'always exists in productive tension with precedents and histories'.[5] I will thus suggest that the unique cultural and political movements of American history will be shown to shape contemporary monologues just as much (if not more than) postmodern or postdramatic notions of performance. As such, these aesthetic strategies emerge in dynamic entanglement with the history of alternative performances of solo speech and oratory in the United States.

Second, I will argue that these aesthetic techniques have a *political* dimension. Chantal Mouffe defines politics as 'the set of practices and institutions through which an order is created'.[6] As the following chapters unfold, I wish to draw attention to how these seminal American monologuists question the dominant practices and institutions that create order and, in doing so, demonstrate the ongoing importance of aesthetic innovation to US solo performance in the twenty-first century. This book will analyse monologues as written texts, live performances and mediatized reproductions and also foreground the spoken and written word, after notions of the body in performance have been given well-deserved attention. Indeed, while vital elements of corporeality and space remain part of this analysis, my work maintains a focus on how monologue solo performance might also deploy text and speech as a critical response to real world historical events: Cold War politics, Reagan-era economic and immigration reforms, the Rodney King riots, Clinton-era political complacency and the aftermath of 9/11.

This book examines American monologue in relation to the history of oratory and solo performance in the United States and examples of monologue performance drawn from Western theatre traditions, in order to explore what Baz Kershaw calls the 'social functioning' and 'political and ideological significance' of these contemporary forms.[7] It draws on the tradition of direct address and the history of oratory and rhetoric as a method through which to critique the formation of political ideology. It also highlights the way in which solo performance has been used by American practitioners as a way of interrupting, or intersecting, or making visible the rhetorical and ideological workings of dominant consensual politics – monologue as a vehicle for agonism.[8] In the closing sections of this work, I examine the political implications of recent monologue performance and conclude that these postmonologues offer a way of constructing effective and affective commentary on world events.

Following the innovations of solo artists from the 1980s to the early 2000s, there are three defining formal characteristics of US monologue that distinguish it from previous uses of the genre as a mode of speech that appears in many different forms in Western dramatic traditions. These features are:

a) Parody – both of the self and of the world. These performances offer self-reflexive, ironic commentary on the historical and political forces that shape the world in which they are embedded.
b) Mediatization – These works engage with popular commodity culture and the technologies of electronic and digital reproduction and are frequently consumed as already mediatized works.
c) Personae – The form privileges the performing persona over the traditional theatrical character.

These common elements are by no means exhaustive, but it is the sophisticated intermingling of these aspects that provides a clear developmental break with earlier forms of solo monologue performance. These features enable critical commentary on the culture in which we live and the politics that shape it. Contemporary monologues can be seen, in this sense, as linguistic, communicational and creative responses to everyday existence in the West, to the dominance of neoliberal economic policy since the 1980s, to periodic waves of social conservatism and to the huge changes in civil liberties and global security in the wake of 9/11.

Performance

The re-emergence of the monologue as a radical genre of performance is deeply connected to developments in the field from the 1960s and 1970s. At the opening of his book *Theatre in the Expanded Field* Alan Read jokes: 'To say what theatre is would be to start an argument. To say what performance is? A fight.'[9] Nevertheless, with Read's warning in mind, the development of contemporary American monologue is underpinned by the period of artistic experimentation, both in the United States and elsewhere, from which the term 'performance' emerges. The notion of performance, as distinct from theatre, includes what Kershaw calls the *limitlessness* of everyday performances: rituals, ceremonies or any cultural presentations with recognizable theatrical components.[10]

The emergence of performance signals a divergence from the traditions of Western dramatic theatre present since the Renaissance. Movements in the historical avant-garde like futurism, surrealism, Dada and constructivism contribute to the notion of performance. Additionally, the importance of the 'everyday' – everyday objects, bodies, movements and voices – increasingly figures in artworks, protests, happenings and live events. Similarly, works not generally included in the academic canon, such as the history of political and religious oratory and popular entertainments – minstrels, jugglers and jesters, circus, vaudeville, medicine and tent shows, the lecture circuit, stand-up and burlesque, street entertainment and the tradition of the raconteur – and one-person shows like those of Charles Dickens, Mark Twain and Ruth Draper, are part of the trajectory of performance.[11]

The new approaches to performance material also prompted reconsideration of the role of the performer in the production of the performance. Writing in 1972, Michael Kirby recognized a significant shift away from 'acting' in performance, towards 'not-acting'.[12] In Kirby's theorization, acting, as it applies to an actor inhabiting a character, is increasingly challenged by performers who are 'not-acting' and by performances utilizing what he calls 'non-matrixed' techniques. Performers who are 'not-acting' are no longer engaged in complex characterizations that relate to imaginary times and places, both conventions encouraged by naturalism and realism in the theatre. Instead, the performers speak as *themselves*, use their real names, relate personal anecdotal material and make no distinction between what they are performing and their own personalities.[13] Importantly, Kirby raised the question – who is performing? – a question that becomes increasingly significant to the types of theatre and performance produced from the 1970s onwards, and one that is integral to the development of monologue as solo performance.[14]

The influence of performance on the monologue genre is particularly relevant to the work of the artists featured in this book because it encompasses alternative utilizations of monologue beyond its traditional position within the dramatic theatre text, particularly through the work of solo artists. Importantly, for Geis, solo artists create works not 'limited to theatrical stagings' and question the boundaries between 'performance and reality, art and life, fiction and autobiography'. They also do not necessarily 'enact' created characters, but rather deliberately confuse their real-life 'selves' with their performance personae challenging the limits of 'enactment' and 'fictionality' and influencing new approaches to monologue.[15]

This generic blurring is partly by design and partly by necessity. As before, emphasis on the broader term 'performance', rather than on the narrow limitations of a specific artistic field, leads to the establishment of several open-ended genres that are inclusive of art and artists working in unique ways throughout the world.[16] The proliferation of electronic and digital multimedia in the late twentieth century also challenged live performance of monologue, as artists began to integrate new technologies that took the genre in new directions.[17] As such, contemporary American monologues take inspiration and stimuli from outside the dramatic context. Emphasis is placed on the subjectivity of the performer of the monologue, the use of the body, the use of media and texts that frequently include material from the personal life of the performer and the everyday.

Indeed, solo performance from the 1980s typically drew on autobiographical or personal experience, and saw a reanimation of spoken and written text in performance.[18] As Marvin Carlson contends,

> One of the trends that encouraged a greater use of language in both solo and group performance from the mid-1980s onward, especially in the United States, was that political and social concerns became one of the main themes of performance activity. ... The importance of political and social content, closely tied to the importance of language in more recent performance art, has not only altered the landscape of current performance, but has changed the views of its historical development.[19]

The work of solo artists who explicitly use monologic speech to engage – either playfully, polemically or po-faced – with political or cultural commentary is a key characteristic of American monologue performance in the last three decades. Though, this phenomenon is by no means limited to the United States. Indeed, while my focus here is on the distinctive emergence of the genre in the United States, it should not be forgotten that rich traditions of solo performance and monologue are also found elsewhere in the world.

However, if we return again to the American context, the art of Anderson, Gray, Smith and Finley and their peers Eric Bogosian, Rachel Rosenthal, Annie Sprinkle, Holly Hughes, Tim Miller, John Fleck, Deb Margolin, Robbie McCauley, Lisa Kron, Dan Kwong, Marga Gomez, Peggy Shaw, Lois Weaver, John Leguizamo, Reno and Danny Hoch among many others, foregrounds the solo voice as a form of critical engagement with American society, exploring issues of race, class, sexuality, gender, ethnicity and personal identity. Moreover, these performers commonly explore the histories and experiences of marginalized subjects, by situating their single live body and autobiographical solo voice alongside an innovative use of media and technology.[20] As such, the process of using monologue to make marginalized experiences visible and audible (often through mediatization) is a key political dimension within the genre.

Conversely, part of the resurgence of monologue solo performance in the last four decades is due to simple economics. Indeed, though solo performance and monodrama has figured as a strong vein in American performance throughout the twentieth century, it is no surprise that the proliferation of one-person shows from the late 1970s coincides with a decrease in public funding for the arts in the United States and an emphasis on individual artists making their work 'financially sustainable'.[21]

Another parallel strand to this recent history of American performance connects to the US higher education system wherein Performance Studies develops as an interdisciplinary field in the 1980s. Beginning at Northwestern University and New York University, it later spreads to other universities in North America, Europe, Asia, Australia and New Zealand. There is also a close relationship between the academic fields of theatre studies, performance studies and autobiographical writing – frequently found in life writing and creative writing courses – and the popularity of autobiographical theatre, performance and writing in the English speaking world.[22]

The growth of these fields, not to mention the popularity of courses that teach written autobiography and biography, all revolve to some extent around the notion of individual voice and expression. This focus connects to the notion that solo performance, which relies on the individual body and voice, may reflect and respond to the ways in which the emergence of performance, in practice and in the academy, also extends the history of civil rights and activist and radical identity politics alive on US university campuses since the 1960s.

Finally, the performance turn means that rather than situating the following analysis neatly within Western dramatic history, this book looks at the contemporary American monologue as a phenomenon that is also fundamentally shaped by the history and politics of the United States. It allows for the conflation of the autobiographic artist/solo performer and places new importance on the performers of monologue, their bodies, their politics, their specific voices and views, and their position as American subjects in the late twentieth and early twenty-first centuries.

Overview

Chapter 1, 'Monologue in Western Drama', outlines theoretical and scholarly approaches to the history and practice of monologue and defines the parameters of the form. This chapter is indebted to the earlier work of Geis, as it briefly reviews existing scholarship on the development of the theatrical monologue as a genre of performance and notes its appearance in classical and modern works, particularly tracing the influence of Bertolt Brecht and Samuel Beckett. In Chapter 2, I then begin to draw attention to the history of American trends in oratory and performance, taking place outside traditional literary or dramatic histories, such as traditions of religious oratory speech, political speech-making, as well as countercultural traditions of speech, including monologue in the one-person show, Beat poetry and solo speech in stand-up comedy and hip hop.

Chapter 3, 'Confessional Monologue', examines the legacy of Spalding Gray by returning to his major work *Swimming to Cambodia* (1984), analysing his last complete monologue *Morning, Noon and Night* (1999), and through contrasting Gray's work with that of monologuist Mike Daisey. Evident in Gray's seminal examples of US monologue is a mode of performance that employs parody, irony and satire in order to problematize elements of post-1960s' US history and identity. Moreover, the unusual conversational style of these performances can be seen to unsettle the traditional power associated with dominant Western narratives and texts. Finally, whereas Gray's performance style might substantially question aspects of American mythology and cultural power, a short contrasting analysis of the scandal over the authenticity of Daisey's *The Agony and the Ecstasy of Steve Jobs* (2010) points to ongoing tensions between historical white privilege and the confessional form.

In Chapter 4, 'Post-punk Monologue', I investigate the performances of Laurie Anderson from the 1980s, including *Home of the Brave* (1985) and *Empty Places* (1989), before tracing the legacy of Anderson's use of voice and text in the work of contemporary American performance company the Nature Theater of Oklahoma. This chapter foregrounds the influence of post-punk culture (poetry and aesthetics) and new technology on the development of Anderson's solo performance as she augments the traditional features of monologue by combining poetic speech with multimedia and technological elements. I suggest that the depersonalized and ironic American voice, routinely associated with Anderson's work, is currently being extended by The Nature Theater of Oklahoma in *Rambo Solo* (2008), *Romeo and Juliet* (2009) and *Life and Times* (2010–). Lastly, through the work's satirical presentation of commonplace images and use of the language of globalization, the sine qua non of American late capitalism, Anderson's work is read as a critique of Reagan-era social and economic policy.

Chapter 5, 'Rights Monologue', reinvestigates Anna Deavere Smith's performance, *Twilight: Los Angeles, 1992* (1993) and the historical use of monologue in the United States as an intervention into civil rights discourse. Deavere Smith uses 'documentary theatre' techniques in conjunction with elements familiar to the monologic form, in her performance of multiple interview texts drawn from discussions with residents of Los Angeles following the Rodney King riots. This work, in its integration of the words of everyday American subjects into a solo performance, considers race, class and gender differences. It particularly reveals the influence of neoliberal and neoconservative ideology in media constructions of race and class in 1990s US culture. Further, when revisited after the surge of documentary theatre and performance of the last decade, Smith's work points to several innovative versions of documentary monologue.

Chapter 6 re-examines the Radical Monologue work of Karen Finley. Finley's performances *Shut Up and Love Me* (2000), *Make Love* (2003) and *The Passion of Terri Schiavo* (2005), suggest an innovative and evolving use of monologue in the new millennium. Indeed, when read alongside a brief analysis of Eve Ensler's popular work *The Vagina Monologues* (1996), Finley's work retains its radical form through her strategic use of black comedy and transgressive speech. These monologues parody aspects of US culture, skewing both conservative 'family values' and individualistic commodity culture. In so doing, Finley's performances will be shown to interrogate elements of dominant ideology in the aftermath of 9/11.

Chapter 7, Future Monologue, examines current theory and trends in twenty-first-century performance in order to situate the contemporary American monologue as a mode of contesting and intervening into politics. I respond to the positioning of monologue within the historical paradigm of postdramatic theatre – a term conceived by Hans-Thies Lehmann in *Postdramatisches Theater* in 1999 – in which dramatic texts are frequently transformed into monologues and non-dramatic texts are also presented through forms of solo speech.[23] And I argue, with references throughout this book to the work of cultural theorists such as Mouffe, Michael Hardt and Antonio Negri and Slavoj Žižek, that monologue engages with and responds to specific US social and cultural environments – in which neoliberal economics and neoconservative politics underpin dominant narratives of nation – through localized discourse, language, speech and parody. Lastly, I identify new trends and potential developments of the monologue form and contend that future works can be read as postmonologues – parodic, mediatized and aesthetically complex solo performances.

1

Monologue in Western Drama

Etymologically, monologue (*mono-logos*) derives from the Greek term for solitary speech. In linguistic terms monologic speech is both univocal and monophonic, meaning that monologue can be broadly understood as being any sustained speech by a single subject that does not require an 'other' to speak to, nor needs a reply.[1] However, 'pure' monologues are almost an abstraction, because solo speech is far more likely to exist in a complicated relationship with dialogue, meaning that even the most isolated monologues (a speech to ourselves spoken out loud or in our heads) tend to address an other, even if that other is the self, and thus implicitly seek a kind of dialogue.

As performances that occur in everyday life, monologues are typically unbroken speeches that are powerfully resistant to interruption. They are also a particularly seductive type of speech in that they, being both sustained and unbroken, allow for a single voice to assert itself. They are heard in the authoritative address, the musings of the bore and the salesman's patter. Historically, many of the first monologues were prayers to a God or Gods, in the hope of a reply.[2] In many religions today, God still continues to be the original and ultimate monologuist.

Monologues are present in oratory speeches, lectures, prayers and laments, in politics, religion, education, business, music and sport. They are integral to our oral storytelling traditions, our confessions and a requisite part of drama school auditions throughout the world. While there are few scholarly books on monologue in performance, there are hundreds of anthologies reproducing selections of the 'best' monologues – classical, modern, postmodern, female, male, queer, African American, Latin American, Shakespearean, comedic, romantic and so on. As a literary mode, the monologue has been traditionally employed in literature, poetry, screenwriting and drama and continues to be mobilized through blogs, vlogs, facebook posts and TED talks.

However, within this overarching term there are lots of different categories and subsections, such as soliloquies and asides, meaning that we might best think of monologue as a *genre* that can employ numerous literary and dramatic devices.[3] Scholar Patrice Pavis sets out a general typology of monologues in his dictionary of theatre terms and concepts. He organizes them according to *dramaturgical function* – to produce narrative, exposition, emotion, reflection and so on – and *literary form* – as an aside, interior monologue, authorial intervention, solitary dialogue, or a play as a monologue.[4] Pavis argues that because the monologue does not depend on a reply from an interlocutor, it establishes instead a relationship between the speaker and the world.

> The monologue communicates with all of society; in theatre, the whole stage becomes the monologist's discursive partner. In fact, the monologue addresses the spectator directly as an accomplice and a watcher-hearer.[5]

This structural capacity for complex and multilayered direct address is both the strength and weakness of the monologue. Monologues frequently take the form of physically and semantically isolated speech acts that can be considered examples of 'deviant discourse' for the ways in which they actively evade 'normal language' (dialogue) through innovation.[6]

Monologues can therefore be creative and playful additions to the dramaturgy. They can also be structurally and formally significant as they may be embedded in the drama – commonly used as a strategic device, a non-linear break, fragment or disruption – or encompass an entire work such as monodrama, or the solo performance subgenre that will be the focus of this book. Moreover, because monologues traditionally subvert narrative linearity, sequential time and dialogue, Pavis notes that they tend to be used in historical periods of drama that are less naturalistic and less devoted to realistic dialogue.[7] The various uses of monologue are widely discussed by historians of Western drama who typically focus on the appearance of the genre in classical Ancient Greek and Roman plays, Medieval and Renaissance drama; Elizabethan drama, Romantic monodramas, the Modern works of Anton Chekhov, Henrik Ibsen, August Strindberg and Americans Eugene O'Neill, Tennessee Williams and Arthur Miller. The genre continues to develop in twentieth-century theatre through its innovative application in the works of Harold Pinter, Bertolt Brecht and Samuel Beckett, not to mention the frequent use of monologue in postmodern and postdramatic theatre.

In the sections that follow I will survey existing scholarship – in a relatively chronological order – on the development of the monologue in Western drama and the various recognized innovations to the genre made by dramatic artists and playwrights. I do this not to suggest a kind of one-after-the-other evolution, or to overlook historical, cultural and geographical specificity, but to point to the key aspects that typically traverse discussion on monologue that will enhance and complicate the forms that I will consider in later chapters. These aspects include the idea of 'forerunner' monologues in classical drama, the notion of the soliloquy as a reflection of complex individual selfhood, the linking of monologue with nineteenth- and twentieth-century expressions of modernity and identity, and finally the recognition that monologue is also a vehicle for ambiguous and multiple personae, along with didactic and persuasive speech.

However, while it is possible to set out a linear trajectory of scholarship on the development of dramatic conventions, this approach also has limitations. I would like to clarify at the outset, then, that this survey is not intended to be comprehensive. It does not, for example, discuss at length the myriad ways in which artists continually reach across and back into history, drawing together multiple influences and aesthetic techniques, in a way that challenges temporal order and linear development. Nor can any survey do justice to the range and possibilities, the many and varied readings and counter-readings, that these dramatic monologues might evoke *in performance*, including their multiple, potentially vivid and affective, effects on spectators. Therefore, while I will endeavour to highlight the multidimensional aspects of the monologue in Western drama there is bound to be, as always, spaces and gaps for you, the reader, to map your own experiences on to this scholarly landscape.

Forerunner monologues

Geis neatly traces the origins of the monologic form and its evolution as a theatrical genre. Indeed, several forerunners of monologue appear in ancient Greek storytelling and drama of which there are two main examples:

- The use of speech as an *expository* device that can provide commentary, explanation or narrative.
- The use of speech by a *character* (typically directed to a chorus that is unable to act), to convey argument, opinion or thought.[8]

The use of exposition can be seen in opening commentaries or during speeches by messenger, or messenger-like, characters. Examples of this type might be the prologue-monologue of Aeschylus' *Agamemnon*, in which a lone Watchman witnesses a lit beacon signalling victory over Troy by his master Agamemnon. It is also evident in Euripides' *Medea* in the solo speech by the Messenger who relates the gruesome burning of Jason's new bride to Medea:

> The golden coronet round her head discharged a stream
> Of unnatural devouring fire: while the fine dress
> Your children gave her – poor miserable girl! – the stuff
> Was eating her clear flesh …
>
> … Save to her father, she was unrecognizable.
> Her eyes, her face, were one grotesque disfigurement;
> Down for her head dripped blood mingled with flame …[9]

This type of messenger speech prefigures later expository monologues that sometimes include the introduction of authorial voice or interventions, historical or documentary material, didactic content and narration. Such persuasive devices are now frequently heard in voice-over for films, radio plays and advertising. One key characteristic of expository monologue is that it frequently transcends onstage events and brings in information from the world beyond the stage, including the ability to alter time and space.[10] The monologue (for *Dr Who* fans) is TARDIS-like in this respect: it can move between relative dimensions in ways that naturalistic dialogue, which is typically wedded to linear time and a particular place, cannot.

The second forerunner example of monologue occurs during an *agon* (debate) between the protagonist and the Chorus such as the famous speech by Euripides' Oedipus, after he blinds himself.[11] Another familiar example might be Sophocles' Ajax, who details his decision to commit suicide following his failure to be given the armour of Achilles:

> The Long unmeasured pulse of time moves everything.
> There is nothing hidden that it cannot bring to light,
> Nothing once known that may not become unknown ...
>
> When next you hear of me, I shall be safe,
> And all this suffering ended.[12]

This speech is bookended by commentary from the Chorus who remain onstage the whole time, but are unable to intervene directly in the drama. While due to the presence of the Chorus these forerunner monologues are not technically solo speeches, they enable speech from a character that voices their inner thoughts. This type of performance has a connection to the use of opinion and argument in political debate and other uses of the monologue in oratory, but in the historical accounts of Western theatre it points most obviously to the development of the Shakespearean soliloquy.

Soliloquy and selfhood

The soliloquy is chief subcategory of the monologue and the form most connected to the writings of William Shakespeare in the Elizabethan period. It is a type of monologue that is commonly associated with introspection and meditation. The term, said to be coined by St Augustine, comes from the Latin *soliloquium* and literally means 'a talking to oneself'. It is broadly defined for drama as 'a locution dominating the stage and the attention of the theatre audience, delivered by a speaker who is alone onstage'.[13] The most celebrated aspect of the device is that soliloquies are directed *inwards*, towards the speaking self and the audience rather than outwards to another character, and are theorized as being expressions of *interior* thoughts, feelings, revelations or decisions.[14] This focus on inward-directed speech frequently results in monologues with a similar type of focus being labelled soliloquies, even if the actor speaking is not technically alone onstage.

However, as Wolfgang Clemen argues, the sheer diversity and scope of Shakespeare's innovations to monologue points to the heterogenenous sources from which he drew. Indeed, the use of rhetoric, colloquial speech and allegorical representation (all techniques associated with Shakespeare) can also be found in earlier forms of drama and performance such as Senecan tragedy, the mystery and morality plays of the medieval period, and the popularity of comedic spectacles, pageants and masques. For Clemen, Shakespeare was not only a creative genius, but an 'inspired borrower' who was able to shape the established tradition of the soliloquy in new ways.[15]

For Lloyd A. Skiffington, the Shakespearian soliloquy contains three often-overlapping features that, although originally based in earlier manifestations of monologue, come to be creatively exploited in Shakespeare's writing. These elements are:

- **Plot exposition**: When the audience may be informed about the overall action of the play, or when a 'persona' alerts the audience to their own presense.[16]
- **Structural function**: Where the soliloquy functions as a lecture or homily to highlight, often didactically, a particular argument or point of view.[17]

- **Character revelation**: Where the soliloquy reveals 'psychology' – that is, the motivation of a character or personae, the intention behind an action, or disclosure and explanation of the inner workings of a character's psyche.[18]

The soliloquy is presented here as a multifaceted device: it can be employed as an opening prologue-monologue, as a didactic tool or, in conjunction with an aside, it can be used as a direct address to the audience to highlight a character's intention.[19] We see this latter use to great effect during *Othello* when Iago reveals his plan to entwine Cassio and Desdemona, Othello's lieutenant and wife, in a clever plot:

> [W]hisper: with as little a web as
> this will I ensnare as great a fly as Cassio.
> Ay, smile upon her, do; I will give thee in
> thine own courtship. You say true; 'tis so,
> indeed: if such tricks as these strip you out of
> your lieutenantry, it had better you had
> not kissed your three fingers so oft, which now
> again you are most apt to play the sir in.
> Very Good; well kiss'd! an excellent courtesy!
> 'tis so, indeed. Yet again your fingers to your
> lips? Would they were clyster-pipes for your
> sake![20]

While Iago is not alone as he delivers this aside, meaning it is not a 'pure' soliloquy, his speech is seemingly directed inward and simultaneously allows the audience to gain insight into his plan. As Clemen notes, the pre-Shakespearean soliloquy was frequently addressed directly to the audience and this tradition helps us to understand the importance of direct address in Shakespeare's work for engaging spectators in the onstage action. In performance, on an open stage with the audience surrounding the speaker, direct address may have created intimacy or a dynamic relationship between spectators and the performer whereby the characters invited the spectators to scrutinize and judge actions taking place in the fictional world of the play.[21]

However, as read aloud by secondary school students all over the world, the soliloquy is most famously embodied in the character of Hamlet. It is Hamlet's performance of monologue – arguably aided by the skull of Yorick held aloft by Olivier, Burton, Branagh, Tennant and co. – that reveals to theatre scholars the *internal* conflict taking place in Hamlet's psyche.[22] This use of the monologue as a means to stage aloud a sophisticated internal debate is no better illustrated than in 'To be or not to be' in which he conducts a so-called 'war within'.[23]

Unlike the soliloquy-as-aside, Hamlet's speeches are regularly performed not as directed addresses, but as if the actor was completely oblivious of the audience – a technique of staging that enhances the notion that the soliloquy is the privileged expression of interiority. Perhaps the ultimate personification of this trend can be seen in Laurence Olivier's 1948 film in which, aided by expressionist images of deserted spiral staircases and a broiling ocean, Olivier's performance of 'To be or not to be' begins as a speech out loud. Then, a few lines in, the soliloquy moves via voice-over to an *internal* speech and a representation of inner thoughts, as the camera moves to close-up on Olivier's face.[24]

Similarly, Hamlet's first soliloquy expresses frustration and sadness over the death of his father, the King, and his mother's marriage to his father's brother within a month of the King's death:

> O, that this too too solid flesh would melt,
> Thaw, and resolve itself into a dew!
> Or that the Everlasting had not fix'd
> His canon 'gainst self-slaughter! O God! O God!
> How weary, stale, flat, and unprofitable
> Seem to me all the uses of this world![25]

Here, Hamlet's speech explicitly draws attention to the interiority of the self as it has the capacity to allow the inner thoughts of a character to find dramatic expression. Moreover, Shakespeare frequently uses the soliloquy as a way of exploring the dialogic potential of the monologue itself, the playful idea of various aspects of human identity being able to converse with one another. This means that, through the soliloquy, the character of Hamlet may temporarily (re)create an interior world and the audience may also be allowed a glimpse into the complicated time and space of the psyche, a place well beyond the onstage world of the play.[26]

Interestingly, Hamlet's soliloquies are frequently characterized as showing a psyche teetering on the brink of madness. Indeed, the monologue is historically approached as much a vehicle for insanity as it is a vehicle for prophecy and genius.[27] Hamlet is said to express inner doubts, confusion and inspiration through monologue. This is a critical feature of writing on monologue as the genre is commonly linked to notions of self, persona and subjectivity that arise in the Renaissance, expand during the Enlightenment, and persist to this day. In particular, theatre historians often approach the monologue after Shakespeare as a reflection of historical conceptions of selfhood: wherein representations of individuality develop alongside literary understandings of the 'I' as a speaking subject; and theorizations of identity are linked to 'modern' understandings of reason, creativity, freedom, liberty, dignity and rights.[28]

Terry Eagleton recognizes Hamlet as an example of the emergence of a different form of subjectivity that signifies the 'dissolution of the old feudalist subject' and the appearance of a self with no inner 'essence'. Instead, Eagleton describes Hamlet's inner world as 'a hollow void which offers nothing determinate to be known'.[29] He thus suggests that Hamlet is a 'radically transitional figure', a character whose behaviour signals the early beginnings of the bourgeois individualism of nineteenth-century modernism:

> It is his [psychological] regressiveness which makes him so modern: eccentric to traditional order but still oppressed by it, unable to transgress its definitive limits into a fully alternative style of being, the resulting 'decentring' of his identity satirically questions the violent closure of bourgeois individualism.[30]

For Eagleton, as for many theorists, Hamlet embodies a new vision of self that is secular and autonomous, bound up with questions of identity, tradition, autonomy and interiority, unshackled from divinity, but in a state of crisis.[31] Emerging from this analysis then, are characters representing a secular individualism and a fragmented, divided self, abandoned by God and abandoning God. The soliloquy can be therefore seen to prefigure the importance of the interior self in the monologues of nineteenth- and early-twentieth-century drama as the historical accounts of monologue move beyond its classical expository application, and towards a privileging of the self.

Finally, however, Hamlet's monologues are open to diverse readings. Indeed, the Shakespearian soliloquy can also be seen as a sophisticated mode of audience manipulation in which sentiments voiced by a character that seem to be true are found to be, in performance, ambiguous, intentionally misleading, exaggerated or simply designed to create further suspense or rhythmic flow.[32] As such, crucial to the history of the monologue is the way in which Shakespeare situated the soliloquy within the dramatic play as a vital part of the dramaturgy and the way in which the soliloquy is ultimately found to be a multidimensional device, capable of combining aspects of epic narration, running commentary, direct address, playful asides and digressions, alongside notions of complex interior expression.

Monologue and modern identity

Subsequent to the flourishing of the monologue in the work of Shakespeare, there is markedly less academic attention given to the genre's use and development in following centuries. Though, as Brian Richardson notes, exceptions such as scholarship on the Romantic form of the monodrama – 'a narrative of the thoughts and experiences of a single character onstage' – and works like Rousseau's *Pygmalion* (1770) or Goethe's *Proserpina* (1778) signals a new subgenre of monologue that is taken to its radical limits in Samuel Beckett's later work.[33]

Studies of modern theatrical works also start to take into account the widespread use of 'dramatic monologue' as a literary device in poetry of the early nineteenth century, by authors such as Alfred, Lord Tennyson and Robert Browning. As Clare Wallace explains,

> Dramatic monologue enables the poet to inhabit a range of personae that may, as opposed to the confidential, earnest lyric 'I', open a space for doubt and ambivalence around the speaker.[34]

Two important strategies emerge from this technique. The first is that the use of multiple personae unsettles the notion of stable self by providing various, often conflicting, points of view within a single work. The second is that these multiple viewpoints allow the poet to draw in broader historical and social material. Browning's *My Last Duchess* (1842), for example, reveals the historical role of gender in determining power relations through the dramatic monologue of the Duke, a character who demonstrates his male superiority by keeping a painting of his late wife concealed behind a curtain on a palace wall. Dramatic monologue can thus be read as expressions of self that are, in the words of Glennis Byron, 'not autonomous, unified or stable, but rather the unfixed, fragmented product of various social and historical forces'.[35] Similar innovations are frequently associated with modern dramatic works and such notions also remain important to analysis of contemporary works of monologue solo performance.

Indeed, Wallace suggests that the prose interior monologue is also an important forerunner to the modern monologue in drama. In novels, interior monologues commonly take the form of unspoken soliloquies and prose narratives also contain monologues of exposition, reportage and stream of consciousness narratives that reveal the inner lives of characters.[36] Thus, the monologue used in modern drama arguably draws much of its inspiration from developments in literary history and this back-and-forth flow of influences between genres continues to this day. The various manifestations of the monologue as a form of authorial commentary, stream of consciousness speech and unreliable narration, also reveals how difficult it is to separate trends into distinct forms of media or linear cultural histories. The blurring between forms and styles – monologue in performance, as prose, as live art, as entertainment – is clearly ongoing and likely necessary for continuing innovation.

Therefore, perhaps partly in response to the development of the prose interior monologue, there is a notable shift in the theoretical accounts of monologue in the modern plays of the late nineteenth and early twentieth centuries. This writing traces an interest in psychology, the birth of Freudian psychiatry and the monologic 'talking cure', to the increasing dominance of a middle-class theatre audience. As such, the work of Henrik Ibsen, August Strindberg, Eugene O'Neill and Tennessee Williams is celebrated for its complex and dreamlike worlds and explorations of individual psychology through poetic and fragmented speech.[37]

Ibsen's *John Gabriel Borkman* (1896) is one oft-cited example of this new modern sensibility because of its illustration of an increasingly solitary self, preoccupied with an inner world. This is evident when the titular character laments his fall from power and wealth:

> I have walked up there on the floor of that room, turning everyone of my actions inside out, and upside down. I have examined them from every angle as ruthlessly and mercilessly as any advocate. And the verdict I reach is always the same; that the only person against whom I have committed any crime is myself.[38]

Borkman also signals a further development that situates the dramatic character as a solitary character. Although still engaged in dialogue, Ibsen's work may even foreshadow the rise of the solo performer who rejects traditional dramatic dialogue in favour of monologue.

The notion of modern isolation also figures in analysis of the solo ruminations of Anton Chekhov's characters. In the work of Chekhov, notably his plays *The Anniversary* (1891), *Uncle Vanya* (1897) and *The Three Sisters* (1901), monologue is seen as being both an insight into character, but also a reflection of a changing Russian society including the impact of industrialization. In post-Enlightenment Russia, the legacy of which is a focus on individual enlightenment alongside the modernization of society, the ageing alcoholic Dr Astrov's frustrated appeal in *Uncle Vanya* can be read as a pointed commentary on the ecological risks embedded in modernization.

> Man is endowed with reason and creative force so that he can increase what has been given him, up to the present he's been destroying not creating. There are fewer and fewer forests, the rivers are drying up, the wild creatures are almost exterminated, the climate is being ruined, and the land is getting poorer and more hideous every day.[39]

Drawing on the genre's capacity for authoritative argument and instructive speech, and the notion of monologue as a vehicle for modern conceptions of reason, freedom and rights, Astrov's monologue begins as a kind of call to arms. Yet, Chekhov quickly undercuts the authority of the speech (and any one dominant view of historical change) by ending the monologue with Astrov being distracted by a glass of vodka and exiting, saying: it is 'probably just my crankiness'.[40] The monologues of Chekhov arguably stage the tension between a frustrated and nostalgic view of the past, the race towards the future, and the parallels between the character's inner lives and the impact of a changing Russian society.

Further, the pairing of Astrov's monologue about the past with Sonya's closing speech to Vanya himself, also suggests that time is not only related to the everyday, but acts as an elemental, tangible and cyclical force.[41] Sonya's monologue begins in the mundane: 'We shall go on living Uncle Vania! We shall live through a long, long succession of days and tedious evenings.' Yet her speech ends in eternity: 'We shall rest! We shall hear angels; we shall see all the heavens covered with stars like diamonds.'[42] Here, the idea that the monologue is a type of speech for performance that can reach across time and space comes to the fore, as both Astrov and Sonya's speeches have a temporal reach that is well beyond the fixed time of the dramatic world. This enables, in part, a kind of longitudinal glimpse of historical events and may even prefigure the kind of ironic commentaries on history often associated with more recent solo performances.

Though, as with the soliloquies of Shakespeare, Chekhov's work also provokes multiple readings. In performance, the scope and diversity of interpretations of Chekhov (not to mention adaptations of his work) by theatre makers, actors and audiences continues to expand. More recent scholarship on Chekhov, for example, has used emotion theory to offer culturally specific and gendered readings of Chekhov's characters and this thinking adds a further dimension to ideas about the form and function of Chekhovian monologue.[43] In light of such scholarship we might then reread the gendered language of Astrov's speech, with its notions of 'Man's reason and creative force', and consider the way it also draws attention to the seemingly emotional (even hysterical) nature of his plea – a trait historically associated with femininity and the framing of environmental issues in gendered terms.

Conversely, scholarship on American playwright Eugene O'Neill suggests that confessional speech is used as the means by which characters convey their individual thoughts to the audience. The most famous of these techniques are the experiments with what O'Neill called 'thought asides' in plays like *Strange Interlude* (1928–9).[44] The opening observations in the play by young novelist Charlie Marsden are indicative of the technique:

> *(He sighs – then self-mockingly)*
> But back here … it is the interlude that gently questions … in this town dozing … decorous bodies moving with circumspection through the afternoons … their habits affectionately chronicled … an excuse for weaving amusing words … my novels … not of cosmic importance, hardly …[45]

In *Strange Interlude*, the features of the soliloquy are embedded within the dialogue, as the speaker is often neither alone, nor wholly engaged in solitary speech. For Mark Maufort, O'Neill's use of monologue is also particularly novelistic wherein techniques such as thought asides allow 'visions of his characters' consciousness' in a 'dramatic equivalent' of the prose interior monologue.[46] As such, the thought asides appearing in an early conversation between Professor Leeds, Marsden and the professor's daughter Nina, impart much information that would normally remain unsaid:

> Professor Leeds: *(thinking distractedly)*
> That look in her eyes! ... hate! ...
> *(With a silly giggle)* Really, Nina, you're absolutely rude! What has Charlie done?
> Nina: *(In her cool tone)* Why, nothing. Nothing at all. *(She goes to him with a detached, friendly manner)* Did I seem rude, Charlie? I didn't mean to be. *(She kisses him with a cool friendly smile)* Welcome home. *(Thinking wearily)*
> What has Charlie done? ... nothing ... and never will. ... Charlie sits beside the fierce river, immaculately timid, cool and clothed, watching the burning, frozen naked swimmers drown at last. ...
> Marsden: *(thinking torturedly)*
> Cold lips ... the kiss of contempt! ... for dear old Charlie! ...
> *(Forcing a good-natured laugh)* Rude? Not a bit![47]

O'Neill's use of the genre suggests that the monologue is an embedded dramatic device for voicing inner thoughts, confessions and memories. In the familiar trajectory of scholarship on classical drama and the Shakespearian soliloquy, O'Neill's 'thought asides' utilize the expository quality of monologue to reveal intention, internal debate, individual alienation and provide background information. Though, narrow readings of O'Neill's works that emphasize character 'depth' over all else are questioned by theorists such as Marc Robinson, who argues that is it also possible that O'Neill 'catalogues varieties of interiority' not to suggest complex character intention and thought, but paradoxically to stress the 'blankness' and unknowability of individual selfhood.[48]

Following O'Neill, writings on monologue in the works of Tennessee Williams and Arthur Miller typically suggest that the monologue is, once again, a privileged vehicle for playing with ideas of psychological interiority and also for characters to reflect upon the illusory nature of the American Dream.[49] In Williams' *The Glass Menagerie* (1945) monologue is used for narration and exposition during the merchant seaman Tom's direct addresses to the audience. At the opening of the play, he explains,

> To begin with, I turn back time. I reverse it to that quaint period, the thirties, when the huge middle class of America was matriculating in a school for the blind. Their eyes had failed them, or they had failed their eyes, and so they were having their fingers pressed forcibly down on the fiery Braille alphabet of a dissolving economy. In Spain there was revolution. Here there was only shouting and confusion.[50]

Tom notes that the play is a 'memory play' and as such 'it is not realistic'. This speech is a fitting frame-introduction for a work built around different types of time-shifting monologues. In performance too, a single actor might play Tom who narrates and the much younger figure of Tom who is represented in the earlier drama, prompting Robinson to state: 'Of course, the conventions of the memory play justify a gap between teller and tale, but Williams exploits its potential for defamiliarization, awkwardness, and even deflating comedy.'[51] Further, as Robinson notes, Tom's memories are then reshaped by Amanda and as Tom steps in and out of the dramatic world to deliver his series of asides, the audience may also begin to reflect upon the unreliability of memory, character and truth.[52]

Staging a tension between the past and present is also an element of the monologues of Blanche DuBois in *A Streetcar Named Desire* (1947). Blanche's confessional speeches are used to evoke memories, while also drawing upon the historical arguments that monologue has the capacity to convey an increasing sense of isolation and mark a descent into madness. Though, as with many of Williams' works, in performance such overwrought emotion also teeters knowingly on the brink between sincerity and kitsch sarcasm.[53]

In Miller's work, including *All My Sons* (1947), *Death of a Salesman* (1949) and *The Crucible* (1953), personal crises are frequently linked to wider critiques of American culture, such as specific historical events like the investigations by the House Committee on

Un-American Activities or overarching questions about class, social equity and the ethos of the American Dream. Miller's plays do not use the monologue mode extensively. However, solo speech in the form of the salesman's banter or the seemingly banal patter between family and friends punctuates his work. In *All My Sons*, Joe Keller lectures his son:

> I'm in business, a man is in business; a hundred and twenty cracked, you're out of business; you got a process, the process don't work you're out of business; you don't know how to operate, your stuff is no good; they close you up, they tear up your contracts, what the hell's it to them? You lay forty years into a business and they knock you out in five minutes.[54]

Similarly in *Death of a Salesman*, Willy Loman attempts to answer the statement 'business is business', from administrator Howard Wagner, by drawing on a nostalgic vision of the past: 'In those days there was personality in it, Howard. There was respect, and comradeship, and gratitude in it.'[55] These monologues can be read as inversions of the traditional authoritative power of the unbroken speech for while they both begin as lectures or instructions they end as pleas, which reveal brittle layers of personal history and psychology.

Miller's plays also explore the balance on stage between dialogue, monologue and silence that precedes a period marked by increasing theatrical experimentation with form, aesthetic style and rhythm, most evident in later twentieth-century monologues in plays by Edward Albee, Sam Shepard, David Mamet, Suzan-Lori Parks and many others. Additionally, the Wooster Group's now infamous use of text from *The Crucible* in their work *L.S.D. (... Just the High Points...)* (1984) demonstrates a further tension between Miller's dramatic exploration of American culture, and the canonization of his work, and the idea of history and performance as multidimensional concepts. As the Wooster Group director Elizabeth LeCompte explained in an interview with David Savran, 'His [Miller's] vision of himself is in the realm of high moral art. But this is a play that most people see in high school productions, with people wearing cornstarch in their hair.'[56] As LeCompte and the final form of *L.S.D* highlights, the way in which a dramatic work appears on the page, the playwright's intention or the historical classification of work, is continually being reshaped by the ways in which artists (be they amateur or professional) perform the work. This potential for reshaping and reinterpretation is a pivotal notion that underpins my re-readings of monologic solo performance in the coming chapters.

While frequently hailed for its innovation, the monologue as it appears in modern dramatic works is also largely integrated into the dramatic text. In analysis of monologue in works from the nineteenth and early twentieth century, brief moments of inward-directed speech, rather than asides or soliloquy, are discussed as the primarily expression of the solitary self in drama. However, with the dramaturgical innovations of mid-twentieth-century pioneers Brecht, Beckett and Pinter, the monologue genre further develops in new and radical ways.

Two key trajectories

> If the actor turns to the audience it must be a whole-hearted turn rather than the asides and soliloquizing technique of the old-fashioned theatre.[57]

In theorizations of the Brechtian use of monologue, solo speech no longer offers insight into the character's interior, nor expresses a psychological truth. Brecht's epic theatre requires the separation of the elements – of verse, song, monologue, dialogue and action – setting each apart for critical contemplation. The significance of this for monologue is twofold:

- First, the monologue emerges from the dramatic text and is foregrounded, once again, as a rhetorical and narrative device.

- Second, the *character* is set at a distance from the *actor*. The epic theatre employs acting that produces *Verfremdungseffekt*,[58] an effort to deny the spectator's unthinking captivation by the character, as the actor refuses to completely transform into the character he or she is representing.[59]

The result, according to Darko Suvin, is that Brecht's work engages the spectator's critical scrutiny:

> [The] Ibsenian well-closed, watertight play cannot do justice to the new public and mass age; it has to be opened up into a series of coordinated paratactic situations, clearly manageable by the actor and the spectator.[60]

Scholarship on Brecht suggests that the dramatic character becomes a means through which the audience can see the inherent artificiality of the performance, and monologue becomes primarily employed as a narrative or didactic tool used as a form of direct communication.[61] In Brecht, the inner world of a character like that typically associated with performances of Hamlet is replaced by an actor who 'explains' or 'quotes' rather than 'becomes' a character.[62]

This is not to suggest that the notion of complex interiority is alien to the Brechtian approach, merely that in the Brechtian monologue the distance between the speaker and what is said (the speech) is highlighted. As Brecht notes,

> To get the full A-effect from the poetic medium the actor should start at rehearsal by paraphrasing the verse's content in vulgar prose, possibly accompanying this by the gestures designed for the verse. A daring and beautiful handling of verbal media will alienate the text.[63]

Thus, for Brecht, monologue exists as a non-dramatic mode that can be used to interrupt the flow of dialogue. Frequently in his work, a character's spoken text shifts from dialogue to a frank 'paraphrasing' aside directed towards the audience. This is evident during Shen Te's address to the audience in *The Good Person of Szechuan* (1948) when, after gaining wealth from the Gods, the young well-meaning prostitute is visited by several greedy neighbours:

> Mrs Shin: And who are these ... ladies and gentlemen?
> Shen Te: They put me up when I first came in from the country. [*To the audience*] Of course, when my small purse was empty, they put me out on the street, and they may be afraid I'll do the same to them. [*To the newcomers, kindly*] Come in, and welcome. ...[64]

Shen Te's address to the audience is, in this case, a 'whole-hearted one'. It also expands the function of the aside because it also serves as a device for estrangement that reveals networks of power in class relations. Indeed, her address explicitly targets the audience, enticing the spectators to question the motives of neighbours and acknowledge their hypocrisy. Such acting techniques are designed to unsettle any spectator 'immersion' in character and to provoke a calm consideration of what is being revealed by the actor.[65] How effective these techniques are in performance is the subject of some debate, yet Brecht's writing on theatre suggests that by re-establishing some of its links to epic poetry and classic theatre, monologue can be employed as a multifaceted quotational and informative device, one designed to enable critical thought.

Further, the interruption of the seamless immersion of the actor in the character establishes a critical distance between the two. When the spectator can no longer trust what the actor is saying they are encouraged to become analytical and deliberative. This is particularly important to theorizations of monologue as it allows for the actor to cast doubt on the reliability of what is being said, and the character saying it, and make visible to spectators tensions and contradictions between the two. Indeed, the use of audience address, multiple performance personae like Shen Te's transformation into her male cousin Shui Ta, the actor who turns to the audience *as themselves* during an aside, and ironic disjunctions between truth, appearance and paradox (parody), all combine in Brecht's unique use of monologue.

These features can also be enhanced, or contradicted, or misread, in performance. During a recent staging of *The Good Person of Szechuan* in Melbourne (2014) the performance of Shen Te was complicated by the casting of Moira Finucane – a cult figure in Australia's alternative live art-scene, well known for her subversive burlesque-drag-performances.[66] Finucane, obviously recognizable to some spectators, was then able to extend the notions of gender subversion and misreadings in ways that drew not only on Brecht's text and theories, but her own legacy and established performance persona. This performance highlighted the ways in which Brecht's ideas on acting, and the slippage between a 'real' figure and a character, might themselves be unsettled and parodied. As such, the underlying importance of Brechtian innovation to the coming chapters is signalled by the way in which the artists under discussion, like Finucane, each employ different interpretations of elements such as personae, parody, quotation and ironic distance in their work.

The second key trajectory of the monologue in the twentieth century is evident in the work of Harold Pinter and Samuel Beckett. While Pinter's work is most famous for its sharp dialogue and the use of silence and pauses, his later work such as *Landscape* (1967), *Old Times* (1970), *Monologue* (1973), *Family Voices* (1981), *Moonlight* (1993) and *Celebration* (2000) also employs solo speech to enable contradiction and disruption. Monologue, as noted, is often described as both a type of 'deviant' discourse and, due mainly to its unbroken speech and an apparent claim to authenticity, a type of authoritative speech with an implicit demand to be heard and believed. Yet, in Pinter's plays monologues are frequently subject to ambiguity and falsification by the characters: memories are shown to be false, perceptions are reversed, hidden motives are revealed and then contradicted.[67]

Indeed, Pinter's monologues – frequently appearing at the end of his texts as a kind of coda – are replete with unreliable narrators and distanced voice-overs, now a common feature in contemporary fiction and cinema.[68] This work undermines the narrative authority of the character, by revealing holes in memory that contradict the monologue's (and character's) claim to authenticity. As such, Pinter's contribution to the dramatic evolution of the genre is frequently underestimated because – in contrast to Brecht's removal of the monologue from the dialogic text as quoted or metatheatrical commentary – he uses monologue to disrupt the realistic drama from *within* the theatrical frame.[69]

However, perhaps the most profound reshaping of the monologue genre comes with the writing of Samuel Beckett. In Beckett, specifically throughout later works such as *Krapp's Last Tape* (1958), *Not I* (1972) and *A Piece of Monologue* (1979), solitary speech takes primacy over dialogue. As Enoch Brater contends, 'The theatre event is reduced to a piece of monologue and the play is on the verge of becoming something else, something that looks suspiciously like a performance poem.'[70] Indeed, in contrast to the integration of monologue as a minor element in otherwise naturalistic dramatic texts, Beckett increasingly privileges the single speaker as the sole catalyst for narrative and dramatic action.

Beckett furthers the tradition of the monodrama, but rather than depicting characters as coherent subjects or narratives as linear stories, his monologues reflect the disintegration of naturalism in the theatre. Within Beckett's later plays characters speak in a cyclical and dissociated fashion. In *A Piece of Monologue* a man called the Speaker narrates fragments of a life story in the third person beginning with the oxymoronic line, 'Birth was the death of him.' Further, in *Not I*, an individual body is reduced to a spotlit Mouth that also speaks in the third person:

> Out ... into this world ... this world ... tiny little thing ... before its time ... in a godfor- ... what? ... girl? ... yes ... tiny little girl ... into this ... out into this ... before her time ... godforsaken hole called ... called ... no matter ... parents unknown ... unheard of ... he having vanished ... thin air ...[71]

In Beckett's monologues, Chekhov's attention to the elemental movements of time is taken to its logical endpoint. In one possible analysis of a work with myriad possible interpretations, the Mouth attempts to narrate a life story from the moment of birth, but the impossibility of the task soon becomes apparent as the speech continually turns back in on itself. According to Geis, the work demonstrates

> monologue taken to its starkest, most 'monologic' and isolated extreme: not only is the primary action of the play reduced to the monologue of one speaker, but that speaker's monologue is in turn reduced to a mouth, a voice, and a third-person narrative.[72]

In Beckett's work the dramaturgy of the monologue is radically reduced to its core components in a way that challenges the coherence of story – as a logical construction in the Aristotlean mode – and identity of the speaking-self. These narrators are not just unreliable, as in the work of Pinter, but seem at times totally unable to emerge from the fragments of memory and the inexorable movement from birth to the silence of death. Similarly, Beckett's tiny piece *Breath* (1969), a thirty-second work containing audio of a single breath and a pulse of light over a stage littered with rubbish, can be read as an extreme compression of the life cycle, with a stripped and cyclic dramaturgy that figures in several of his texts.

Yet, as Brater makes clear, to experience Beckett's late work in performance is also to be confronted with the visceral, hypnotic and experiential aspects of language, silence, image and affect. The Mouth, disembodied and suspended above the stage, spitting and droning serves to challenge the listening capacity and eyes of the spectators.[73] Additionally, there is also the challenge to the performer of the monologue, not only because of the work's pace, duration and constant (maddening) repetition, but because of the way the performer's mouth must be strapped or held exactly in place as they themselves are strapped or held eight feet up above the stage.

Krapp's Last Tape too, offers an interesting variation to the monologue form as it contains solo speech that is filtered and altered through technology. The work, a kind of duet between Krapp and a tape recording of his younger self, might also be considered a kind of 'transhistorical' monologue for the way in which the solo voice and text remains unbroken. For Brater, the use of technology, the rumbling, spooling and clicking of the tape recorder, draws attention to the precise moments of contrast between silence, the solo voice, the image of the solitary presence onstage and, simultaneously, disrupts sentimentalism.[74]

> Here I end this reel. Box – (*pause*) – three, spool – (*pause*) – five. (*Pause.*) Perhaps my best years are gone. When there was a chance of happiness. But I wouldn't want them back. Not with the fire in me now. No, I wouldn't want them back.
> *Krapp motionless staring before him. The tape runs on in silence.*
> CURTAIN[75]

Yet, while the later works explore the possibilities of monologue, even in earlier work such as *Waiting for Godot* (1953) and *Endgame* (1957) the boundaries between duologue and monologue are thin. Laurens De Vos, who positions Beckett's drama alongside the almost-monologic text of British playwright Sarah Kane's *4:48 Psychosis* (2000), argues that Beckett's work troubles the entire idea of the monologue as a single isolated voice.[76] Such a vision of interiority is different from earlier naturalistic approaches to character, for it lacks not only a coherent subjectivity, but also any possibility of dialogue or of change.[77] The legacy of Beckett's work that De Vos finds in Sarah Kane, is in the 'juxtaposition of several voices within a monologic structure' wherein the narrative and persona take the form of fragments.[78]

The work of Brecht, Pinter and Beckett is seen to radically and distinctly alter previous conceptions of monologue. These artists use solo speech to create and encourage a distance between the 'speaker' of the monologue and the spectator, though with vastly different effects. Beckett establishes this distance by foregrounding the theatricality of the narrative and reducing the stage action to the words of a single speaker. From within the world of the dramatic play, Pinter uses monologue to show contradiction and the ambiguities of memory and character. In the epic mode, Brecht achieves a distance by drawing attention to the narrative and theatrical process, and using monologue as a metatheatrical device capable of imparting a critical or political message. Importantly, however, in each case it is increasingly difficult to link the 'speaker' of the monologue to any stable theatrical character or any stable 'self', an innovation that becomes integral to more recent solo performance.[79]

The work of Beckett thus marks the end of this survey of scholarship on the Western theatrical history of monologue. Two major trajectories emerge: the first monologic tradition gives voice to the solitary inner self and the modern subject, though the narrative authority of this subject is increasingly undermined as personified by the work of Pinter. This tradition is, to a large degree, brought to crisis in the work of Beckett. Beckett wholly separates the monologue from the dialogic text so that it gains uninterrupted focus, and employs a self that is fragmenting and radically alienated. The second is the epic tradition of monologue, developed by Brecht, which positions solo speech as a mode of direct communication using quotation as a didactic, dialectical political tool. Though the monologue in Brecht exists in conjunction with dialogue and the drama, the form regains its expository potential and increases its ability to alter the narrative world through the use of parody and by breaking the fourth wall.

These two trajectories feature strongly in more recent monologue, as the form begins to take on a diverse array of influences, splits into numerous trajectories and emerges as a truly multifaceted genre enlivened by experimentation and play. In the twentieth century influences from outside dramatic history increasingly see the genre branching out and expanding as a form of solo performance. After the dynamic period of the 1970s, monologue is a rejuvenated genre that begins to influence, irritate and challenge the traditional notions of theatre.

2

Monologue in American Performance

I would now like to move away from accounts of the monologue in Western drama, that are necessarily informed by largely British and European traditions of theatre, and begin instead to explore the notion of the monologue as it might intersect with historical accounts of diverse American performance cultures. As I mentioned in the introduction to this work, my experience of American art, politics and entertainment suggests that the solo performance monologue is a historically privileged type of speech and performance in American culture. I am therefore interested how the idea of a 'contemporary American monologue' might also be contextualized by performance traditions related to the use of oratory speech, rhetoric and solo performance in social and religious discourse, and political performance. Further to this, I will consider the monologue as a possible mode of anti-mainstream twentieth-century American performance, arguably visible in the history of the one-person show and alternative stand-up comedy, the writing of the Beats and the music of hip hop.

As with the preceding chapter, this material is presented in a roughly chronological order and with awareness that this concentration on monologue in US culture may give the impression of linearity and cohesion when historical and cultural progression is clearly far more dynamic and complicated than any broad enquiry can do justice. Rather, as Brecht noted, history is a 'zig-zag' progression and with this image in mind the following sections trace a kind of zig-zag line through American performance, from early constructions of a national imaginary and conceptual beginnings of the American Dream, to more recent examples of countercultural performance from the twentieth century.[1] This chapter does not attempt to describe the immense breadth of US performance, to unpack the many degrees of cultural specificity, or intend to suggest that American performance develops in a kind of isolated national context, but highlights instead several key trends in which oratory or solo performance is widely visible, documented and frequently mediatized. By drawing out these aspects I will examine how the monologue may have developed as a prototypical American performance mode and explore how solo performance traditions in American culture might inform the work of contemporary practitioners.

US oratory and performance

In order to explore the notion of an American monologue we need to examine not just the influence of Western history and theatre traditions, but also the distinctive features of oratory and performance that are commonly associated American culture, history and politics. Monologue performance, and its relationship to rhetoric and speech, has been a foundational aspect of politics and oratory since its application in the civic discourse of ancient Greece and Rome and so there is nothing essentially American about the European origins of solo performance. The classical features of rhetoric lists 'performance' or 'delivery' as a key component in the craft of oratory.[2] Indeed, for the great orator Cicero (106–43 BC) the importance of demeanour, voice, deportment, gesture, vocal and body training, even grooming and attire, were vital elements of early manifestations of speech-making and political performance. However, in moving from this catchall notion to the emergence of a specific American national identity, the influence of oratory traditions on US culture is profound. Oratory speech, for example, can be seen as a source of cultural meaning-making that developed within the colonies and early republic.[3] The birth of the nation, as conceived by the founding fathers and clearly drawing on European and British examples, also required a persuasive rationale and this design was debated and then proclaimed through speech and performance. Part of this rationale is arguably reiterated through the frequent use of oratory performance in US history and the traditional use of monologue in political speeches, stump speeches, town hall addresses and sermons from the pulpit.

In his study of the New England Puritan Jeremiad or *political sermon*, Sacvan Bercovitch argues that the early speeches of the colony began to provide the initial rhetorical framework for what we now understand as the American Dream. The traditional European jeremiad was a lament whereby preachers hoped to teach moral lessons about the natural depravity of humankind. In contrast, the American Puritan version of the jeremiad revised the form by attaching a sacred mission to colonization. In the words of Bercovitch, 'In explicit opposition to the traditional mode, it inverts the doctrine of vengeance into a promise of ultimate success, affirming to the world, and despite the world, the inviolability of the colonial cause.'[4] As such, a far more optimistic use of jeremiad developed, which promised a New World of both spiritual and worldly growth.

The American Jeremiad is important to the contemporary vision of the American nation as it links religious and political speech to conceptions of nation, optimism and personal freedom as the basis for US-style capitalism. Through this unique style of sermon, the Puritans connected the economic growth of the individual and community to an overarching spiritual narrative. Therefore, these foundational oratory traditions established an interdependent relationship between religious, political, cultural and economic rhetoric – a narrative that arguably defines the Nation – and the history of American solo performance. The emergence of the American Jeremiad also suggests that aspects of US oratory traditions are distinct from the rest of the world and may even continue to contribute to the types of speeches and modes of performance that are produced throughout US history.

American oratory traditions are also important to the foundation of alternative forms of political, religious and cultural movements, such as evangelical Christianity and African American and Native American civil rights. Early civic performances such as the Gettysburg address, and groundbreaking speakers: from George Washington, John Adams, Abraham Lincoln, Fredrick Douglass, Sojourner Truth and Harriet Tubman to name but a few; employed monologic speech to examine issues of race, suffrage, war, citizenship and social crisis. In particular, exploration of the now famously conflicting accounts of Truth's speech 'Ar'n't I a Woman?' (1851) confirms the significance of not only speech, but also aesthetic representation, performance, media framing and persona, to early oratory traditions. I include below the two accounts of the speech made to The Ohio Women's Rights Convention, the first by Marius Robertson editor of the *Ohio Bugle* (1851) and the second 'invented' report written twelve years prior by Frances Dana Gage, a (white) women's right advocate and abolitionist.

> Marius Robinson: One of the most unique and interesting speeches of the Convention was made by Sojourner Truth, an emancipated slave. ... It is impossible to transfer it to paper, or convey an adequate idea of the effect it produced upon the audience.
>
> > 'I want to say a few words about this manner. I am a woman's rights. I have as much muscle as any man, and can do as much work as any man.'"
>
> Frances Dana Gage: Slowly from her seat rose Sojourner Truth, who, till now, had hardly lifted her head.
>
> > Well, chillen, whar dar's so much racket dar must be som'ting out o'kilter. ... And ar'n't I a woman? Look at me. Look at my arm. ... I have plowed and planted and gathered into barns, and no man could head me – and ar'n't I a woman?[5]

The striking differences between these two accounts, the first written in 'standard' English and the second in an invented dialect thought to be modelled on an idiom of Southern black plantation speech,[6] reveals the multiple elements of performance at work. These accounts foreground text and speech, and also attribute ideas of symbolic staging, gesture, audience reception and embodied presence to Truth's speech (invented or not). Further, as Nell Irvin Painter points out, Truth's performance, during her lectures and speeches over forty years as an itinerant preacher (1840s–70s), typically combined preaching, song, witty speech, innovative phrasing and physical presence to reaffirm her persona (both real and symbolic) as an empowered and intelligent black woman.[7]

Similarly, Douglass considered speech and performance to be a vital component of civic and political life and his addresses, such as 'What to the Slave is the Fourth of July?' (1852), drew on a variety of rhetorical techniques, including irony and satire, in material that foregrounded personal experience, literature, history, and Biblical metaphors and quotations.[8] As John Stauffer puts it,

> Douglass believed that true art could break down social barriers. True art for him meant accurate and 'authentic' representation of blacks, rather than caricatures such as blackface minstrelsy. Through speeches, writings, and images, he created a black public persona that became one of the most famous in the nineteenth century.[9]

As such, the importance of constructing compelling performance personae and the connections between rhetoric, representations and aesthetics, in the tradition of Truth and Douglass, is also visible in later speakers who employed public oratory in the services of dynamic social change and to re-inscribe national values. Indeed, Martin Luther King's 'I Have a Dream' – one of the world's most famous and most loved speeches – reflected earlier examples of speech and performance in the tradition of the political sermon as he drew attention to African American protest being 'deeply rooted' in the promise of the American Dream in which 'all men are created equal'.[10]

Further, current US presidential campaigns and religious addresses deal with issues of politics and faith in ways that resemble early civic solo performances, though now of course with increasing layers of mediatization. Enthusiastic debate over the performance style of President Barack Obama also points to the continuing links between oratory and politics.[11] Indeed, while many nations are defined to some degree by their oratory histories, American history reveals a particular entanglement between notions of freedom, prosperity, media and virtuoso solo performance.

The public performance of political figures relies on recognizably theatrical components such as costume, scripting, staging, persona and dramaturgical framing. We might also read the speechifying of modern campaigns and the American presidential address to nation as monologues. According to Michael Heale, the notion of a 'Presidential image' was codified after the 1820s as part of the emergence of mass political society in the United States. The constructed appearance of the archetypal president personifies the nation and reinforces the values of patriotism, piety and 'rugged self reliance'.[12] This trend has been firmly represented in campaigning and elections in the United States since the early nineteenth century and links the constructed appearance of the leader with their ability to employ the authoritative and seductive solo voice.

Indeed, the codification of the State of the Union address (formerly the President's Annual Message to Congress) in the early twentieth century, as a ritualized performance of rhetoric and argument, also points to a unique type of US presidential speech and solo performance.[13] Similarly, the intimate fireside chats of Franklin D. Roosevelt allowed the president's voice to be projected through the radio into the lounge rooms of the citizenry. And the televised speeches and press conferences of John F. Kennedy combined constructed performance, and a youthful image, with optimistic and ambitious speeches on the future of the United States.

More recently, presidential performance has been embodied in the figures of Presidents Ronald Reagan, Bill Clinton, George W. Bush and Barack Obama, all of whom have relied to varying degrees on notions of authenticity, charm and authority conveyed in part through oratory and public address. It has become more obvious than ever that American politics now relies on skilful public performance, celebrity and persona wherein current political figures employ a sophisticated use of performance and media techniques.[14] Indeed, theorists such as Timothy Raphael and Brian Massumi have argued that Reagan's harnessing of affect in performance – through voice, scripting, staging, rhetoric and media training – situated political speech outside traditional political debate and discourse, and firmly inside the realm of mediatized popular culture performance.[15]

Additionally, the effective use of ritual theatricality and monologic performance – often attached to major addresses during campaigns, inaugurations and at the State of the Union – are central elements in the construction of the contemporary presidential image. In this way we can trace the notion of the presidential image and the effective use of monologue in major speeches and solo performances as being part of a civic, religious and political history that extends from the American Jeremiad to the current State of the Union address. However, after concentrating on accounts of American oratory and performance that might be seen to reaffirm the elements of the American Dream (freedom, liberty and individual economic success through capitalism), I will now begin to note the ways in which oratory traditions also inform a critical narrative in American performance cultures: the notion of an antagonistic and alternative American voice.

Anti-mainstream American voices

It is with an awareness of the importance of monologic speech to aspects of American politics, culture and identity formation that I return to the notion of the monologue and its resurgence as a genre of contemporary artistic practice. Wallace argues that two major strands come to characterize contemporary monologue in live performance.[16] The first strand is *monologue drama*: work that remains embedded, to some degree, in the world of the theatre, the world of the play and the notion of the dialogic script. In the tradition of monologues on the American stage, playwrights such as Sam Shepard, David Mamet, Marie Irene Fornes, Ntozake Shange expand upon earlier innovations, as do more recent artists Sarah Ruhl and Shelia Callaghan. Further, the overlapping voices frequently appearing in British playwright Martin Crimp's writing, the intertextual incursions of Austrian Nobel laureate

Elfriede Jelinek, the popular comedy of *Buyer and Cellar* (2013) and recent works by Tony Kushner, are all examples of contemporary monologue drama.

However, monologue drama remains distinct from the second strand of contemporary monologue, the *solo performance*. The solo performance monologue is work that collapses the roles of author/performer and playfully negotiates the concept of the autobiographical and performing self in a manner that remains at odds with monologue as composed by a playwright and performed by an actor. Of course, the boundaries here are not always distinct as when playwrights Wallace Shawn or David Hare appear in their own monologic works. Shawn in particular, in plays such as *The Fever* (1991) and *The Designated Mourner* (1996), explores the boundaries between monologue as drama and a kind of almost-autobiographic solo performance persona with significant formal sophistication. That Shawn's persona is likely already familiar to viewers of Louis Malle's cult film *My Dinner with André* (1981), in which he and his friend André Gregory appear as 'themselves', provides a further layer of interest. Additionally, performances such as *The Vagina Monologues* (1996) also cross borders as they draw upon multiple texts and an explicitly activist agenda, while being primarily monologic works.

As mentioned in the introduction, the solo performance monologue can also be linked to the exploration of the term performance in experimental artwork from the 1960s onwards. As Richard Schechner argues, the 1960s countercultural slogan 'the personal is the political' may be actualized by solo performance, as emphasis shifts to the 'artist/person present performing right in your face'.[17] Moreover, while related traditions of solo performance exist elsewhere, it is from the 1980s American performance scene (often originating in New York) that a particular type of contemporary monologue solo performance develops and thrives. As Wallace explains,

> The use of persona as a means of social critique, the undermining of gender stereotypes through role-play, blurring the outlines of the autobiographical, 'authentic' subject, are recurrent features of,

in particular, a genre of solo performance that has developed in the United States (and beyond) since the 1980s.[18]

Indeed, the artists/performers featured in this book are critically engaged with their American historical context, from the 1980s to the early 2000s. The work of Anderson, Finley, Gray and Smith is telling in this regard because they actively assert creative control over their material and its performance, and each respond to US culture and politics in a variety of ways. It is this type of solo monologue, combining influences from Western dramatic traditions with the notion of performance as linked to American culture, history and politics, which thrives in the United States.

Alternative twentieth- and twenty-first-century solo performers owe much to the relationship in American culture between innovative oral performance, literature, religion and politics. Indeed, a tradition of anti-mainstream and countercultural voices has been frequently noted throughout American history. Such performances relate to the tradition of early oratory for, as Sandra M. Gustafson explains, 'oratory proved so vital to the dynamic world of the colonies and early republic because it permitted the staging of a variety of social and cultural relations'.[19] As such, from the early speeches of abolitionists, to the suffragettes and civil rights campaigners of later centuries, black nationalists like Martin Delany, Marcus Garvey and Malcolm X, American solo speech frequently draws on a radical tradition of using political and social critique to reveal tensions in US culture around freedoms of speech, race, gender and abuses of power.

Other examples of solo performance such as the raconteur performances of Mark Twain and Charles Dickens from the late nineteenth century also suggests a lineage that includes the macabre musings of German-American Brother Theodore, authors as celebrity solo performers and social commentators such as Truman Capote and Gore Vidal, to more recent American chroniclers like Garrison Keillor or David Sedaris. Additionally, the legacies of early-twentieth-century performers Beatrice Herford, Jackie 'Moms' Mabley, Marjorie Moffett and Ruth Draper can be seen in the contemporary work of

Lily Tomlin, Whoopi Goldberg and Sarah Jones. As Jo Bonney argues, in her anthology of twentieth-century American solo performance *Extreme Exposure*, the profusion of 1980s solo performance needs to be understood in relation to the flourishing of solo performance in the United States throughout the twentieth century.

> Solo performance ... is very much a product and reflection of a century that has given rise to the hedonism of the twenties, the radical individualism and activism of the sixties and the so-called 'me decade' of the eighties. The nineties finally made room for the previously marginalized diverse voices of this society, and the solo form has tracked these developments.[20]

The solo performance monologue, then, can be seen as mode of American performance that responds swiftly to movements in contemporary culture and politics. It folds in idiosyncratic speech and performance techniques drawn from music, art and popular entertainment: from the satirical monologues of Herford and Draper on the intricacies of social mores, the rhythms of black jazz musicians and African American culture in the work of Moms Mabley and Lord Buckley, to more recent parallels with the culture and cadences of punk, post-punk and hip hop.[21]

Lastly, the American exemplars of alternative stand-up – personified by the groundbreaking work of Lenny Bruce, Richard Pryor, Sandra Bernhard, Andy Kaufman, Eddie Murphy, Robin Williams, Chris Rock and Sarah Silverman – provides a form of twentieth-century solo performance that can be linked back to both the polemics of early orators and to the more theatrical tradition of one-person shows in the United States.[22] In particular, the radical, challenging, offensive and frequently improvised performance of Bruce typifies the tradition of anti-mainstream American voice, as in this excerpt from *How to Talk Dirty and Influence People* (1963):

> To me, if you live in New York or any other big city, you are Jewish. It doesn't matter even if you're Catholic; if you live in New York you're

Jewish. If you live in Butte, Montana, you're going to be goyish even if you're Jewish.

Evaporated milk is goyish even if the Jews invented it. Chocolate is Jewish and fudge is goyish. Spam is goyish and rye bread is Jewish.

Negros are all Jews. Italians are all Jews. Irishmen who have rejected their religion are Jews. Mouths are very Jewish. And bosoms. Baton-twirling is very goyish.[23]

Bruce delighted in exploring the complicated historical taboos embedded in such a diverse society and revealing the everyday hypocrisies and lies that he found endemic to American political culture. The legacy of this kind of anti-mainstream American voice can be found as much in the performances of Karen Finley as that of stand-up comedians who perform a more conventional Borscht Belt version of Bruce's shtick, such as Jackie Mason.

Moreover, the countercultural writing of the Beats from the 1950s frequently employs radical solo voices in both prose and poetry. Using autobiographic, individualistic and anti-mainstream American characters, and drawing influences from jazz, bop, drugs culture and European literature, the Beats responded to the aftermath of World War II, the Cold War, civil rights movements and anti-communist hysteria in the United States. In many ways, Allen Ginsberg's *Howl* (1956) – which famously begins, 'I saw the best minds of my generation destroyed by madness, starving hysterical naked, dragging themselves through the negro streets at dawn looking for an angry fix ...' – prefigures later poetic, autobiographical monologues.[24] The legacy of Jack Kerouac's spontaneous confessional prose, particularly seen in *On The Road* (1957), also stands as an important example of alternative American voice. Finally, the experimental writing techniques of William S. Burroughs, including non-linear cut-ups, is a notable influence on the work of Laurie Anderson and many other postmodern, punk and post-punk artists.

The emergence of hip hop in the 1970s – with its roots in African American culture: the black diaspora, the music of jazz, blues, soul and bop, performance of gospel, and the civil rights movement of the 1950s and 1960s – is another significant form of lyrical American solo performance. According to Imani Perry,

> Orality and verbal dexterity are highly appreciated skills in black American culture, and that appreciation has spilled over into the mainstream through black American voices since the civil rights era. Charismatic black leadership of the past forty years has largely depended on the spoken word.[25]

Indeed, the narrative strategies of hip hop such as the use of Call-Response, first-person narration, sampling and quotation and direct address to an audience points to the importance of the spoken word and solo voice in African American culture. The narrative form of hip hop can also be likened to the dramatic monologue in poetry, for its use of persona and dramatic character, and as an extension of early storytelling traditions.[26] These same strategies are also frequently found in contemporary American monologue performance.

Additionally, hip hop also frequently combines monologic speech with political critique. This form is used by artists such as Public Enemy, De La Soul, Mos Def, Talib Kweli, Nas and Jay Z (among many others) as a form of critical commentary on both the world of hip hop and wider US and global culture.[27] As Jay Z puts it, in the introduction to Michael Eric Dyson's *Know What I Mean? Reflections on Hip Hop*:

> Yes, our rhymes can contain violence and hatred. Yes, our songs can detail the drug business and our choruses can bounce with lustful intent. However, those things did not spring from inferior imaginations or deficient morals; these things came from our lives. They came from America.[28]

As Jay Z makes clear, hip hop artists draw on a unique history, geography, culture and politics that produces a particularly American type of solo performance. These voices come from America. Indeed, traces of the 'personal is political' perspective that is often connected to post-1960 politics can also be found in the lyrics of contemporary hip hop. Similarly, Jay Z frequently raps his individual narrative from teen hustler to successful artist, such as in 'Renegade' from the album *The Blueprint* (2001): 'I chose my own fate/I drove by the fork in the road and went straight.'[29] As with earlier forms of American alternative solo performance, Jay Z and other hip hop artists use their solo voices as a mode of individual self-fashioning and a method of social commentary.[30]

Another common element linking together this alternative history of American monologue is the ongoing legacy of the American Dream. From the Puritan Jeremiad through to Rap's call and response, these styles of monologue typically draw in notions of economic prosperity and ideas of individualism that emphasize personal choice and freedom. Though, paradoxically, while this perspective is progressive in many ways, such narratives also find their ultimate expression in neoliberal economics, dominant since the 1980s and a subject of critique by many contemporary monologuists.[31] As Mouffe points out, the folding of formerly counterculture aesthetic strategies into the texture of neoliberal capitalism and notions of individual autonomy and productivity, remains in ongoing tension with ideas of contemporary art's capacity for political critique.[32] Yet, crucially, the American artists central to this book respond as much to historical trajectory of these essentially *antagonistic* US traditions of monologue, which privilege oratory, the production of affect and alternative forms of political solo speech, as they do to the histories of Western drama and theatre. Indeed, contemporary performance in the United States – in the theatre, as live art, in music, on the political stage or in the everyday – can continue to be seen as a central site in which ideological debates around race, citizenship and identity are staged and come to shape the national imaginary.[33]

As we have seen, throughout the twentieth century, US monologue is influenced by an alternative history of art and American performance. We see new artistic forms such as jazz, bop, pop, conceptual and postmodern art, happenings, Beat poetry, rock music, punk and hip hop, radio, television culture and rapid advances in new media. These diverse aesthetic interests also coincide with various countercultural movements: the Beats, hippy culture, civil rights movements, anti-war movements and the rise of alternative subcultures.

Additionally, while American performance is influenced by Western dramatic and literary histories and while artists from the UK, Europe, Canada, Ireland, Australia and Latin America have strong traditions of experimentation with contemporary monologue, the rise of solo monologue performance also recalls the tradition of oratory speech in US culture. This innovative version of monologue arises as much as it does from Beckett, Brecht, O'Neill, Williams and Miller as it does from the traditions of the sermon to political speech-making and modern campaigning, to civil rights, women's rights and countercultural movements. It is the combination of these multiple elements integral to US performance and cultural history that results in the appearance of the contemporary American monologue.

Therefore, from the 1970s onwards, the American monologue can be seen to emerge as a genre of performance that is not only linked to dramatic history, but also informed by a panoply of art movements and media, not to mention influences drawn from US society, culture and politics. As such, in contrast to its sombre presence in the work of Beckett, monologue appears in the 1970s, and 1980s as a far more exuberant, joyful form, unleashed from the dramatic text and capable of considerable innovation. As the following chapters will reveal, the monologue – as a form of confession, as mediatized art, as a form of civil rights discourse or as a radical speech – is also a paradigmatic type of contemporary American solo performance.

3

Confessional Monologue and the Legacy of Spalding Gray

On 20 April 1979, in the Performing Garage theatre in Soho, New York City, Spalding Gray rambled his way through a monologue entitled *Sex and Death to the Age 14*. The monologue begins:

> I can remember riding beside the Barrington River on the back of my mother's bicycle and she was shouting out and celebrating because we had just dropped the bomb on the Japs in Hiroshima, and that meant that her two brothers were coming home. A lot of people died in World War II. I didn't know any.[1]

These opening three sentences hint at many of the elements that would come to constitute Gray's solo career. His focus on the events in the life of a white American male, born in the middle of an American century, and his ironic reflection on the relationship between self, privilege, family, nation and history were themes that continually informed his work. Following *Sex and Death,* Gray became known for a series of iconic monologues in which he chronicled his life over the subsequent twenty-five years.

In early 2004, suffering from severe depression, Gray died after (it is assumed) he leapt from the Staten Island ferry into New York Harbor. For an artist whose monologues were based on the minutiae of the daily life of 'Spalding Gray' his passing also prompts reconsideration of his performance persona. Gray's autobiographical and confessional performances are seminal examples of the flourishing of the monologue genre in the United States during the latter years of the twentieth century. A re-evaluation of his legacy is therefore vital when considering the development of the solo monologue as a prototypical American form.

As Gray notes of his early performances, 'I really felt like I talked to the audience and that felt good – kind of like a preacher, poet, comedian, all mixed together.'[2] Indeed, this self-described performance style draws on several strands of American performance – the political oratory found in the American Jeremiad, the legacy of performance poetry from Walt Whitman to Ginsberg and the anti-establishment rants of alternative stand-up comics like Lenny Bruce – that are as much part of Gray's work as the traditions of monologue from Western theatre.

His major monologues include *Sex and Death to the Age 14*, *Swimming to Cambodia* (1984), *Monster in a Box* (1990), *It's a Slippery Slope* (1996), *Morning, Noon and Night* (1999) and the posthumous *Life Interrupted: The Unfinished Monologue* (2005). A documentary about Gray's work made after his death, *And Everything is Going Fine* (2010), was directed by Steven Soderbergh. Other celebrations of Gray's life include performances of unpublished material in *Leftover Stories to Tell* (2006) and former New York mayor Michael Bloomberg's decision to name the fifth of June 'Spalding Gray Day'. His diaries were also edited by Nell Casey and released to critical acclaim as *The Journals of Spalding Gray* (2011). In the introduction to the journals, Casey suggests that Gray's work reformulated the ancient idea of confessional storytelling and 'transformed the theatre world' by imagining a new version of the autobiographical monologue in the United States.[3] While I believe it is true that Gray's monologues partly inspired a reinvigoration of the genre, it is also important to situate his work within the larger trajectory of monologues and solo performances throughout US history. Gray's work has a lot to tell us about the innovation and sophistication that underpins the contemporary American monologue.

Gray's first extended attempts at using autobiographic material and the autobiographical monologue took place under the direction of Elizabeth LeCompte, artistic director of the New York based Wooster Group. LeCompte included Gray's recollections in the Rhode Island Trilogy: *Sakonnet Point* (1975), *Rumstick Road* (1977), *Nayatt School* (1978) and the later *Point Judith* (1979). During his performances in the Trilogy, Gray began to develop a monologic style based around the recounting of his life events in a first-person address to the audience. *Rumstick Road* and *Nayatt School* both contained instants where Gray would address the audience as himself: 'My name is Spalding Gray' (*Rumstick Road*). These moments became the genesis of his later, expanded monologues and his signature autobiographical mode of performance.⁴

Gray's work was performed live, but was also often electronically recorded and reproduced. Several monologues, such as *Swimming to Cambodia*, *Monster in a Box* and *Gray's Anatomy* (1993), were made into films directed by Jonathan Demme, Nick Broomfield and Stephen Soderbergh. Others, such as *It's a Slippery Slope*, were released as audio recordings (1998). *And Everything is Going Fine* also contains footage of many of Gray's live performances, with the 2010 edition including the reproduction of a 1982 version of *Sex and Death*. The mediatization and the mass production of these monologues has been examined for the way they break down distinctions between high art and popular commodity culture.⁵ Gray's work is thus widely disseminated across a number of popular media: books, films, audio recordings and in the theatre. Testimony to Gray's oscillation between 'downtown' performing artist and mainstream popular entertainment were his appearances on talk-shows, sitcoms and work on several major motion pictures. Yet, the confessional format of his monologues always allowed Gray to fold experience back into his solo work. Indeed, his minor role in Roland Joffe's *The Killing Fields* (1984) became the subject for *Swimming to Cambodia*, just as his role in a Broadway version of Thornton Wilder's *Our Town*, was relived in *Monster in a Box*.

William Demastes argues that Gray's monologues spanned 'the postatomic, 1950s glow of America', the Vietnam War, the failure of Johnson's Great Society and the revolutionary movements of the 1960s, the cold war, Reagan-era free markets, Clinton's scandals, the Iraq wars and the events of 9/11.⁶ In short, Gray's work provides a longitudinal glimpse of American cultural, economic and political power through the eyes of a self-consciously privileged persona: a white, middle-class, Anglo-Saxon male.

Two of Gray's monologues from both ends of his career, *Swimming to Cambodia* (1984) and *Morning, Noon and Night* (1999) provide insight into the huge influence his work has had on the recent history of monologue in US and Western performance. *Swimming to Cambodia* establishes a sophisticated form of confessional solo speech that employs parody, mediatization and personae, to problematize aspects of post-1960s American history and identity. In contrast, *Morning, Noon and Night* shows the parodic tensions of contemporary monologue performance in its exploration of an ironically nostalgic view of American history. These seminal examples of US monologue reveal Gray's innovative use of the form to substantively challenge aspects of American mythology and cultural power.

Swimming to Cambodia

Premiering in 1984 at the Performing Garage in Soho, *Swimming to Cambodia* details Gray's role in the Hollywood film *The Killing Fields*. In the monologue, Gray brings together historical details of the American bombing of Cambodia (from 1966 on) and the rise of the Khmer Rouge, with his own experiences during the production of the picture. Gray recounts historical facts, observations and utilizes visual aids such as maps of Cambodia and scenes from the movie projected on to a screen behind him.

The eighty-five-minute film version of *Swimming to Cambodia* (1987) – ostensibly the first half of the original four-hour monologue – begins with Gray walking along a New York street in an overcoat and entering the Performing Garage. There is a shot of the seated audience and the unassuming entrance of the performer through a door to the side. He seats himself at a wooden table, in front of a microphone and notebook, and moves a glass of water from one side of the table to the other. Interestingly, while Gray's work is widely recorded, published and distributed the monologues themselves are dramaturgically minimal. The common elements of Gray's monologues include a wooden table and chair, microphone, single glass of water, and Gray's 'costume' of a plaid shirt. As *New York Times* critic Vincent Canby once noted, 'It would be a coup de theatre if he just stood up.'[7]

The title of the film appears, 'Spalding Gray's … Swimming to Cambodia', after which Gray opens the notebook and takes a sip of water. Gray has silver flecked hair, angular features, and he is relaxed. Indeed, he appears so relaxed as himself in front of an audience that it draws attention to the inherent self-reflexive layer in Gray's work. He is about to confess, and conveys a sense of purpose and consummate ease. Spalding Gray's job is to perform as Spalding Gray.[8]

Figure 3.1 Spalding Gray (*Photo:* Ken Regan, Camera 5).

The initial narrative fragment sets the scene: 'Saturday, June 18th ... Gulf of Siam, Thailand.' Gray describes 'the first day off in a long time'. He remembers watching, from the side of a pool in a modern hotel 'a pleasure prison', Thai waiters bringing him and other foreigners, many of whom are working on *The Killing Fields*, their Kloster beer.[9] This beginning juxtaposes the relaxing Westerners with the obliging waiters. It also makes clear Gray's cultural authority, as foreign, and his narrative authority as the teller of the tale. Gray's voice is melodic and it retains much of the Rhode Island accent of his youth:

> The waiters were running and jumping over hedges because they couldn't get to us fast enough. They were running and jumping and smiling – not a silly smile but a profound smile, a deep smile. There was nothing idiotic about it because the Thais have a word, *sanug*, which, loosely translated, means 'fun'. And they never do anything that isn't *sanug* – if it isn't *sanug* they won't touch it.[10]

The monologue is framed as 'authentic' and 'true to life'. This ensures that no matter what deviations Gray's narrative may take he is always in control. The monologue is obviously framed as *his* story where, by referring to himself as 'I', Gray enacts what Ken Frieden suggests is the monologue's 'consummate sales pitch'.[11] Gray demands his confession be heard and believed.

Throughout his career, Gray adopted the self-effacing persona of the 'neurotic' White Anglo-Saxon Protestant (WASP). He is a self-proclaimed narcissistic Oedipal male, obsessed with his mother's suicide, and worried about his own tenuous grip on life and reality. At the beginning of *Swimming to Cambodia*, 'Ivan (Devil in My Ear)' the Mephistophelian South African and Gray's colleague on *The Killing Fields*, offers Gray a joint on the day before his 'Big Scene' in the movie. This causes Gray to ruminate:

> Now, every time I've been in a country where the marijuana is supposed to be really good – Mexico, India, Northern California and now Thailand – I've always felt that I should try it. Maybe this time it

would be different. ... Maybe this time I'd have a sense of well-being and feel at one with the world.[12]

According to the monologue, Gray's response to the marijuana is one of heightened paranoia. He panics and fights with his girlfriend Renée, who wants him to return home or to get married. He becomes increasingly hysterical and ends up vomiting and hallucinating on a beach. Gray's anxious persona is clear as he struggles against Renée's pleas to return home to New York and the lure of the exotic intoxicated East.

Throughout *Swimming to Cambodia*, Gray is searching for what he calls a 'perfect moment', an epiphany that will provide a natural closure to his journey. The ever-elusive moment is a reoccurring theme in Gray's work:

> You see, I hadn't had a Perfect Moment yet, and I always like to have one before I leave an exotic place. ... Also, I was beginning to get this image of myself as a kind of wandering poet-bachelor-mendicant beating my way down the whole coast of Malaysia, eating magic mushrooms all the way, until I finally reach Bali and evaporate into the sunset in a state of ecstasy. But I wasn't telling Renée that.[13]

The suspense of the perfect moment, along with his neurosis, are such frequent elements in Gray's monologues that his performing persona begins to resemble a caricature of himself.[14] He radically conflates his persona with his 'real-life' self and refuses to distinguish between the two. As Gray himself states, 'I became a kind of inverted Method actor. I was using myself to play myself ... a kind of creative narcissism.'[15] However, though theorists have occasionally positioned Gray's work within a discussion of mental illness and depression,[16] to pathologize Gray's performance would be to radically misjudge the sophistication with which Gray continually experimented with his performing persona in each monologue.

Indeed, a particular innovation in Gray's work is his use of a kind of epic autobiography. The monologue is partly a mode of direct communication in the traditions of Brecht and Pinter, in which Gray utilizes parody and plays with the notions of authenticity and unreliable narration in performance. It is also epic in terms of both its length – the work started as a four-hour piece – and because each monologue is merely one piece of a much larger performance project. Gray performs a version of Spalding Gray, but we are unsure how truthful this persona and the stories he is telling us might be, or when these stories will end. However, because the work is also autobiographical and privileges the self as the primary inspiration for the monologue, Gray also draws on the history of confessional storytelling – which includes oral and religious traditions as well as significant works of literature such as St Augustine's *Confessions* (397–400) and Jean-Jacques Rousseau's *The Confessions* (1782) – as an authentic means of telling-the-truth. It is the combination of these elements that makes Gray's persona so difficult to categorize.

Indeed, in *Swimming to Cambodia*, Gray goes as far as referring to his work as a 'talking cure' reflecting on the modern obsession with individual selfhood and its self-conscious exploration through self-administered psychoanalysis.[17] By using monologue as a linguistic form that relies on the single speaker, Gray places the solitary self centre stage. However, *Swimming to Cambodia* is also a narrative in which Gray takes a mainstream acting job. In *The Killing Fields*, he plays the role of the Ambassador's aide. In the monologue then, he not only plays 'himself' but also shows footage of himself performing a character in a Hollywood movie. Additionally, he performs both these versions of Spalding Gray in a monologue that is eventually filmed and becomes a successful film in its own right. This begs the question: 'Where does the "fictive" persona end and "reality" begin?' Later in the monologue, following a request to participate in a radio interview, Gray suggests that it is time to 'make himself up' and he proceeds to inform the interviewer of a nonexistent film-biography, including his imaginary role as a ski instructor in a movie set in Toronto.[18] Fittingly then, the performer and persona of Spalding Gray become largely interchangeable.

The implication here is that even though Gray's sophisticated play with notions of authenticity and persona might suggest an inherent inauthenticity, his work remains underpinned by his personal charisma and the power of the monologic sales pitch. Part of the richness of such work is the way in which it situates these traditional features of monologue – the authoritative voice and unbroken speech – in a performance that is profoundly ambiguous in terms of its story and voice. The tension exists in the chance to see Gray make himself up while simultaneously wanting to believe in the truth of autobiography and the body performing before our eyes.

Gray's persona, which plays with the terms of reality and fiction, is echoed in the improvised, perpetually unfinished quality of his monologues and the absence of any 'authentic' text. Gray's work is not just epic in scope, but epic in its dissemination across media. The electronic reproduction of Gray's work is another element that disrupts the artist's authentic presence.[19] The text of *Swimming to Cambodia*, for example, resists any attempt to claim an origin or closure as we are presented with numerous texts: the performances, which often changed from night to night; the film (1987); the book, published separately (1985) and in his collected works (1987); the DVD (1996); and Gray's own wish to re-perform the monologue in 2002.[20]

Figure 3.2 Spalding Gray with Laurie Anderson and Jonathan Demme (*Photo:* Ken Regan, Camera 5).

There is no longer any discernible original. In the words of Henry M. Sayre,

> There is no 'script,' only an evolving story [and] the plurality of performances. Nor can we locate, in the hall of mirrors between performance and reality, the 'original' Spalding Gray.[21]

Swimming to Cambodia, therefore, sees multiple versions of each text, multiple layers of the persona 'Spalding Gray', all of which claim to be 'real' but which can never be authenticated. Gray's use of this ironic performing persona radically expands the scope of the monologue genre by questioning the confessional self in performance across an entire career built of autobiographical works. In a Western world in which confession has become a ubiquitous site of cultural and personal expression,[22] Gray's work positions the monologue as an important means of engaging with contemporary life.

Persona and politics

Throughout *Swimming to Cambodia,* Gray distributes historical 'facts' that exist alongside his own unreliable recollections and observations. Early in the monologue he describes the establishment of Viet Cong outposts along the Cambodian border during the 1960s. These outposts are eventually used as justification for the United States' secret bombing of Cambodia after 1965, or 'Operation Breakfast' as it was known. Gray rolls down a number of maps that are suspended behind him and gestures with a pointer to assist his story. Gray highlights the bombing campaign on one of the maps as well as describing the aftermath of the bombings that saw the rise of the Khmer Rouge and the withdrawal of American troops from Cambodia:

> But instead of driving the Vietcong back, Operation Breakfast had the opposite effect. It drove them further into the Cambodian jungles where they hitched up with this weird bunch of rednecks called the

Khmer Rouge, run by Pol Pot. ... They had been educated in Paris in the strict Maoist doctrine, except someone threw a perverse little bit of Rousseau into the soup.²³

Swimming to Cambodia contains a number of these historical segues through which Gray provides a context to the filming of the motion picture, and outlines the historical relationship between Cambodia and the United States. The details of Cambodian history are presented as an abridged version of history that serves as background and context to the story of *The Killing Fields*, and also to Gray's search for a perfect moment. The monologue performs an expository function, familiar in this sense to its classical incarnations, as an informative commentary.

However, these reflections on history also offer a critical view of America's aggressive and secretive foreign policy. The monologic exposition suggests that the United States and/or the CIA was politically self-interested and short-sighted in relation to Cambodia. It suggests that five years of secret bombing carried out by the United States, helped, in the words of Gray, 'set the Khmer Rouge up to carry out the worst auto-homeo-genocide in modern history'.²⁴ *Swimming to Cambodia* slips between subjective and objective viewpoints, contains narrative fragmentation, and 'quotations' from multiple texts. As Gray noted in his journal, 'It was the first monologue in which I spoke of events not directly experienced in my own life. Some of it was made up from stories and reports from other lives and therefore open to vast opinion and interpretation.'²⁵ In summing up this tragic period of Cambodian history and the American engagement, Gray references conversations with *The Killing Fields* director Roland Joffe, the finished movie, William Shawcross' *Sideshow*, from which Gray 'draws' much of his historical material, and powerful 'eyewitness' accounts.²⁶

> Then the mass murder began. Eyewitnesses said that everyone who had any kind of education was killed. Any artist, any civil servant was butchered. Anyone wearing glasses was killed. ... Little kids were doing the killing, ten-year-olds, fifteen-year-olds. There was very little ammunition left so they were beating people over the head with ax

handles or hoses or whatever they could get hold of. ... It was a kind of hell on earth.²⁷

Upon closer reading, any 'factual' information is filtered through the various layers of retelling and the explicit reconstruction of historical narratives. Gray appears critical of America's involvement in Cambodia, but this is not a fixed position. This ambiguity is made more so by the mode of representation which also serves to deny historical authority. Gray thus enacts, through his 'autobiographical' account and through the monologic sales pitch, a claim to 'truth' that simultaneously undermines itself. Gray's use of the form becomes, as John D. Dorst puts it, a depiction of the 'complex undecideability of ... storytelling as it operates under current cultural conditions ... [including] the breaking down of the old stabilities of teller/tale/told to'.²⁸ Indeed, the monologue form comes to echo Gray's own persona as fragmented, and frequently in the process of questioning its own construction and authenticity.

In performance, Gray presents himself as the typical insensitive tourist and white American male. He has a Thai girlfriend called Joy who sits on his lap and he indulges in recreational drugs to try to increase his enjoyment and personal pleasure.²⁹ Gray's role in the motion picture also provokes his lust for material success, to be rich and a desire to be a 'serious' actor. Indeed, Michael Peterson, along with Peggy Phelan, puts forward the argument that, while Gray's work does focus upon the politics of *The Killing Fields* and US military power, it 'privilege[s] charm and naiveté (or neurosis and bemusement, or wonder and appreciation) over analysis'.³⁰ As Phelan writes,

> He has not faced the truly radical innovative edge in his project. To face this edge in *Swimming* would require that Gray abandon his boyish unconsciousness and explore his own misogyny, racism, colonialism, and economic imperialism, which run like sludge throughout his text. Such an exploration would not abandon irony, but it would add to it a more challenging intelligence. I don't care one bit that Gray has all of these embarrassing attitudes toward other people and other cultures, most of us do; but what I find disappointing is his assumption that this

can be glossed over without comment in favor of some boyish charm or political naiveté.[31]

Here, the ability of Gray's employment of ironic autobiography to make a substantive critique of aspects of American history is questioned as, for Phelan, *Swimming to Cambodia* demonstrates that Gray's privileged persona as a white American undercuts much of the ironic speech Gray performs.[32] His position as the white American male surrounded by the 'running and jumping' Thai waiters is a telling one. It relegates the tangible tragedy of Cambodia's past to mere padding in the life of Spalding Gray. It may also reconfirm the presence of a powerful global American identity that no amount of irony or self-deprecation can erase.

This tension is typified in the case of performer Mike Daisey. Daisey, whose solo performances include *Invincible Summer* (2007) and *American Utopias* (2012), performs monologues in a style closely reminiscent to that of Spalding Gray, including the use of a bare stage, desk, microphone and glass of water. His work received notoriety in 2012 after his autobiographical monologue about technology, globalization and dubious labour practices in China, *The Agony and the Ecstasy of Steve Jobs* (2010), was aired on radio programme *This American Life* and later found to contain several exaggerations and inaccuracies.[33] Daisey's monologue included descriptions of Shenzhen, China's first Special Economic Zone and home to the Foxconn factories that produce many Apple products. The work was also consistently critical of the Apple brand and its exploitation of workers, particularly in China, that guarantees the steady flows of consumer products to the West.

However, following the revelation that sections of the monologue were fabricated – something Daisey initially denied – *This American Life* aired a 'Retraction' episode in which Daisey stated, 'The mistake that I truly regret is that I had it on your show as journalism and it's not journalism. It's theatre.'[34] Putting aside the notion that a lot of contemporary journalism increasingly resembles opinion or memoir dressed up as fact – Fox News has popularized the right-wing monologic rant that is frequently as fantastical as any dramatic fiction – the Mike Daisey scandal draws attention to the ongoing tension in monologic performance between truth, representation and politics. As Shannon Steen notes, Daisey's use of a confessional style that blends autobiography with elements of documentary was one of the key reasons the work was assumed to be factually accurate in the first place.[35] At the heart of the scandal then, was that the piece was framed as journalism in which the monologic sales pitch was used to support a pointed and sometimes didactic critique.

In contrast to Daisey's work, however, Gray's performance persona in *Swimming to Cambodia* resists didacticism by playing significantly with notions of authenticity and parody. Linda Hutcheon defines parody as a means of enabling critical questioning of the present and the past in order to critique the production of historical and ideological narratives.[36] Throughout the monologue, Gray contrasts 1960s Cambodian history with his experiences filming *The Killing Fields*. It is the juxtaposition of these two separate historical contexts that facilitates his use of irony to explore the cultural ramifications of America's involvement with Cambodia's past. Indeed, Gray's description of American involvement in Cambodia constitutes a telling political commentary.

Gray's critique is effective because, and not despite the fact, his almost naïve retelling of the Cambodian past is placed in direct contrast to his own, more hedonistic adventures. This seeming naïveté should not be taken at face value however, for just as his persona as the white American male questions its own authenticity and privilege, Gray's performance also ironically restages the (neocolonial) assumption that it is possible to know 'facts' about a foreign country yet impossible to know one's own self/nation. Indeed, it is through the juxtaposition of Gray's search for a utopic perfect moment and the horrors of Cambodian history, that the performance creates parody. First, *Swimming to Cambodia* parodies Gray's identity as a travelling American white male, insensitive to cultural difference. Secondly, he parodies the Western, specifically American, culture in which the monologue is embedded by setting notions such as sex tourism and genocide side by side and allowing spectators to draw critical connections and find sudden parallels between Gray's self-indulgence and American imperialism.

According to Demastes, the historical cultural privilege attributed to Gray as a self-proclaimed middle-class WASP leaves two options open to him in pursuing a political agenda in his work. The first is that Gray might reject his personal history and attempt to enact change from a position of 'without', 'a "have" joining in with the "have-nots"'. The second option given to Gray is to accept, at least rhetorically, his position of authority and attempt to address his location in history and culture from 'within', through the tools of that system, namely language. Thus, for Demastes, 'while Gray's work *appears* supportive of the status quo, it presents a persona who ironically utilizes an empowered naivety to undermine itself and the authority it seems to uphold'.[37] However, Gray's work not only undermines the status quo, it also engages in a substantive critique of American incursions into South East Asia. It evokes the events of the Vietnam War and also recalls the Hollywood reproductions of the conflict such as Francis Ford Coppola's *Apocalypse Now* (1979). Indeed, Captain Willard's (Martin Sheen) monologic voice-over is also a kind of hallucinogenic journey into the jungle in which the vestiges of Western civility rapidly fall away. Similarly, in *Swimming to Cambodia*, Gray uses monologue, as a primarily linguistic form that historically privileges the self, in order to parody that self and, in doing so, offers a parody of American cultural dominance in South East Asia.

This critique is consolidated, following his search for a perfect moment on the beaches of Thailand, when Gray returns to America with the idea of going to Hollywood. He parodies the self-absorbed attitude of the tourist returning home believing himself to be a changed man or the enlightenment fantasy made popular by the Beatles which sees rich celebrities seek spirituality in the exotic East. 'I'd adopt a Cambodian family, I'd have my teeth taken care of, pay my taxes, clean my loft, try to put it at perfect white, right angles.'[38] Through this parody of the self, Gray also satirizes the 'perfect white, right angled' world of the white

American male and American culture in general. As Demastes argues, Gray moves 'toward criticizing America's one great flaw: its willingness to perpetuate a world unequally divided between haves and have-nots even while propagandizing a doctrine of equal opportunity'.[39] Gray articulates his own consumerist impulse with irony, contrasting it with the search for a perfect moment, the relative glamour of the film shoot, and most importantly the overarching narrative of Cambodian and American history. *Swimming to Cambodia* exploits, therefore, the historical capacity of the monologue as an autobiographical device as an expression of the inner self and simultaneously parodies this performative process and the process of historical narrativization.

Similarly, in Gray's descriptions of flying in a helicopter above an artificial war zone for *The Killing Fields*, another moment that suggests a parallel with Coppola's epic film, as the monologue reveals the great distance between the world of the motion picture and that of the Thai peasants paid to lie on the ground pretending to be dead. Once again, Gray parodies himself by describing his fears of falling from the helicopter mid-flight just as he is distracted by the fake war zone beneath him:

> I was looking up the Chao Phraya River and I saw, my God, how much area the film controlled! Twenty miles of Thai jungle, all the way up the river, there were Thai peasants throwing more rubber tires on the fire to make black smoke, to make it look like war, and I thought, of course! WAR THERAPY. Every country should make a major war movie every year. It would put a lot of people to work, help them get their rocks off. And when you land in that jungle you don't have to Method-act. When those helicopter blades are whirring overhead, you shout to be heard. You don't have to Method-act when you look down and see a Thai peasant covered with chicken giblets and fake blood in 110-degree weather for fifteen hours a day for five dollars a day. (If they're real amputees they get seven-fifty.) It's just like the real event![40]

Gray's observation that the film is 'just like the real event' highlights the gulf between the artificial film environment and tragic historical reality. It draws attention, not only to the film as an historical replica that is simulated, but also to the performance of the monologue as a constructed entertainment. Like the fake war, *Swimming to Cambodia* claims an 'authentic' reality, a truth telling 'just like the real event'. As before, Gray's seeming naïveté and enthusiasm for 'war therapy' provides a critical juxtaposition between the powerful narratives of American history, including a 'global' American identity that is white, capitalist and insensitive to cultural difference, and the events of Cambodia's past.

It should not be forgotten that this monologue was performed in the midst of a period characterized by muscular American foreign policy in the dying days of the Cold War, and a renewed sense of American self-confidence both at home and abroad. However, Reagan's social legacy, a rise in poverty, homelessness and economic inequality – the gap between the haves and have-nots – is also part of the historical background for Gray's work. As neoliberal economic policies (sometimes called Reaganomics) emphasized individual wealth creation over public spending on social health and welfare – overwhelmingly privileging a white middle class – *Swimming to Cambodia* is a playfully critical monologue about a male WASP. The Performance thus provides a critical reflection on the mobilization of US power during the middle of the Reagan administration and in the context of the Cold War. I argue that Gray's parodic employment of the monologue form and his confessional persona allows him to launch a critique of American culture from within.

The conflation of the performer and persona in Gray's work eschews the traditional dramatic character and, thus furthers the potential of monologue to become an increasingly self-reflexive mode of dramatic representation, a kind of ironic jeremiad for the late twentieth century. *Swimming to Cambodia* extends the traditional features of monologue by placing them alongside trajectories found in American performance history: the sermon, the confession and the comic rant; and through these aesthetic innovations establishes a critical re-reading of dominant American mythology and cultural hegemony.

Morning, Noon and Night

Fifteen years after *Swimming to Cambodia*, *Morning, Noon and Night* was first performed in 1999. The monologue begins with Gray waking beside his infant son Theo and partner Kathie and looking out the window of his new home in the coastal village of Sag Harbor, Long Island.

> My eye stops at the old Whalers' Church, where I see the first of the sun's rose-colored light build up behind it and seep out at the edges. This beautiful church was built in 1844 and had an incredible one-hundred-and-sixty-five-foot steeple that the whalers could see in the distance as they rounded Montauk Point. The steeple guided them home after two or three years at sea.[41]

He recollects their recent purchase of a house, and the birth of Theo as *Morning, Noon and Night* takes up the theme of tranquil family life. This monologue was the final major completed work before Gray's passing and it offers a 'day in the life' narrative with a nod to James Joyce's *Ulysses*.[42] In this piece, Gray's trademark hysteria is tempered by the calm of his relationship with Kathie, stepdaughter Marissa and young boys Forrest and Theo. The frenetic setting of New York, which had provided the background to Gray's tales up to this point, is also absent. As he describes their move to Sag Harbor, he says, 'I wondered if I would miss New York City after thirty years there and not be able to live without that crazy hustle and bustle that had become such a natural part of my life.'[43] However, in *Morning, Noon and Night* it is as if Gray, like the whalers at sea, has come 'home'.

This monologue marks an intriguing phase in Gray's career. Produced during the final years of Democrat Bill Clinton's presidency, the work seems far removed from Gray's earlier performances. Gray's voice is less cynical and the text has a consciously structured beginning, middle and end (morning, noon and night). Here, an artist often associated with postmodern innovation performs in a style that, at first encounter, contains little overt manipulation of the monologue form. Indeed, theatre theorist Alisa Solomon argued that it was a fundamentally conservative work in which the monologue's 'cornball happiness makes Gray's abiding dread seem disingenuous, even embarrassing'.[44] This critique prompts exploration into Gray's arguably nostalgic view of American culture in this late 1990s monologue. However, just as *Swimming to Cambodia* offers a critical counterpoint to Reagan-era rhetoric, I suggest that *Morning, Noon and Night*'s combination of cornball charm and family bliss can also be read as a revealing depiction of cultural insularity during the Clinton period. And with hindsight, of course, this nostalgia for inward looking 'village life' is also radically undercut by the attacks on the World Trade Centre that would take place in 2001.

Much of *Morning, Noon and Night* concentrates on Gray and Kathie's children, such as a visit to the Sag Harbor Elementary Assembly as Kathie, Spalding and toddler Theo join Forrest at school.

> They have class theme skits, show-and-tell, songs of all sorts, but mostly patriotic songs. And then there is the salute to the flag of the United States of America. ... On Fridays all the children link arms and sway together as they sing the Sag Harbor Elementary School Song. The first time I witnessed this, I cried.[45]

Gray expresses parental pride as he watches his children. 'It was the children', he says, 'who finally got me out of New York City'.[46] And throughout the work he recounts his conversations with Forrest, confrontations with Marissa, and describes in detail his delight at watching Theo wake. Gray's description of the quaint setting of the town is also peaceful.

> Now, as I pan Theo from west to north, we sweep past the corner of Robert Lowell and Caroline Blackwood's last home. Through the autumn foliage we catch only a little corner of it, which looks like a giant piece of wedding cake.[47]

However, as if to counter any notion that he has 'settled down', the monologue is interspersed with recognizably neurotic fantasies. The

Spalding Gray persona is in this regard relatively unchanged, as he details several instances of imagined trauma and disease that are typical of his earlier performances. Though Gray's paranoia is now also framed by the gothic imagery of the churches and cemetery in Sag Harbor:

> My fantasy was that, just as I was about to escape at last from New York, after thirty years of relatively good health, I eat some salad fixed by a food handler who has just a little bit of poop under his fingernail and I come down with this bad case of hepatitis. ... I see myself getting out of bed in a delirious state and wandering, in a late November wind and rain, in my long underwear across the street into the historic cemetery.[48]

When he is not contracting hepatitis, Gray self-reflexively charts his career up until *Morning, Noon and Night*. He alludes to his first monologue in the Rhode Island Trilogy and the Trilogy's exploration of family history and his mother's suicide. He also recalls his tales of growing up from *Sex and Death to the Age 14* onwards until he begins to witness the growing up of his own children in *Morning, Noon and Night*.[49] Gray also gently mocks his compulsion to continue telling this ongoing story to an audience:

> I am terrified and rigid, looking for a branch, a tree, anything to grasp and save us from this black river that leads us to that fall into the endless abyss of something that is not nothing which is also not us. It is the endless negation of us and I cry out for a reprieve and grab for one last story, one last memory that will be the branch that will save us. ...[50]

However, as distinct from *Swimming to Cambodia*, *Morning, Noon and Night* contrasts Gray's neurosis with the intimate, almost homespun, details of family life in small-town America, rather than with a broad historical scenario. *Morning, Noon and Night* describes, instead, the traditional patriotic markers that make up everyday American life. Gray watches Forrest and the children of Sag Harbor Elementary singing, swaying and saluting the flag. His claim that upon initially witnessing this event he cried seems ironic in light of his earlier work. Indeed, it is significant to observe the persona of Spalding Gray weeping at this obvious display of American patriotism when in *Swimming to Cambodia* he is critical of all things 'white and right-angled'. Indeed, in an inversion of *Swimming to Cambodia* in which the experiences of the privileged Westerner were contrasted with historical tragedy and genocide, in *Morning, Noon and Night*, Gray juxtaposes everyday happiness in the United States with a profound terror of the unknown:

> I see rogue asteroids hovering in dark space all around us. I think of all the new drug-resistant bacteria. I see a vision of the Islamic Jihad burning American flags. I see the scrotal arteries being crushed by bicycle seat. I hear Theo falling down the attic stairs. ... I worry about Kathie coming down with chronic fatigue syndrome. Oh my God, save me from that. I almost find myself trying to actually pray. How would I ever get the children off to school each day over and over again until death do us part?[51]

Three things should be noted here. The first is the ironic listing of mishaps typical of the Spalding Gray persona, a kind of Woody Allen-like *kvetching*. The second is that Gray's fears for his family are closely linked to his fears for the nation. And finally, there is the foreshadowing of the events of 9/11 as Gray panics and fantasizes that bacteria may become resistant to drugs, and sees a vision of Islamic Jihad burning the American flag. The productive tension in *Morning, Noon and Night* is between Gray's sincere embrace of family and the insularity of small-town existence, which is placed in sharp distinction to global threats, bugs and burnings.

There is also a measure of black comedy in Gray's hysteria as he reinvigorates his neurotic persona once again. Indeed a similar section of *Monster in a Box*, Gray's 1990 monologue, details an incident where Gray believes he may have contracted AIDS:

> The whole situation has triggered in me this irrational, off-the-wall, out-of-control AIDS hysteria. I am now convinced that I am carrying the virus and that I'm about to explode at any minute like a disease bomb.[52]

Yet, while Gray's paranoia is undoubtedly a mainstay of his persona throughout his monologues, *Morning, Noon and Night* places greater emphasis on the stability of the family unit and threats entering from outside of the nation. In contrast to these threats, signs of American patriotism seem to be almost multiplying in the monologue. Gray rides his bike through the town spotting American flags – 'I pass the fire station on my right, which gives me a clear view of my first American flag of the day'[53] – and he explains that the flags are everywhere:

> Sag Harbor has more American flags flying. When I first went there I thought it was a national holiday, until I saw them everyday. Now I've come to love our flag. It is, I think, the most beautiful of all the flags in the world.[54]

However, there is a subtly ironic tone to Gray's descriptions of Sag Harbor in which all the flags, anthems and celebration become almost as overwhelming as the threat of drug-resistant bacteria. There is also irony in Kathie and Spalding's choice to hang thrift-shop portraits of George Washington in their Sag Harbor home. With its numerous American flags and paintings of Washington – both 'a little campy and a little patriotic-real' – hanging above the mantel, Gray's version of Sag Harbor is a tongue-in-cheek illustration of the American Dream.

This monologue also offers a glimpse into a version of US complacency after the End of History thesis, in which the great ideological battles of the twentieth century – capitalism versus communism, fascism versus democracy – saw the triumph of Western liberal democracy.[55] With this in mind, the reoccurring presence of notions such as patriotism, traditional family values and the American flags in *Morning, Noon and Night* are elements that draw attention to wider changes in taking place in American culture during the late 1990s. Part of the social trajectory of this period saw a reanimation of neoconservative 'values' across the nation.

In broad terms, neoconservatism is a political ideology that offers traditional conservatism an intellectual framework that goes beyond social and cultural stability and instead concentrates on economics.⁵⁶ Irving Kristol, often described as the godfather of the neoconservative movement, encourages '[the] conservative ideal of the normal household – the household that exemplifies "family values"' and advocates a socially conservative view on cultural production, education, relations of Church and State, censorship and the regulation of pornography.⁵⁷ Similarly, on matters of foreign policy, neoconservatism promotes 'patriotism as a natural and healthy sentiment [that] should be encouraged by both public and private institutions'; a suspicion of international institutions; and the capacity of 'statesmen' to distinguish friend from foe.⁵⁸ The election of George W. Bush in 2001 and the so-called War on Terror, including the Iraq and Afghanistan incursions, arguably signalled a period in which neoconservative thought began to dominate aspects of American domestic and foreign policy.

In *Morning, Noon and Night*, Gray parodies this insular vision of the world through his depiction of partner Kathie. 'I see, through the kitchen French doors, Kathie, the mother, in the kitchen. There she is, doing her cooking and cleaning and cleaning and cooking.'⁵⁹ With the repetition of 'cooking and cleaning and cleaning and cooking' Gray pokes fun at a robotic 1950s portrayal of the housewife. The thriving diversity of New York is nowhere to be seen. In its place, Gray depicts Sag Harbor as an idyllic rural hamlet that from above looks, 'like a Norman Rockwell Monopoly town ... just nestled there with its off-season population of 2,009, about the size of the population of an average New York City subway at rush hour'.⁶⁰ As such, Gray's Sag Harbor as an unchanged relic, a Stepford community, one where patriotism is alive and well and where the mother cooks and cleans and cleans and cooks with no thought other than her chores and her family.

Similarly, in Gray's depiction of prosperous family life – a kind of agnostic version of the American Jeremiad and its focus on freedom, wealth accumulation and spiritual growth – an irony rests alongside images of nostalgia. Gray contents himself by cutting his lawn with a hand mower and rather than running off to join an 'experimental theatre company' as in his earlier days, he fantasizes that, lawn mower in hand, he is now playing a different role:

> It's as if I'm on a stage, or a movie set, waiting for the action to begin. I feel like Ozzie Russo, who is being played by Spalding Gray, who is playing at being a family man here in the Let's Pretend yard of Life.[61]

There is an alienated version of the American Dream in Gray's 'Let's Pretend yard of Life' as the mythologies of 'family' and 'nation' reappear through nostalgia for 'old America'.

According to Frederic Jameson, the appearance of nostalgia is, in the postmodern context, incompatible with 'genuine historicity'.[62] In short, nostalgia is one element characteristic of contemporary life that denies experience of historical reality and our current political situation. Nostalgia clouds the ability to see past its own terms and address concrete historical problems. Jameson argues that without the experience of 'real history' a loss of critical distance takes place, a loss that ensures the ineffectiveness of cultural politics.[63] He notes that the concept of 'real history' is a contested term, but it can be said that in the context of this study the active experience of history and our current experience is 'real' to some degree.[64]

For Solomon, Gray is so enamoured with nostalgia for the 'comfy cocoon of the old grand narratives' that he has little interest in questioning them.

> His new nuclear family is cozily intact and wrapped in the flag ... in this astonishingly conservative new monologue, which follows a day in his life as a dad in his new Long Island home, replete with lawn mower.[65]

This reading suggests that Gray's persona no longer questions the themes of 'family' and 'nation', but is in danger of being subsumed by them. Conversely, a counter-reading suggests that the nostalgia and Americana present in *Morning, Noon and Night* needs to be read in contrast with the aspects of ironic confession in Gray's performance. Indeed, critiques of Gray must also take into account the wider cultural and political context that continually sits in tension with his performing persona.

This monologue highlights the degree to which American culture in the late 1990s may have become inward looking. The Clinton presidency saw an extended period of US economic expansion and wealth creation. It was also interrupted by a case for impeachment in 1998, following the Monica Lewinski scandal, which served as a clarion call for the conservative right. Interestingly, in *Morning, Noon and Night*, neoconservative signifiers of 'family', 'God' and 'country' thrive and the monologue often knowingly reveals an undercurrent of ideologically loaded 'values' that figure in the everyday lives of contemporary US subjects. Similarly, while Gray gently mocks Sag Harbor, it is through ambiguity and parody that his performance begins to undermine the nostalgic view of American culture:

> Once I get my first drink made, I go into the living room to get a fire started in the fireplace. ... I fantasize that I am in my study drinking and reflecting on the manifestations of my genius. Then, when this fantasy bubble breaks, I go out into the kitchen and play at being the 'family man'. I mix and intermingle with the children. I stir Kathie's lamb stew with a long wooden spoon. I squeeze Theo's cheek. Then I go back into the living room to sit down again by the fire.[66]

In *Morning, Noon and Night*, Gray plays at being the 'man'. However this persona is also embedded in the family. Gray 'plays' at being the father, the 'family man'. It is his wife who makes the stew and Gray who sits by the fire drinking his Bloody Marys and wine. This may read as politically regressive, of course, but the persona performed by Gray also continues to self-consciously reflect upon the culture and world in which he exists. As Gray notes in his journals of this time, 'The well told PARTIAL TRUTH to deflect the private RAW TRUTH.'[67]

With hindsight, the raw truth of *Morning, Noon and Night* may be that Gray's parody of himself – the naïve cornball whose personal anxieties are never far away – also describes embedded ideology in American 'patriotic family values' in the days before September 2001. The flag, the anthem, the idyllic setting of Sag Harbor with its old American charm, its freedom from the lights of cities and shopping centres that might 'obliterate the night sky' is an insular vision.[68] It is, according to Gray, a Pretend yard of Life. Arguably the return to 'traditional values', to certainties such as Gray's relationship to his children, his family and the patriotism in the Sag Harbor School Assembly are nostalgic. However, Gray also made a career by shaping a persona that was sceptical of its cultural formation and the problematic hierarchies that exist in American and indeed Western culture. Thus, an alternative reading suggests that Sag Harbor is, metaphorically, the nation and that the repeated appearance of flags, family and freedom in *Morning, Noon and Night* raise questions about the degree of insularity that characterized American cultural power at the close of an American century.

The contrast of these two monologues at either end of Gray's career reveals his innovative and radical manipulation of the solo form. As Gray wrote in his journal, 'The monolog form is more open. It is not set in print. It is a wheel that spins in a new way each night. It is more true to how reality is.'[69] His legacy is essential to understanding the reassertion of monologue as a genre of contemporary American performance because of its characteristic combination of playful aesthetics and politics. Gray's impact on the development of monologue leaves the genre uniquely positioned to be politically insightful for, in the tradition of the Jeremiad, he offers a rhetorical vision of the United States in the late twentieth century. Gray's work situates the autobiographical confession as an unlikely mode of critical contemplation and reflection on history and ideology within Western, and specifically American, culture.

4

Post-punk Monologue and the Performances of Laurie Anderson

In November 1984, in the same year Spalding Gray first performed *Swimming to Cambodia*, President Ronald Reagan was elected to a second term, following the Los Angeles Olympics and a successful campaign in which he proclaimed it was 'Morning again in America'. Reagan combined rigid patriotism and hokey charm with a sophisticated use and understanding of visual forms of communication and the possibilities of the television medium.[1] His performances were cinematic: carefully location scouted, stage-managed, scripted and filmed with the TV audience in mind; the presidential image was provided to the news media and public as a polished product. As key media adviser Mike Deaver noted of this approach to televisual politics, 'We understood one thing that the evening news wouldn't admit. And that was they weren't news they were entertainment.'[2]

Television dominated the cultural sphere too, as the popular influence of media phenomena like MTV (first introduced in 1981) was changing music, visual style and entertainment with songs from innovative post-punk bands such as Talking Heads and Devo played on high rotation. Seminal theatre artists such as the Wooster Group were also drawing on televisual culture in their works. This world of New York City avant-garde performance was gaining significant mass exposure through events such as Robert Wilson's *the CIVIL warS*, which was created for the 1984 Summer Olympics and included music from Talking Heads' David Byrne.

It is from this context that the work of Laurie Anderson – including music, visual and conceptual artwork, sculpture, film and live performance – arises. Similar to her contemporaries Gray and Karen Finley, Anderson was part of the New York art-scene in the 1970s and early 1980s. Famous for her high-tech performances featuring avant-garde electronic music, Anderson is an accomplished musician who provided the soundtracks for the film versions of Gray's monologues *Swimming to Cambodia* and *Monster in a Box*. She was signed to Warner Brothers for a six album deal after the success of her song 'O Superman' in 1981, making her one of the first performance artists to 'cross over' from downtown New York City into the world of popular entertainment.[3] Indeed, following the success of 'O Superman', Anderson was a symbol of art-scene 'cool' with her spiked hair and oversized tuxedo jacket. In Australian high school art classes in the 1980s it was not uncommon to hear her voice issuing from a mix-tape.

Anderson's major solo performances include *Americans on the Move* that later became *United States* (1983), *Empty Places* (1989), *Songs and Stories from Moby Dick* (1999) and the recent trilogy *Happiness* (2002), *The End of the Moon* (2004) and *Dirtday!* (2012). These works invigorate the history of American monologue from the 1980s through the way they combine a post-punk monologic voice, and notions of sampling and quotation, within a multimedia environment.

United States is a particularly significant work as it brought together several disparate techniques into an epic performance that situated the lone human body and autobiographical material within an environment of sophisticated technologies.[4] Indeed, Anderson has engaged with new technology in performance over four decades. Her use and invention of elements such as the 'tape-bow violin', which enables the playing of cut-up texts and tape loops, high-powered lights placed in her mouth or mounted onto her hands, and the electronic amplification and modification of her voice and body parts, are surreal post-punk experiments.

In addition to her use of multimedia in performance, Anderson's works are built around the simplicity of the solo voice, which is extrapolated, illustrated and enhanced by music, images and technology. Her monologues typically employ an ironic, whimsical and deadpan voice and reflect upon American culture and the technologically mediated lives of Western subjects. Yet, monologue has rarely been at the centre of the discussion of Anderson's performances, though theorists have previously noted Anderson's use of anecdote and solo voice.[5]

Anderson's monologues frequently incorporate cut-ups and found texts. In this way, they recall dada, the music of John Cage, and Robert Wilson and Philip Glass' landmark opera *Einstein on the Beach* (1975). Her performances also developed alongside the work of other US avant-garde punk and post-punk artists such as Patti Smith, Talking Heads, Devo and her partner the late Lou Reed. This work sees crossovers between art, rock music, punk, post-punk, and poetry that is indicative of the New York scene of the late 1970s, supported by venues and institutions such as CBGB and the Brooklyn Academy of Music (BAM). Beyond their New York specificity, Anderson's monologues also bring to mind other related traditions of American storytelling and music, such as the use of quotation, sampling and the Call and

Figure 4.1 Laurie Anderson, in *Empty Places* 1989 (*Photo*: Linda Alaniz-Hornsby).

Response that can be heard in the playful direct address of much hip hop and rap.

In Anderson's monologues, reoccurring motifs include the influence of militarization, mass media and large-scale advances in technology on contemporary culture.[6] Anderson once described her view of America as 'off-shore', meaning she performs from a perspective that comes from disconnected positions, such as above from planes or satellites.[7]

This interest in evoking a wide-angle view on various social narratives is an important feature of her work. Anderson has a strong American and international profile – she is a frequent headliner of international festivals and has been artist-in-residence at NASA (2003). As such, the dissemination of her work across a range of media gives her monologues a global presence both as artistic products and as commodities.

The inclusion here of two examples of Anderson's work: *Home of the Brave* (1985) and *Empty Places* (1989); will revisit her performances from the 1980s to explore how Anderson expands the core features of the monologue – solitary speech and a single figure alone onstage – by incorporating spoken text within an experimental technoscape. I concentrate exclusively on Anderson's performances from this period, because of their critical response to the economic and social policies of Reagan-era America and their links to the countercultural history of spoken word and music in American culture, such as influence of the Beats, post-punk and hip hop.

Home of the Brave

Home of the Brave premiered in 1985 as a concert film of the earlier live performance *Mister Heartbreak* (1984). The film is comprised of text, songs, instrumental sections, dance and movement sequences, and large-scale film and still projections. Anderson performs the bulk of the material and is assisted by a backing band, supporting singers and a cameo from cult figure and Beat writer William S. Burroughs.

The performance is a sequence of short scenes and does not contain a clear unifying narrative, although themes including the complexities of language and the influence of electronic products and services on the lives of Western subjects feature repeatedly.

The film opens on a silhouette of a figure wearing a white suit with white gloves, shoes, a full-faced mask and a black shirt with a white tie, dancing against a dark blue backdrop. A futuristic violin rests near its feet. Several other masked figures enter the space as the dancing figure picks up and plays the electric violin, Anderson's own invention, which emits electronic hoots and hums. The figure, Anderson, speaks:

> Good evening. Now, I'm no mathematician but I'd like to talk about just a couple of numbers that have been really bothering me lately, and they are zero and one. Now first, let's take a look at zero. To be a zero means to be nothing, a nobody, a has-been, a zilch.
>
> On the other hand, just about everybody wants to be number one. To be number one means to be a winner, top of the heap, the acme. And there seems to be a strange kind of national obsession with this particular number.
>
> Now, in my opinion, the problem with these numbers is that they are just too close – leaves very little room for everybody else. Just not enough range.[8]

This solitary speech draws upon the traditions of the introductory monologue with the formal greeting of 'Good evening' and a presentation delivered directly to the audience like a lecture. The single speaker, the 'I', is obvious. However, in this case the identity of the speaking I is confused because (though the central figure is assumed and eventually shown to be Anderson) the voice is electronically altered so as to sound deep and distorted, and the costume and gestures of the body give an initial impression of androgyny and anonymity.

Indeed, the potential for the voice to enable an expression of coherent individuality is confused because Anderson's voice both is and is not her own. Her disembodied voice can be altered, from high pitch to low and through variations in between, dislocating to some extent her (gendered/fixed/authentic) vocal identity.⁹ Therefore, at the beginning of *Home of the Brave*, Anderson performs a persona that is not recognizable as either masculine or feminine.

Vocal processing was first used by Anderson in 1978 and still reoccurs in her work. In earlier decades, she often referred to the voice heard in *Home of the Brave* as the 'Voice of Authority' and it is only in recent years that Anderson's partner, the late Lou Reed, reportedly ascribed the voice with a gender and a name, Fenway Bergamot.¹⁰ The naming of Fenway suggests a kind of familiarity with the vocal technique, because it is one that has developed over years of use and improvisation.

At the time of *Home of the Brave* however, the '0s and 1s' monologue uses this new technology to call for gender heterogeneity and more 'range'. It might even be read as a kind of post-human figure, a theory popularized by Donna Haraway's *A Cyborg Manifesto* (1985) that continues to be used as a productive site for exploring the hybridization of the human through the erasure of traditional species categorization.¹¹ Anderson's work can also be linked to explorations of hybrid-forms, and the subcultural experimentation with video and electronics as part of the post-punk scene of the mid-1980s and the cyberculture aesthetic typified by Ridley Scott's *Blade Runner* (1982).¹² The binary code of computing – entirely reliant on different combinations of zeros and ones – is seen to be too much of a closed circuit just as Anderson, through the modulation of her voice and her body, confuses the similarly closed circuit of binary gender codes. These gender binaries are present, but Anderson wilfully contradicts the hierarchies implicit in them by performing in a voice that is neither quite male, nor female, nor the individual voice of 'Laurie Anderson'.¹³

Anderson's self-conscious use of digital technology in performance of monologue is an integral part of this shifting version of the self. According to media theorist Sean Cubitt:

> Anderson's constantly remodulated vocals not only enact the decay of individuality that accomplishes its ossification; they also continue the

estrangement of the voice from the body in which we can recognize the theft of knowledge under the guise of information. Our speech is not our own.[14]

Home of the Brave sees an opening monologue that creates hybrid voices that stand in stark contrast to earlier forms of the genre that rely upon the notion of the individual speaking self.

Moreover, as the text progresses Anderson becomes dwarfed by a projection of multiplying 0s and 1s that quickly fill the entire screen behind her. 'What we are actually looking at here', she suggests, 'are the building blocks of the Modern Computer Age.' The speech and voice marks a significant deviation away from the traditional introductory monologue – the prelude that invites the audience into the dramatic or autobiographic world through a seductive and intimate use of solo speech – as it brings a synthetic flatness to the speaking I. It is particularly indicative of the performance persona that Anderson creates, which is ironic and frequently altered by technological means even as it seems to draw on personal anecdote or observation as the basis for the spoken text.

From the 1980s on, Anderson consistently employs cutting-edge voice modifiers, invented instruments, multiple projections and synthesizers, all used on a scale more closely associated with a rock concert than a monologue performance. In *Home of the Brave* Anderson, as the androgynous figure, distances herself from the speaking I of the opening monologue because her voice and body are both modified. The electronic modulation renders her expression flat and strips away much of the 'individuality' of Anderson's 'normal' voice that is heard soon after. Moreover, that Anderson is known for her continuing use of complex large-scale technologies, reliant in part upon the system of 0s and 1s, is a further deliberate irony.

This work draws heavily on the theatre, music and new technologies of the 1980s. In the theatre, artists such as the Wooster Group, Richard Foreman and the work of Robert Wilson, such as the previously mentioned *Einstein on the Beach* and *the CIVIL warS* (1984), use a kind of non-expressive narration and stand as notable influences on *Home of the Brave*. In particular, Wilson's operatic performances include architectural design motifs, the visualization of language and texts by Christopher Knowles that employ 'non-dramatic, often banal conversational passages' in performance.[15]

Concurrently, American bands such as Talking Heads and Devo began to use a similar 'deadpan' quality in their textual delivery. Interestingly, the post-punk artists in the period of 1978–84 also borrowed heavily from modernist literary, art, dramatic and performance histories as inspiration for lyric style, expression and performance personae. Bands like Talking Heads make a more oblique treatment of politics, wherein mordant sarcasm works to critique contemporary apathy and dysfunction, in contrast to punk's declamatory rage.

Further, the Wooster Group experiments with televisual and video technology to fragment and enhance narrative and voice onstage. No longer is the complex inner world of the character at the centre of these monologic texts, but a decaying individuality and estranged voice that recalls the work of Samuel Beckett and also the kitsch synthetic voices familiar to the music of Devo.

One way of reading this style of deadpan speech is through the notion of 'cool' in performance. According to Hans-Thies Lehmann, writing here on West-European theatre:

> Cool is the name for emotionality that has lost its 'personal' expression to such an extent that all feelings can be expressed only in quotations marks, and all other emotions that drama was once able to show must now pass through the 'irony filter' of a film or media aesthetic.[16]

While Lehmann is responding to primarily European examples, the notion of cool as it appears in the 1980s art-house scene in New York can readily be applied to the work of American artists like Blondie and the performances of Wilson and Anderson. Perhaps most similar to Anderson's work are the lyrics and performance of Talking Heads' David Byrne, whose songs frequently use a kind of plain-spoken interior monologue, almost expressionless delivery, and explore objects of contemporary culture: cars, buildings, TV, appliances, cities; rather than subjective emotions or personal revelation.[17] As Byrne sings in the opening to *Once in a Lifetime* (1981), 'And you may find yourself behind the wheel of a large automobile' and ask 'How did I get here?'[18] Similarly, in the second text from *Home of the Brave* (that follows a song) Anderson stands alone in a spotlight dressed in a silvery-white full-body suit and tells a story of her 'last birthday' in her 'normal' voice. She narrates:

> A while ago, on my last birthday, I had a couple of people read my palms and, oddly enough, they both said the same thing about my past lives. They said, in your first life on this planet you were a cow, and then you were a bird, and then you were a hat. And I said, hat? And they said, yeah. The feathers from the bird were made into a hat and that counted as a kind of half-life. And then I was hundreds and hundreds of Rabbis. This is my first life as a woman, which explains quite a few things. Anyway, if any of you have any Rabbinical questions I'll be out in the lobby, after the concert, and I'd be happy to try to dredge up some answers.[19]

In comparison to Gray's at times frenzied pace, Anderson delivers this speech slowly. Indeed, her monologues are dryly observational and allegorical rather than confessional, peppered with deliberate pauses and characterized by a wry poetry. While the material for the text is often autobiographical – Anderson's birthday recollection encourages a conflation between the performing persona and the 'real-life' self, as she refers to 'the concert', 'the lobby', 'my last birthday' and 'my first life as a woman' – there is also distance between the persona and the autobiographical provenance of the spoken text. The first-person narration, along with Anderson's now unaltered voice, emphasizes the autobiographical and truthful content of the text. However, like David Byrne's songs for Talking Heads, there is a lack of emotive or subjective signifiers – we simply do not know why Anderson chose to have her palm read on her last birthday or how she feels about being hundreds and hundreds of Rabbis in her past lives. This means that the strangely depersonalized narrative and almost sardonic delivery makes it difficult to gauge how authentic her stories are, or whether they have merely been carefully constructed to give an impression of autobiographic reality.[20]

The use of depersonalized voice and deadpan style continues to figure in more recent works of American theatre. Indeed, the work of Young Jean Lee or the Nature Theater of Oklahoma extends the history of the American deadpan voice in performance, in which Anderson, Wilson, Byrne and others remain as key figures. The work of the Nature Theatre in their epic *Life and Times* (2010–) is particularly interesting as it uses monologue, based on recordings of extended phone conversations with company member Kristin Worrall, as the basis for a multilayered durational performance in which verbatim transcriptions constitute the text. *Life and Times* is a Spalding Gray-like attempt to chronicle an entire life, from birth to thirty-five years of age, that takes the form of an exact verbatim script with pauses, ums, ahs, likes, repetitions, deviations and even toilet breaks intact. Episode one revisited the travails of early childhood and schooling:

> Reading groups – reading groups yeah, we're separated in all these different tiers and I guess I was a very, even though I didn't fashion myself as this, but I was very quiet and um, a very quiet child and so they ... put me into the lowest reading group which was like, I was with like the re ... two other really like ... dumb kids.[21]

Life and Times demonstrates two familiar strategies of recent writing for performance that I will return to in the closing chapter of this book: first, the attention on the minute and mundane details of the everyday and the capturing of everyday speech with its unique lexicon intact; and second, the interest in making dialogue – or in this case an interview – into a series of monologic texts that reject naturalistic notions of character and dialogue.

Similar to these more recent uses of monologue, the performing persona in *Home of the Brave* avoids creating a coherent dramatic character. Instead, in a manner that foreshadows the epic use of depersonalized speech in *Life and Times*, the text seems self-consciously 'quoted' and encourages playful reflection upon the authenticity of the persona performing, the idea of memory, and the material performed. Anderson's idiosyncratic asides perpetuate a style of almost banal quotation. Indeed, the two opening texts of *Home of the Brave* draw upon the epic traditions of monologue with elements of formal presentation, introduction, direct audience address, 'personal' memory and quotation. Whereas monologues have historically been used as vehicles for authoritative speech and voice, Anderson uses her Voice of Authority to trouble notions of the gendered speaking subject. Moreover, Anderson's second monologue also begins to push at the bounds of the genre as it draws in the deadpan speech of post-punk to challenge notions of a fixed, authentic and cohesive individual self.

In *Home of the Brave* the distinctions between the '0s and 1s' monologue, with its exploration of language in a digital age, and the seemingly autobiographical 'Birthday' monologue is keen. According to Gunter Berghaus, Anderson's monologues contrast 'futuristic high-tech modernity and very personal feeling, of cool factualness and surreal dreamscapes'.[22] Again in a manner that recalls the songs of Talking Heads, Anderson describes moments of everyday American life and engagement with ubiquitous objects such as TVs, telephones and computers. However, she enhances these monologic texts by juxtaposing her small human body and the single voice with the epic scale of the technological apparatus surrounding her.[23]

The numbered world of digitization is far from the recollection of Anderson's birthday monologue that stresses the human contact of the hand upon hand through the palm reading. There is a contrast too between the rational and mathematical world of computerization and the metaphysical and vaguely hippyish culture of the Shaman. In these two monologues, the combination of the autobiographical everyday is placed against the operation of contemporary technology. Indeed, the complex amalgamation of synthesizers and projections with the solitary speech from a human body establishes Anderson's performance as a hybrid product. The innovation of these monologues is their inclusion within this multimedia environment: as speech acts they are fully integrated into the performance and encourage consideration of their mediatized context.

The relationship of Anderson's monologues to one another is ambiguous, as is their ultimate message or politics. However, the notion of building unconnected stories, one on the other, can also be seen as a method of avoiding narrative linearity.[24] Further, Anderson's disjointed monologues resemble media sound bites that could almost be rearranged in performance.[25] While this might recall Brechtian episodic techniques, it more closely resembles the sampling and mixing of quotations that is typical of hip hop. Through the construction of her high-tech persona, and the episodic structure of the texts, Anderson develops monologues that are detached and ironic. This form radicalizes the excesses of confessional or 'personal' narratives prevalent in earlier modes, as seen in the modern traditions of monologue in drama, and draws instead on alternative American traditions of the solo voice such as the techniques of the cut-up found in Beat poetry, the synthetic deadpan voice of post-punk and the hip hop tactic of stylized quotation seen in the actions of rap or DJ'ing.

Yet, while Anderson's monologues deflect formal unity, her texts do not ignore the American cultural and political context in which they are produced – in which the rapid advancement of technology during the Reagan era that saw the rise of MTV and television culture alongside the development of the 'Star Wars' strategic missile defence system. The 0s and 1s monologue ironically indicates the commodity status of the performance of *Home of the Brave* and the status of performance in the 1980s as mediatized, mass cultural commodity. The second example Anderson gives of the digital code demonstrates this:

> It is an expression of the first two numbers of my home phone. The remaining digits are available in a limited edition of autographed floppy disks on sale at the souvenir stand in the lobby.[26]

In the 1980s context, the era of market boom and 'Greed is Good', art and performance pieces became increasingly entangled with the technologies of mass consumption. Anderson's transference of parts of her performance and its 'aura' to floppy disc, at once easily copied and disposable, ironically situates her work, along with her status as a popular artist, as reproducible mass commodities. This monologue also comments on the increasingly prevalent electronic reproduction of artworks in 1980s culture, as it draws attention to the removal of the artwork from the non-reproducible realm and its more sophisticated relationship with new media.[27]

Anderson's monologue persona figures across a number of media. This means that her performance is no longer specifically tied to its live version onstage, but is replicated and remediated.[28] Yet, solo speech remains a critical element in Anderson's hybrid approach. Her conflation of new technologies and a 1980s post-punk aesthetic into texts that use a detached performance persona expands the capabilities of the monologue genre. Moreover, as in her later work *Empty Places*, her use of monologue continues to situate the genre as a means of alternative address, reflection and commentary on contemporary American culture.

Empty Places

Premiering in 1989 *Empty Places* is composed of a series of monologues and songs. As in the earlier *United States* and *Home of the Brave*, the monologues are performed in conjunction with numerous other multimedia and performance elements including the projection of a collection of images; film and slides of New York City taken by Anderson.[29] The songs also feature on the album *Strange Angels* (1989). The performance was a large-scale technological event, with twenty-foot projection towers, forty-five slide and film projectors and high-tech gadgetry of MIDI keyboards and voice altering electronics. Super-titled in ten different languages, *Empty Places* toured to fifty cities in the United States and Canada, had a brief series of five concerts in South Africa and was performed in thirty-three European cities.[30] It is also an overtly political work that Anderson created after claiming that she had 'slept through the Reagan Era politically'.[31] The monologues in *Empty Places* critique, through a 'cool' performance of solo speech, the influence of neoliberal economics on 1980s US society.

In *Capitalism and Freedom* (1962) economic theorist Milton Friedman argues that 'competitive capitalism', the organization of economic activity through a free market, is a necessary condition for political freedom, because it privileges economic freedom and encourages an individual consumer's right to diverse choice.[32] Friedman's theories are a key influence in the displacement, in the mid-1970s, of previously dominant social democratic political ideas and policies with a number of market-orientated ideologies. These free market approaches, though they are not distinct to the United States, begin to dominate political and economic policy throughout much of the West from the 1980s onwards. These approaches also take on various titles: Reaganomics in the United States, Thatcherism in Britain and economic rationalism in Australia, though they can be grouped under the term that will be used here: neoliberalism.

Neoliberalism encourages private capital, competition and the consumer's right to 'choice' where the individual consumer is the ultimate manifestation of difference. A particular emphasis on personal responsibility and a lessening in the role of government in administering social programmes is characterized by then British Prime Minister Margaret Thatcher's oft-quoted interview with *Women's Own* magazine in 1987:

> Who is society? There is no such thing! There are individual men and women and there are families and no government can do anything except through people and people look to themselves first. ... There is no such thing as society. There is living tapestry of men and women and people and the beauty of that tapestry and the quality of our lives will depend upon how much each of us is prepared to take responsibility for ourselves.[33]

According to Thatcher, governments should no longer be held responsible for 'society'. Instead, the responsibility falls on the people, with the inference being that the government's chief domestic role is not to manage large-scale institutions such as health or education, but rather to encourage freedom of choice for individuals through increasing privatization and the free market. It is the intersection of such neoliberal economic thinking with neoconservative social and foreign policy that informs much commentary on American politics during the last three decades.

Empty Places can be read as a critical commentary on the effects of neoliberal ideology on 1980s US culture, as Anderson employs her cool style of monologue to reveal a growing economic and social inequality. In the monologue 'Falling', Anderson recounts tripping into an open manhole on a New York street and meeting a homeless woman in an emergency room:

> A couple of months ago I was getting out of a cab
> and I turned and fell right down
> into an open manhole.
> Yeah, right into the New York City
> sewer system.[34]

The monologue is autobiographical, yet distant: a familiar feature of earlier works. In its strange mix of the banal and the extraordinary, the anecdote also makes the spectator doubt its veracity, as Anderson goes on:

> And when I was down there, I looked around
>   and said to myself:
> This is exactly like one of my songs!
> And then after I'd been down there
> a little longer
> I thought:
> No, it's not.
> So the ambulance took me to the hospital and parked
> my wheelchair in the emergency room.
> And I sat there ... [35]

As distinct from the monologues in *Home of the Brave*, 'Falling' concentrates on Anderson's lived local social context: the homeless

Figure 4.2 Laurie Anderson, in *Empty Places* 1989 (with Globe) (*Photo*: Linda Alaniz-Hornsby).

and disenfranchised subjects of New York City. Previously, Anderson's monologues explored wider social questions about the influence of technology and the mass media yet, in *Empty Places*, the texts focus on the heightened everyday.

> I sat there watching this long line of misery
> passing by. Gunshot wounds, stabbing victims,
> and as the night wore on,
> the old people started to come in.
>
> And there was this old woman sitting next to me.
> She was a bum and her feet were bleeding
> and swollen up like grapefruits
> and she kept saying:
> 'Look at my feet! Look at my feet!'
> And I couldn't ... [36]

Anderson's meeting with the homeless woman is a documentation of an unlikely urban experience. However, the cool, almost calculated, delivery with which Anderson speaks also creates a sense of her detachment from the situation. Anderson's anecdote about the 'gunshot wounds and stabbing victims' is told from a removed position. Her vocal pitch and ironic retelling once again distances the reality of the event from its retelling in performance.

Anderson's description of the swollen feet of the woman beside her passes through the 'irony filter', that Lehmann links to 'cool' performance, along with the media aesthetic that characterizes Anderson's monologues. Yet, this 'cool' style does not necessarily indicate either social insensitivity, or the ideological blindness of the petty bourgeoisie. Rather, it arguably demonstrates, in Lehmann's words, 'a desire for new forms of communication' that confront social and political conditions, while taking into account the 'mass dissemination of mediatized reality'.[37] Therefore, while commenting upon the situation of the homeless in a detached manner, 'Falling' is also depiction of rarely glimpsed American subjects (the 'long line of misery') that reflects social inequity in 1980s US culture.

Anderson's reluctance to look at the homeless woman's swollen feet operates as a larger metaphor too, one in which the affluent artist and comfortable Westerner, is unable to react to the uncomfortable 'reality' of his or her surrounds. Indeed, the juxtaposed images of Anderson's accidental descent and the homeless woman's pleas to 'Look at my feet', which Anderson cannot do, reprises her monologic tactics of irony and ambiguity. After all, Anderson only ended up in hospital because she was figuratively incapable of watching her own feet. Again, as Lehmann suggests, cool performances are those in which 'moral indignation does not take place where it would have been expected; likewise dramatic excitation is lacking, even though reality is depicted in ways that are hard to bear'.[38] As such, the 'Falling' monologue also reveals the dynamic impact that the calculated use of a performance persona that is detached rather than active may have.

Similar to the post-punk artists working around the same time, ambivalence towards grand salvational or revolutionary narratives of history and polemical politics is part of the texture of this work. The personal as political is refigured here, not as a form of subjective autobiography, but as the juxtaposition of Anderson's cool style with the poignancy of her narrative underlines the homeless woman's position as a forgotten by-product of individualized global capitalism. Individual freedom, choice and financial growth in the United States is shown to overshadow the human figures in Anderson's monologue.

In 'Falling', the last observation does not come from Anderson, but rather from an old homeless man who, unlike Anderson, is able to look at the old woman's bleeding feet.

> There was an old man sitting on the other side of her
> and she kept saying:
> 'My feet. Look at my feet!'
> And he did.
> And he said:
> 'That must really hurt'.[39]

The elderly man's words close the piece. This final image of the monologue depicts his 'ordinary' caring reaction towards the homeless woman. The final line of 'Falling', 'That must really hurt', is also multilayered because it has meaning beyond the New York hospital setting and reflects upon the social climate of the 1980s. *Empty Places* suggests that the legacy of the Reagan administration – so often portrayed as a period characterized by American confidence, patriotism and economic power – was also characterized by intolerance and self-interest that manifested in growing social and economic inequality. The performance of *Empty Places* critiques the excesses of the neoliberal, market-orientated approach wherein the individual is primarily responsible for paying for health and welfare services. The homeless addressed in 'Falling' are indicative of those subjects who are economically unable to do so.

The homeless woman is a single human subject placed in contrast with the great wealth and financial power of New York. The monologue reflects upon the city that never sleeps and a city that is divided between wealth and poverty. *Empty Places*, while it contains little didactic or polemical political commentary, returns to the theme of social disenfranchisement throughout. Again, it is the seeming simplicity of the solitary voice and the details drawn from the almost banal everyday that gives 'Falling' resonance in the wider American culture. Anderson's coolness enhances this effect, because the texture of the monologue is not wholly individual or subjective: instead, it is ambiguous and multilayered.

Moreover, any reading of Anderson's work must also take into account the interrelation of the monologues throughout *Empty Places*. This is because her monologues typically build in significance through bumping and rubbing up against each other, dodgem-car-style. In this way, the performance of *Empty Places* only enables full reflection on the contemporary social context after consideration of all of the monologues included.

Indeed, critical consideration of American culture continues in *Empty Places*, through the monologue 'Pobre Mexico'. This monologue returns to the theme of economic and social disenfranchisement by drawing a distinction between the affluent United States and the poverty of Third World Mexico. 'Pobre Mexico' contrasts the wildness of the Rio Grande river, which 'just keeps flooding and changing course and messing up all the maps', with the rigidity of a signpost on the Mexico/American border that reads: WILD RIVER – REASONABLE MEN. As Anderson states, the sign is a reminder of flows of history and power:

> How often the river moves
> and property changes hands
> and Mexico becomes America
> and America, Mexico.[40]

The monologue highlights too, the significant gap between the West and the rest of the world. The suggested meaning of the sign is to remind all concerned how easily the river can alter and restructure the border. Yet it also makes clear that 'reasonable men' would never allow any substantial change: Mexico will never be America; America will never be Mexico. This monologue also alludes to ongoing historical tensions in the relationship between the United States and Mexico.

In the 1980s these points of potential conflict included the War on Drugs taking place across central and Latin America, the weakness of the Mexican economy (exacerbated by neoliberal austerity measures), and the reframing of Mexican immigration as a matter of national security. In 1985 President Reagan argued that the United States had 'lost control of its borders' and was now subject to an 'invasion' of illegal immigrants. Subsequently, the 1986 Immigration Reform and Control Act saw increased funding for border security and a crackdown on employers who hired undocumented migrant workers, alongside an amnesty for illegal immigrants that had lived in the United States since 1982.[41] As such, Anderson's monologue reflects upon gaps in wealth and power that are framed by US hegemony.

> The sign that should really be posted
> at the border is
> > that old Mexican proverb,
> > the one that goes:
>
> > POBRE MEJICO
> > TAN LEJOS DE DIOS
> > TAN CERCA DE LOS
> > ESTADOS UNIDOS
>
> > ----------------------------
>
> > POOR MEXICO
> > SO FAR FROM GOD
> > SO CLOSE TO THE
> > UNITED STATES[42]

As distinct from 'Falling', there is less of a personal narrative in 'Pobre Mexico'. Instead, Anderson plays the role of an observer in this piece. As such, 'Pobre Mexico' utilizes the informative capacity of the monologue. It offers critical contemplation of American historical dominance placed in opposition to the moveable Mexican border.

Finally, further demonstration of the sophisticated irony employed in Anderson's monologues can be observed in the 'Listen, Honey'. This text depicts a protest outside the Playboy Bunny Club in New York where Anderson (and others) were demonstrating against the economic exploitation of women and their treatment. The protestors argued that Playboy was treating women like animals:

> I had drawn up some pamphlets to illustrate this:
> pictures of chicks and bunnies
> and foxes and pussycats and other animals
> that had come to symbolize women
> and I was handing them out ... [43]

The politics of gender, economic and racial inequality are present in both 'Pobre Mexico' and 'Listen, Honey'. 'Listen, Honey' focuses upon the New York context of the monologue, however, and Anderson also exhibits a performing persona that rather than simply observing is engaged in the protest march. Indeed, the monologue describes Anderson's encounter, mid-march, with a Playboy bunny on her way to work:

> I gave her one of the free pamphlets.
>
> > And she said: 'Listen, honey,
> > I make eight hundred dollars a week at this job.
> > I've got three kids to support.
> > This is the best job I've ever had.
> > So if you want to talk about women and money,
> > why don't you go down
> > to the garment district
> > where women make 10 cents an hour
> > and why don't you go and march around
> > down there?'
> >
> > And I said:
> > 'Hmmmmmmmmmmmmmmmm[44]

In 'Listen, Honey' there is a disjunction between the ethical imperative of the marchers and the economic imperative of the Playboy Bunny. Indeed, the Playboy Bunny contends that her employment is necessary because she has three children to support. The didactic aspects of the protestor's approach, which assumes that exploitation is taking place, is clear only after the Playboy Bunny provides this unexpected perspective. 'Listen, Honey' evokes the multiple perspectives present in political debates regarding individuals, where a Playboy Bunny draws attention to the mistreatment of women who are far worse off financially than herself. Anderson's work highlights that the politics of gender (like that of race, class and identity) are complex and that the primacy of the notion of individual wealth creation, a key element of neoliberal economics, is deeply intertwined with other aspects of everyday American life and the historical mythology of the American Dream. As she adds in a later monologue,

> You know, for every dollar a man makes,
> a woman makes 62 cents.
> Fifty years ago, it was 62 cents.
> Soooooooo ... with that kind of luck,
> it'll be the year 3888
> before we make a buck [45]

In considering the interrelationship between Anderson's texts we are invited to make links, for example, between economic inequality and the realities of poverty, homelessness, border security and sexual exploitation. Ending 'Listen, Honey' with a contemplative 'Hmm ...' however, neither discounts nor celebrates the opinion of the Playboy Bunny. This ambiguous ending makes no claim to the ultimate truth in any moral or ethical sense, instead the monologue is left to brush up against the musings of the Mexican proverb and the feet of a homeless woman. Anderson's monologues change perspectives between a range of Western subjects in a way that ensures critical insight into 1980s American culture and the social effects that are inevitably caused by politics and ideology at work.

In Anderson's aesthetically complex works, monologue is continually privileged as a fundamental element operating within a hybridized and technological mode of performance. Situating these works in relation to post-punk aesthetics, alongside the strategies associated with postmodern solo performance, shows that Anderson's monologues combine cool aesthetic techniques, ironic autobiography and multimedia technology to enable a reflection on the commodity culture characteristic of global capitalism in the United States. Drawing on quotation and ideas of sampling and mixing that are common to hip hop and post-punk, her monologues reflect upon the changing nature of communication, language and individuality in the contemporary Western context. Anderson uses monologue to comment on 1980s American culture and society, in which her use of ironic fragments and new technology furthers the sophistication of contemporary American monologue.

After Anderson, the solo monologue performance can be both intimate speech and large-scale event. This radical shift in scale reaffirms the rejuvenation of the genre from the 1970s and draws on the rich history of the solo speaker in the United States as a countercultural figure who provides alternative and artistic commentary on everyday life and world events.

5

Rights Monologue and the Work of Anna Deavere Smith

After twelve years of Republican leadership, the last decade of the twentieth century saw the election of Democrat Bill Clinton as president following the 1992 election. The 1990s were characterized by a period of extended economic prosperity in the United States, Clinton's centrist third-way approach to economics, an impeachment scandal, as well as attempts to reform welfare and to achieve peace between Israel and Palestine. It was also in 1992 that writer/performer Anna Deavere Smith rose to prominence through her one-person show *Fires in the Mirror: Crown Heights, Brooklyn, and Other Identities*, in which Smith builds upon the history of American monologue by combining documentary materials, techniques and research in solo performance.

Earlier, in 1982, Smith had begun researching a project entitled *On the Road: A Search for American Character*. Initially, *On the Road* was conceived as an investigation into the development of an acting technique based around a re-enactment of different 'manners' of speech and voice, as the basis for being able to understand the essence of a character's individuality. It is also, through its reference to Jack Kerouac's Beat classic *On the Road*, immediately situated within the unofficial canon of American counterculture literature and Kerouac's own earlier performance of (distinctly American) subjectivity. In the words of Smith,

> If we were to inhabit the speech pattern of another, and walk in the speech of another, we could find the individuality of the other and experience that individuality viscerally.[1]

During these investigations, however, the project has evolved into a series of solo performances as Smith creates theatre texts from the words of the everyday subjects she interviews. Smith's process includes interviews and research into the lives and stories, the unheard oral history of 'ordinary' Americans from a variety of economic and ethnic backgrounds. The interviews, or parts of them, are then re-performed by Smith as verbatim monologues. Her major solo works include *Fires in the Mirror* (1992), *Twilight: Los Angeles, 1992* (1993) and *Let Me Down Easy* (2008). Sometimes based on a single occurrence or situation of conflict, such as the Brooklyn Heights riots in 1991 (*Fires in the Mirror*), or an important national topic such as the health system (*Let Me Down Easy*), Smith's work explores notions of race, class and community in American society.

Explicitly focusing on the words of others, rather than her own, Smith's performances engage with the complex narratives, multiple identities and ethnicities present in the American social and cultural context of the 1990s and 2000s. Her work gained a significant US audience following the translation of *Fires in the Mirror* into a nationwide PBS television special in 1993 and has been well documented ever since.[2] However, her work has been rarely situated in relation to the US history of monologue and performance traditions that use solo speech – through the modes of oratory speech, sermon, music, poetry or protest – as an engagement with civil rights discourse.

Twilight: Los Angeles, 1992 is an important social document of American culture at the close of the presidency of George Bush, and the end of a Republican era that began with Ronald Reagan's election in 1981. Smith's work expands the monologue genre by situating solo performance techniques alongside the traditions of 'documentary' or 'verbatim' theatre. Documentary theatre, a form that has become increasingly prevalent during the last decade, is frequently monologic, non-dramatic and part of an oral traditional rooted in social, political and cultural issues.[3] It also extends the tradition of the monologue as a form of activist speech that highlights racial tension in American society – from Sojourner Truth to Frederick Douglass to Malcolm X to Jesse Jackson – as Smith's performance reveals a gap between individual social experience and the workings of dominant historical and ideological narratives of race and class in American culture. *Twilight: Los Angeles, 1992* responds to issues of race and class politics in a manner that foregrounds the radical disenfranchisement of numerous Americans during the 1990s, through the use of verbatim quotation and multiple personae.

Twilight: Los Angeles, 1992

Twilight: Los Angeles, 1992 began as a commissioned theatrical work centred on the Los Angeles riots that took place in response to the notorious police beating of Rodney King in 1991 and the subsequent trial of the police officers involved. Despite widespread public outrage and the media circulation of the videotape evidence, the officers were pronounced not guilty on 29 April 1992. The riots that took place following the verdict bore witness to the discontent of the predominantly poor, urban community. It has often been argued that, following the apparent failure of the courts to prosecute the white police officers for crimes against King, the case revealed an inherent racism in American society.[4] Indeed, while Smith's performance is now over twenty years old, the fatal shooting of St Louis teenager Michael Brown by a white police officer in August 2014, which saw protests throughout the United States, suggests that underlying tensions in race and class, visible in the 1992 riots, still pervade contemporary American life.

Premiering in May 1993, just over one year after the events it explores and in the city in which the riots occurred, *Twilight: Los Angeles, 1992* contains approximately twenty-five monologues derived from initial interview texts.[5] The published text encompasses fifty monologues, with a prologue and timeline, all of which are taken from the nearly two hundred interviews conducted by Smith in the wake of the riots. The interviews include bystanders, gang members, Hollywood agents, TV personalities, religious leaders, shopkeepers, activists, academics, actors and theatre directors. Even the former president of the Los Angeles Police Commission, Stanley K. Sheinbaum, presents his views on the potential reasons and ramifications of the civil unrest.

At the start of the performance, ominous music rises and the, by now iconic, grainy images of King being assaulted are projected onto a large screen. A barefooted Smith moves towards the front of the stage. She wears black pants, a white business shirt and a tie. Smith performs each monologue in this minimal costume, though in later monologues she trades the tie for other small additions. These additions assist in the differentiation between subjects: a bowtie for the former police commissioner; a baton and protective glasses for a riot policeman, a cap and jacket for accountant Katie Miller.[6]

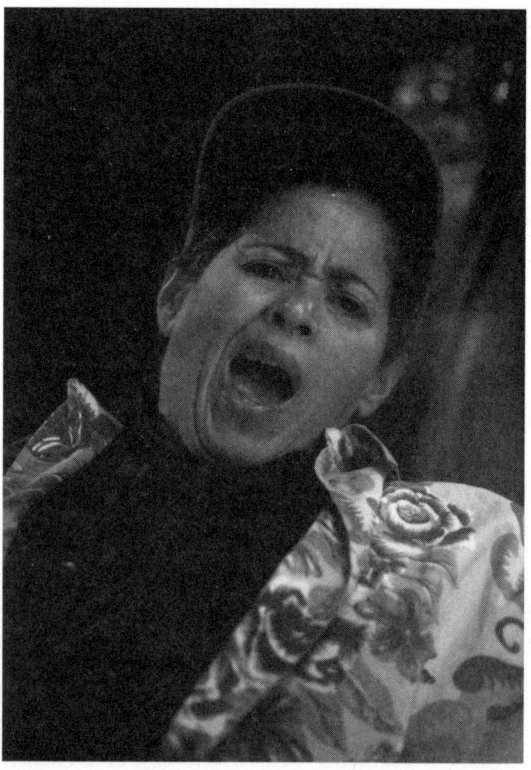

Figure 5.1 Anna Deavere Smith as Katie Miller (*Photo*: Adger W. Cowans).

This minimalist staging is consistent throughout all her performances, including the more recent *Let Me Down Easy* in which Smith appears once again with bare feet, a white shirt and black trousers.

Close to the beginning of *Twilight: Los Angeles, 1992* is Smith's rendering of a man known as Rudy Salas in a monologue titled 'My Enemy'. On the printed page the text offers a detailed description of Salas, including his occupation as a sculptor/painter and the setting in which the interview took place:

> (A large very warm man, with a blue shirt with the tails out and blue jeans and tennis shoes. He is at a dining-room table with a white tablecloth. ... He has a hearing aid in his left ear and in his right ear. He is sitting in a wooden captain's chair, medium-sized. He moves a lot in the chair, sometimes with his feet behind the front legs, and his arms hanging over the chair.)[7]

In performance this description is projected, along with the name – RUDY SALAS SNR – above the performance space. On stage, Smith sits at a desk scattered with newspapers and her live body is juxtaposed with the projected description of Salas above. In the published text, Salas's physical gestures are noted and his speech is meticulously transcribed, as can be observed in the following:

> And then at school,
>   first grade, they started telling me
>   I was inferior
>   because I was a Mexican,
>   and that's where
> *(He hits the table several times, taps, twenty-three taps until line 'the enemy' and then on 'nice white teachers' his hand sweeps the table)*
> I realized I had an enemy
> and that the enemy was those nice white teachers.
> I wonder what is it,
> why
> did I have this madness
> that I understood this?

It's not an enemy I hated.
It's not a hate thing,
the insanity that I carried with me started when I took the
    beating
from the police.
Okay, that's where the insanity came in ...[8]

The monologue in performance illustrates the physical characteristics and gestures of Salas: Smith taps her hand on the desk, and makes the sweeping gesture on cue. She also takes on both the vocal and gestural characteristics of her subject. The result is that the performance demonstrates a seductive form of imitation and mimicry. However, though monologic, Smith's work is neither self-consciously ironic nor self-reflexive, both features of the monologues of Gray and Anderson. As Carol Martin argues, while Smith's work uses a number of innovative techniques, 'pastiche, appropriation, multivocality, discontinuity, quotation, gender changes [and] lack of closure ... her work is not ambiguous'.[9] As such, the Salas monologue is performed as a 'truthful' documentation of the interview and the interview subject. It can be understood in this way as being a 'mimetic' performance.

Mimesis, as Elin Diamond states, 'denotes both the activity of representing and the result of it' taking into account both the 'embodied activity' of representing and the representation or replication of a (true) model.[10] Similarly, Smith's performance is an embodied replication of a true event. This is not to suggest, however, that Smith performs Rudy Salas as a traditional modern dramatic character with a psychological interior. Indeed, Smith's body and gender are never subsumed by the 'characters' she re-performs. Her costume, though nondescript, is different from the depiction of the subject projected above, bringing attention to the difference between Smith, the person/actress and her performance subject 'Rudy Salas'. Similarly, while her costume has masculine associations as the designated uniform of the businessman, Smith does not hide her femininity, foregrounding an obvious disjunction between Smith's body and the physical description of her subject.[11]

As such, while Smith does not perform the 'character' of Salas in a naturalistic way, the inclusion of the desk, the newspapers and Smith's costume having associations with a masculine identity, creates a different kind of accuracy or reality of the representation of Salas. Additionally, the published text of the performance not only transcribes the monologues as they would have been recorded but also shows which words or phrases were stressed. In the published work, these texts are laid out on the page much like poems. The sentences are often broken up by line breaks to preserve the rhythm of the speech, and notes on any movements made by the interview subject, or idiosyncrasies of a unique vocal pattern or pronunciation, are also included:

> I'm not a racist!
> But I have white friends, though,
> but I don't even see them as whites!
> I don't even see them as whites! And my boys,
> I had a lot of anxiety, I told
> them, 'Cooperate, man,
> something happens,
> your hands ...
> *(Puts his hands up)*
> let them call you what they want,
> be sure tell me who they are'.[12]

The introduction of these details and idiosyncrasies draws further attention to Smith's mimetic techniques. The monologue does not rely upon autobiographical material in the manner of Gray or Anderson, who confuse their real-life selves with their performance personae. Rather, the virtuoso quality of Smith's mimicry recalls the traditions of the American one-person show. Indeed, there is a significant trajectory of US solo performers – from Beatrice Herford to Lily Tomlin to Eric Bogosian to the work of Sarah Jones in *Bridge and Tunnel* (2004) – that all use the features of a 'monopolylogue'.[13] These artists adopt multiple characters throughout a single show and rely on their skills in vocal and physical imitation, along with their frequent use of comic lampooning.

They also typically imitate a range of often stereotypical and exaggerated characters from various classes and ethnicities in American culture. However, these voices and ethnicities are also frequently missing from mainstream entertainment. Smith's work, as with Tomlin's performance as a New York bag lady from *The Search for Signs of Intelligent Life in the Universe* (1985), or John Leguizamo's semi-autobiographical account of his Latino family in *Freak* (1998), also belongs to the history of the one-person show that uses the virtuoso solo work as an important means for US artists to explore historically marginalized subjects or communities.

Moreover, while Smith's work contains both elements familiar to the traditions of the American one-person show, it is further distinguished by its use of documentary theatre techniques. Indeed, it is the combination of monologic techniques within a documentary theatre approach that frames Smith's critical contribution to the monologue genre.

Documentary monologue

As Alan Filewod argues, documentary theatre may be examined as both an 'historical phenomenon' and as a 'genre of performance'.[14] Documentary theatre emerged in Germany during the 1920s, particularly through the work of Erwin Piscator. Historically, in documentary forms, the notion of factual authenticity through a dramatic re-enactment based on primary source material was paramount. The documentary process typically involves research and testimony from a variety of subjects and progressively shapes these stories into a theatrical text. It is created, often collectively, for a specific community and frequently explores the experience of minority communities rather than stories from the dominant culture. In privileging its presentation of evidence and actuality the documentary approach also puts itself forward as an antidote to the contemporary cultural environment in which media, PR and politics are seen to lack a basis in truth or authenticity.[15]

It is clear that *Twilight: Los Angeles, 1992* utilizes these traditional conventions of documentary theatre. It draws upon the testimony of subjects, in their vernacular, and investigates a specific community, though admittedly the 'community' under examination is a large one. Thus, the work reflects upon wider cultural issues of race, class and gender in the American context. Smith's performance of Stanley K. Sheinbaum, former president of the Los Angeles Police Commission is, for example, both informative and didactic. It gives an account of Sheinbaum's meetings with gang members and the police, and details the antagonism between the two groups. However, it also reflects upon problems within the wider community where each group is the 'enemy' of another:

> I knew I hadn't won when they said,
>   'So which side are you on?'
>   When I said, I said, it's ...
>   my answer was
>   'Why do I have to be on a side?'
>   Yu, yuh, yeh know.
>   Why do I have to be on a side?
>   There's a problem here.[16]

This monologue highlights the various tensions existing between social and cultural groupings in the context of the Los Angeles riots. In contrast to the epic trajectory of monologue, Smith's style does not use quotation as a technique aimed at breaking through the fourth wall and she does not offer commentary through asides or comic rants. Instead, her performance of Stanley K. Sheinbaum stresses its veracity as a documentation of personal experience. The reliability of what is being said or the speaker saying it is never under interrogation.

However, more recent diversifications of the documentary genre point to a far more self-consciously reflexive and multilayered approach to truth claims and 'reality'. As Alison Forsyth and Chris Megson note:

> The once trenchant requirement that the documentary form should necessarily be equivalent to an unimpeachable and objective witness to

public events has been challenged in order to situate historical truth as an embattled site of contestation. Indeed, documentary performance today is often as much concerned with emphasizing its own discursive limitations, with interrogating the reification of material evidence in performance, as it is with the real-life story or event it is exploring.[17]

As such, the complicated ethics of the documentary approach – who has the right to speak for which community and why – raises questions about the politics and efficacy of Smith's monologues. Further, the notion of 'participatory art' in which artists engage with the social environment and where the 'authenticity' of the stories and experiences of real-life subjects is a key element, has also recently undergone extended debate.[18]

With hindsight, one key feature of Smith's performance that foreshadows later innovations and debates on the documentary form, performance and social engagement, is her use of monologues and one-woman show.[19] Indeed, while her work clearly stresses the veracity of the stories collected and the interview process, the ultimate arbiter is Smith's own performance in which she reanimates the stories of these everyday subjects to reveal a more complex and shifting relationship with notions of truth, memory, identity and authenticity.

Indeed, while the diversity of the social experience is vital to Smith's work it is, unavoidably, a *curated* diversity. The monologues are first subject to a selection and editing process. Therefore, Smith's choice of interview subjects is of great consequence. Similarly integral to the construction of the performance is the part or fragment of the interview selected for performance, as well as the order of the monologues.

Furthermore, the choices made in this process directly impact on the material chosen and the monologue fragments appearing in the stage performance or published text are testimony to Smith's editing process. As noted earlier, these monologues are selected from approximately two hundred taped interviews, consequently paired down by Smith and a dramaturgical team.[20] The monologues are, as she discusses, chosen with their theatrical qualities in mind, with those that are especially evocative or 'performable' more likely to be selected. And while Smith's use of a dramaturgical team to assist with the process of arrangement and editing certainly diffuses a level of subjection it is, of course, impossible to include *every* story or even to imply that any text provides such a total, objective view.

As such, Smith's work relies heavily on the material she collects and the order she chooses to perform it, meaning its ultimate effect is both tied to the text and her performance and, simultaneously, at its mercy.[21] Indeed, all of the monologues included in *Twilight: Los Angeles, 1992* make a claim for the veracity of the work's truth and the mimetic performance of Smith serves to reinforce this 'truth'. This may create, as Timothy Brennan writes on *Fires in the Mirror*, a potential for over-simplification and cleanliness in Smith's work that belies the complexity and 'ideological strictures' inherent in its creation:

> The truth of this play is deeply mixed, and like other recent triumphs in the ethnic arts it contains ideas of extraordinary democratic and critical force. But along with them came certain timidity: a large sign reading 'this far, and no further' In this way the play also creaks with untold stories.[22]

Brennan contends that Smith's work is too neat and too balanced: 'Identity in the real drama of the social is much messier that even Smith is able to make it.'[23] As such, because her performance persona is presented as a conduit, one careful to express the words of selves in positions of power as well as minority voices, *Twilight: Los Angeles, 1992* arguably exhibits an implied objectivity that is problematic due to the documentary form's simultaneous reliance on 'authenticity' and 'diversity' when in fact both these terms are questionable.

Yet, in *Twilight: Los Angeles, 1992*, Smith's use of the solo form resists privileging any one viewpoint, or ideological position, as the performance continually contrasts different elements of the story. Indeed, a clue to Smith's negotiation of the ethics of the documentary approach can be found in the published of *Twilight: Los Angeles, 1992*, which includes a monologue from the eminent postcolonial scholar Homi Bhabha. Through the metaphor of 'twilight' Bhabha reflects upon the Los Angeles riots and suggests that, rather than being dictated to by the 'hard outlines' of daylight, a state of twilight may provide a more inclusive, interpretative basis from which to consider the riots. To quote Bhabha at length:

> (Phone interview. He was in England. I was in L.A. He is part Persian, lived in India. Has a beautiful British accent.)
>
> This twilight moment
>   is an in-between moment.
>   It's the moment of dusk.
>   It's the moment of ambivalence
>   and ambiguity.
>   The inclarity,
>   the enigma,
>   the ambivalences,
>   in what happened in the L.A.
>   uprisings
>   are precisely what we want to get hold of.
>
> We have to interpret more in
> twilight,
> we have to make ourselves
> part of the act,
> we have to interpret,
> we have to project more.[24]

The Bhabha text, though not included in the mediatized version of the performance, explores the twilight metaphor that gives the work its title and emphasizes terms such as 'ambivalence' and 'ambiguity' to provide a starting point for investigation of the nuances and complexities of the civil unrest. However, it also lends itself to analysis of *Twilight: Los Angeles, 1992*, by providing an illustration of the innovative elements Smith's performance brings to the tradition of monologue in order to question 'daylight', or normative, notions of identity and the politics of race and class.

Included in the performance, for example, is the testimony of Reginald Denny, a white victim of the riots, along with the alternative viewpoint of Paul Parker, an advocate for the four men arrested for the beating of Denny. The Reginald Denny monologue provides a depiction of the riot up to his eventual loss of consciousness, his gratitude to those who extricated him from the violence, and his perspective on what he calls the 'color problem'. The monologue moves from Denny's relative ignorance of the events following the King verdict until after his recovery in hospital. By this time his wish was for people to 'wake up. It's not a color it's a person.'[25] In contrast, the Paul Parker monologue considers the reaction to Reginald Denny's beating as testament to the unequal treatment historically delivered to African American subjects, or indeed non-Anglo-Saxon subjects:

> Because Denny is white,
> > That's the bottom line.
> > If Denny was Latino,
> > Indian, or black,
> > They wouldn't give a damn.[26]

The divisions between the two perspectives in these monologues are clear. Each explores a single event in the riots and also its wider ramifications. The points of view of Denny and Parker are largely held in opposition to one another, though both monologues stress the inequality of race relations in American society. However, Smith's compression of these two perspectives into a single solo performance also impacts upon the meaning of Denny and Parker's words, as it draws upon the notions of ambiguity, inclarity and ambivalence that Bhabha signals is so important to the metaphor of twilight. Thus, the notions of 'truth' and 'authenticity' are shown to exist not in one dominant point of view, but in the complicated and changing negotiation between viewpoints.

This privileging of the monologue form as a method of documentary created and performed by a solo artist fundamentally alters the meaning and politics of the performance as Smith engages in fluid movement between the identities of the multiple subjects she performs.[27] According to Carol Martin, Smith's 'hypernaturalistic mimesis' is deceptive because 'the authority of one group over another, of one individual over others, is undermined by the presence of Smith as the person through whom so many voices travel'.[28] Thus the politics of race and class are explored, not through self-reflexivity, but by the fluidity of Smith's performing persona as it foregrounds, in the terminology of theorist Judith Butler, the contingent, temporal and performative nature of identity.[29]

Indeed, Smith's performance has been likened to a critical version of 'passing' – a tactic historically used by subjects to assume different race, ethnicity, gender or class to gain acceptance in a different social group.[30] However, where passing relies on its successful concealment of the original body or voice or identity, Smith's performance always shows a little bit of the seams in the process of character transformation. As such, there is a very important distance between Smith, the performer, and the subject that she performs.

Therefore, while Smith's style of acting foregrounds mimicry and imitation her swift movement between performances of many different identities, from Reginald Denny to Paul Parker to academic Cornel West, ultimately contradicts the stability of identity itself.

This disjunction has the continual effect of unsettling any normative notions of character and, more importantly, of showing that ideas of authenticity and truth are both vitally important but also subject to contingency, change, performance and ambiguity. Whereas Gray and Anderson employ ironic and self-reflexive personae to trouble the notion of authenticity, Smith creates ambiguity through multiple transformations of the solo voice and body.

Indeed, by engaging with acting practices that present identity as changeable, performative and negotiated Smith can, in the words of Debby Thompson, 'question the fact of race without discounting racism's very real effects'.[31] Smith's performance as Hollywood agent Anonymous Man #2 reveals these 'twilight' tactics at work. The 'Anonymous Man' monologue begins with a depiction of Hollywood

Figure 5.2 Anna Deavere Smith as Cornel West (*Photo*: Adger W. Cowans).

agents having lunch in Beverley Hills. Smith knots a dotted tie around her neck, a small distinction in the costume to mark the beginning of her imitation, and sits relaxed in a revolving chair. The Anonymous Man describes the rising racial tension that has the 'upper class, upper middle class – whatever your definition is – white successful …' patrons in an increasing panic. He has a vision of 'aging or aged yuppies, Armani suits … fleeing like wild-eyed' as the riots begin:

> The spark –
>   was the verdict.
> which was
> *absurd.*
> But that was just the spark –

this had been set
for years before.
But maybe,
not maybe,
but, uh, the
system
plays unequally,
and the people who were
the, they,
who were burning down the Beverly Centre
had been victims of the system.[32]

Critical to this monologue are the categorizations of 'them' and 'us'. The testimony of the Anonymous Man is particularly conscious of these distinctions, indeed he starts 'fearing' for the safety of his family, but at the same time is aware of the inequality of the 'system'. Here, Smith's solo performance monologue creates a heightened disjunction between her race, class and gender, and the content of the stories she re-performs.

The irony of the Anonymous Man's words – an illustration of a culture divided along economic, racial and gender lines – is heightened because Smith's performance ensures an ongoing tension which exists between the words and identity she performs and her presence onstage. As before, Smith does not make her gender ambiguous using lighting or costume. Therefore, no matter the prowess of her mimicry there remains a deliberate disjunction between Smith's live body and the testimony of the subject for whom she speaks.[33] This tension between the solo documentary speech and the solo body complicates notions such as 'them and us' and demonstrates the problem of representing historical events in such simplistic terms.

Twilight: Los Angeles, 1992 is particularly interesting when Smith, an African American woman, speaks the words of this non-black male body. This moment creates a Brechtian *Verfremdungseffekt* by providing ironic reflection on the privileged social and cultural position from which the Anonymous Man speaks. The mimetic performance of Smith, commensurate with the documentary approach, situates her performance as neutral and objective. However, as Schechner has noted, it is at the points at which this mimesis breaks down or reveals differences and contradictions between Smith and the words of the interview subject, that a calculated tension is produced. The potential for her performance to consciously 'fail' in its attempt at 'smoothness' and in order to create humour and irony, is also indicative of a style makes visible oppositions and hierarchies (self/other, black/white, rich/poor and so on).[34]

A brilliant successor of Smith's approach can be found in the headphone verbatim theatre of Australian theatre-maker Roslyn Oades. In performances such as *Stories of Love and Hate* (2008), *I'm Your Man* (2012) and *Hello, Goodbye. Happy Birthday* (2014), Oades uses audio recordings of interviews, stored as MP3s, as paperless scripts. On stage, actors simultaneously listen and re-perform the 'voiceprint' of the interview subjects. While clearly removed from the American context, Oades was nonetheless inspired by a 2001 workshop with Mark Wing-Davey entitled 'Drama Without Paper'. Davey had combined the use of headphones with documentary interview techniques after previously directing Smith in her work *House Arrest* (1997).[35]

As such, Oades' work (and others who use audio-scripting techniques such as UK artist Alecky Blythe) is an extension of Smith's earlier attention to capturing the idiosyncratic patterns of voice in performance. Similar to Smith's work, juxtapositions between the vocal print and the bodies of the performers gives rise to fruitful tensions between evident signs of gender, race, ethnicity and class. In her most recent work, *Hello, Goodbye*, Oades interviewed subjects at opposite ends of their lives, contrasting those aged eighteen and eighty. Here, the sophisticated use of audio technology and an audio script provided additional layers of Brechtian-like estrangement as the obvious use of the headphones placed emphasis on the process of ageing, forgetting, the act of listening, retelling and a reflexive approach to memory and identity in a culture dominated by phenomena such as smart phones and social media, that are used to document and augment our experiences.[36]

Twilight: Los Angeles, 1992, then, can be read as an earlier example of innovative documentary performance that not only privileges difference and heterogeneity, but that uses the juxtaposition of monologues to leave space open for ironic contradiction. Yet, in a way that prefigures these later trends, *Twilight: Los Angeles, 1992* develops a form of monologue that shows the dominant historical and ideological narratives within American culture to be deeply contradictory. Primarily through its structure of juxtaposition, this documentary monologue form enables critical consideration of these divergent points of view from within the contemporary cultural and political context in which it is embedded.

Indeed, the monologues typically encounter one another with an inherent friction between them. Interviews such as Anonymous Man (Juror in Simi Valley trial) are contrasted with those of Allen Cooper, a.k.a. Big Al (Ex-gang member, ex-convict, activist in the national truce movement).

> Anonymous Man: We've been portrayed as white racists.
> One of the most disturbing thing, and a lot of the jurors said that
> the thing that bothered them that they received in the mail more
> than anything else
> more than the threats, was a letter from the KKK
> saying,
> 'We support you, and if you need our help, if you want to
>   join
> our organization,
> we'd welcome you into the fold.'[37]
> Allen Cooper: Rodney King ...
>   It been –
>   it's been twenty, thirty years,
>   and people suffered beatings from law enforcement.
>   It ain't nothin' new.
>   It was just brought to light this time.
>   But then it showed what –

it showed that it doesn't mean a thing.
Now if that was an officer down there gettin' beat,
it would a been a real national riot thing –
you hear me? [38]

The formerly quoted monologue of Anonymous Man is largely defensive in tone. It details personal difficulties as a juror in the King trial, including his fear or disgust evoked after receiving a congratulatory letter from the Ku Klux Klan. In contrast, the Allen Cooper monologue puts forward a damning view of a history of police brutality visited upon the African American community in Los Angeles and throughout the wider American society. Indeed, while the Anonymous Man is justifiably upset at being compared to the KKK, Allen Cooper reveals that the historical legacy of violence and intimidation visited on African American's 'ain't nothin' new':

You gotta look at history, baby,
you gotta look at history.
  It wasn't ...
  Anything is never a problem 'till the black man gets his
    hands on it.
  It was good for the NRA
  to have fully automatic weapons,
  but when the Afro-American people get hold of 'em,
  it was a crime!
  Aww.[39]

These monologues provide two very different accounts of the Los Angeles riots. The juror is concerned specifically with the Rodney King case while Allen Cooper, by comparison, situates the Rodney King case within the context of African American civil rights throughout history.

Further, the monologues in *Twilight: Los Angeles, 1992* frequently diverge from one another, subsequently drawing attention to both the differences and similarities contained within them.[40] This strategy stages the sites of contention between identities, subjectivities and ethnicities. By engaging with notions of community, Smith's work also points to the dominance of American narratives that position individualism and personal wealth creation at the heart of contemporary social and economic interactions. Her most recent work on the crisis in American health care *Let Me Down Easy* (2008) similarly explores the tensions between individual economic choice, civil rights and the collective good.

The monologues in *Twilight: Los Angeles, 1992* thus challenge the 'hard outlines' of day and offers instead a performance persona that embodies Bhabha's theorization of 'twilight'. Rather than merely reiterating the ideological hierarchies implicit in the construction of race and class, Smith's performance in *Twilight: Los Angeles, 1992* encourages consideration of the Los Angeles riots that does not ignore the complexity of social and cultural identities. In this way while her work belongs to the traditions of documentary theatre, it also draws upon the use of solo speech in the United States as a mode of speaking back to historical oppression. It belongs to the trajectory of American oratory, from Sojourner Truth's *Ar'n't I a Woman?* in 1851 to Barack Obama's 2008 address *A More Perfect Union*, for the ways in which it explores the multiplicity of contemporary American life and uses public performance of solo speech as a powerful means by which to examine sociopolitical realities and attempt to (re)define the nation.

In *Twilight: Los Angeles, 1992* Smith's performance acknowledges the vast diversity in contemporary American society. The monologues explore this complexity as they enable consideration of largely forgotten narratives. One such inclusion is Smith's performance of gang member Twilight Bey, an organizer of a truce between gangs in Los Angeles, as the closing monologue of the performance. This monologue is integral. Its placement in the performance ensures that it provides a kind of encapsulation of the work, but the monologue is also significant because Twilight Bey is a subject who is on the edge of what the Hollywood agent calls 'the system'.

Twilight Bey's speech recalls Bhabha's earlier notion of twilight identity because it is an expression of the creative potential that can be found in ambiguity. The monologue details the bargaining of the gang truce and also provides a perspective from within the disenfranchised African American community in Los Angeles. Twilight recollects seeing 'little kids between the ages of eight and eleven out at three in the morning ... beating up a old man on the bus stop, a homeless old man'. He also depicts driving through his neighbourhood and seeing the 'living dead', 'the base heads, the people who are addicted to crack' who are up at night trying to get money 'to get the hit'.[41] As such, this monologue reflects on subjects that are forgotten by both the economic ideology of neoliberalism and the 'family values' of the 'conservative ideal of the normal household' that underpins neoconservatism.

Twilight Bey is conscious of his position 'in limbo', removed from dominant social and cultural narratives. However, his monologue, while illustrating social disenfranchisement, also maintains an optimistic acknowledgement of the task of working towards 'understanding others' and seeks openings for social dialogue in a manner typical of documentary works:

When I talked about the truce back in 1988,
    that was something they considered before its time,
yet
in 1992
we made it
realistic.
So to me it's like I'm stuck in limbo,
like the sun is stuck between night and day
in the twilight hours.

I am a dark individual,
and with me stuck in limbo,
I see darkness as myself.
I see the light as knowledge and the wisdom of the world
    and
understanding others,
and in order for me to be a, to be a true human being,
I can't forever dwell in darkness,
I can't forever dwell in the idea,
of just identifying with people like me and understanding me
    and mine.[42]

The Twilight Bey monologue is an illuminating perspective on the future of race relations in the United States. The metaphor of twilight is once again central to this monologue. It highlights the potential for conscious movement away from binary categories, towards an opening of a gap from within which critical reflection upon historical and ideological narratives is possible. The inclusion of the monologue at the closing of *Twilight: Los Angeles, 1992* also serves to reinforce the importance of the metaphor to the work as a whole. By shifting between the performance of police officers and activists, between members of the Simi Valley Jury and the aunt of Rodney King, Angela King, Smith's performance foregrounds narratives of difference. Through the performance of monologue in *Twilight: Los Angeles, 1992* Smith reiterates identities and viewpoints that are often in contrast to the dominant 'daylight' narratives of race, class and gender.

Indeed, through the performance of often varied, contradictory monologues, Smith enables a performance of a 'twilight' persona of her own, one that is aware of the complexity inherent in the construction of these narratives and identities. This persona combines the truth claims indicative of the documentary theatre approach with a performance of monologues that is open to perspectives not generally recognized in the American culture. As Deavere Smith's rendering of theatre director Peter Sellars highlights,

> Dad ... he won't replace the burnt-out light bulbs.
> You know, he yells at the family for complaining and
> condemns everyone
> to live in darkness.
> 'Cause he's too cheap
> to put in light bulbs.
> That's what America feels like right now.[43]

In comparison to the economic necessities of neoliberalism or the patriotic narratives of neoconservatism, issues such as police violence, urban poverty and disenfranchisement are at risk of being overshadowed. Such issues are difficult to see in the 'hard outlines of day' yet *Twilight: Los Angeles, 1992* reflects upon both the hierarchies that support these ideologies and the complex and contrasting viewpoints that characterize the American social and cultural context of the 1990s.

Twilight: Los Angeles, 1992 demonstrates the documentary monologue as an important record of social experience. However, the legacy of Smith's approach is in the way she combines documentary with solo performance monologue to create productive tensions and ambiguities in performance. It is through the juxtaposition between contrasting and often contradictory texts that Smith's performance enables ironic consideration of the influence of neoliberal and neoconservative ideology on American subjects. A return to her work gives an impression of the complex narratives of race, class and gender in American society in the 1990s and suggests that innovative performances in the tradition of civil rights discourse remain ever vital to our understandings of contemporary life and cultural memory.

6

Radical Monologue and the Performances of Karen Finley

Following the Clinton era of the 1990s, and coming soon after the turn of the millennium and the election of George W. Bush, the events of 11 September 2001 were to fundamentally alter life in the United States and across the globe. Whereas the 1990s might have been framed by debates about the 'end of history' and the dominance of Western liberal democracy, the next decade witnessed invasions of Iraq and Afghanistan, a War on Terror, a global financial crisis, and increasing rates of climate change and ecological devastation. Reflecting on this time of radical change, it is fitting to now turn attention to the use of monologue as a radical form of alternative speech and politics in the new millennium.

Karen Finley rose to prominence during the mid-1980s as her cabaret-style monologues, part comic rant and part performance art, were gaining a modest popularity. However, wider attention was drawn to Finley's art with the publication of C. Carr's 1986 feature article in New York's *The Village Voice* on her show *I'm an Ass Man* (1984).[1] The subsequent labelling of Finley's art as 'obscene' saw her work placed under greater public scrutiny, including its censorship in London in 1986.[2] In 1990 Finley, along with fellow artists Holly Hughes, John Fleck and Tim Miller, had her National Endowment of the Arts (the US federal arts body) funding withdrawn.

The NEA 4 artists, as they became known (or, as Hughes quipped, 'Karen Finley and the three homosexuals'), tried to appeal this groundbreaking censorship decision, a process that ultimately saw the case dismissed by the Supreme Court. Finley's involvement with the NEA 4 case had the effect of creating a substantial public profile, arguably ensuring her position as a 'controversial' and 'censored' artist. Jill Dolan later contended that Finley and her colleagues became the unfortunate scapegoats of a conservative backlash against the arts in the United States.[3]

Finley's work has delved into such issues as women's rights, AIDS, censorship, the politics of race, gender and class, along with the effects of physical and emotional abuse, all of which are contained within a diverse examination of American capitalist culture. Her monologue performances subvert the iconography of the American Dream, including the 'safe' 'nuclear family', in a manner that is at once sad and humorous in major works such as: *I'm an Ass Man* (1984), *A Constant State of Desire* (1987), *We Keep Our Victims Ready* (1990), *American Chestnut* (1993), *Shut Up and Love Me* (2000) and *Make Love* (2003).

The scholarly debates framing Finley's work particularly recognize her use of a feminist politics that privileges women's perspective, voice and position in society. Additionally, Finley's work is also examined for its interrogation of the social effects of commodity capitalism.[4] Such analyses commonly stress Finley's explicit use of her body in performance, though Finley's texts are also typically monologic. From the early *I'm an Ass Man* to more recent works *Make Love*, *The Passion of Terri Schiavo* (2005) and *The Jackie Look* (2008), Finley's work integrates influences from experimental avant-garde performance and visual art within performances of monologue that directly critique aspects of American society.

Finley's use of solo speech is a radical one. In *Shut Up and Love Me*, she joyfully deploys and subverts multiple personae, non-linear texts and the wholesale rejection of coherent dramatic character to critically reflect upon American culture at the turn the millennium. Subsequently, her performance *Make Love* reflects on American culture and politics in the aftermath of 9/11. Finally, Finley's privileging of the solo voice in *The Passion of Terri Schiavo* strategically positions monologue as an alternative form of expression operating within global capitalist culture.

Fragmented persona

Finley's performance *Shut Up and Love Me* contains seven to eight spoken texts. The texts are playful and outrageous, and focus on the themes of sex, intimacy and dysfunction. In the Melbourne performance of 2001, Finley enters the stage in a sheer dressing gown and, seemingly offhand, talks directly to the audience:

> Are there more people out in the lobby? Should they turn on the light? Or ... I didn't eat really good today. All I had was a croissant and toast. ... I just did alotta carbs, and ... the other thing is ... I walked the gardens last night ... through, to get over my fear, because I would never walk through a park in the United States ... in the dark ... and ... Let's see what else I did. ...[5]

The Finley persona in the opening of *Shut Up and Love Me* is acerbic and erratic. The 'introduction' includes improvised impressions of Australia and comments about previous Australian performances. She makes continual references to Australian slang and her love of the use of the word 'feral' as a substitute for vagina and touches herself, 'this is my feral', in a self-consciously silly play with taboo. 'Finley' speaks as 'herself' to the audience, combines ribald humour with improvisation, and in doing so adopts an approach familiar to the formal and generic features of stand-up comedy.

The distinctions between alternative stand-up, such as that by Lenny Bruce and Sandra Bernhard, and the monologues of Finley, Spalding Gray and Laurie Anderson are blurry. In many ways each of these artists draws upon American traditions of countercultural solo speech, found in the comic rambling of German-American Brother Theodore, the exploration of the abject in American stand-up, or the anti-establishment writings of the Beats in the 1950s and 1960s, as much as they do the history of monologue in Western theatre.[6] Finley begins *Shut Up and Love* Me with a direct addresses to the audience, 'Let's see what else I did,' and this serves as a 'personal' introduction or even a type of prologue-monologue.

Following this introductory speech, Barry White-type music begins playing as Finley strips off her gown and, now dressed only in lingerie, moves through the crowd. She playfully interacts with seated audience members by performing an absurd send up of a lap-dance, gyrating, tripping over their feet and falling from their laps to the floor. Finley then moves to the stage where a vintage chaise longue is positioned and sardonically states:

> I am just TOO MUCH of an exhibitionist and I ... I know ... no, no. ... There's a REASON why I take my clothes off. It's for the OPPRESSION OF WOMEN. FOR THE OPPRESSION OF WOMEN. But I have to accept that ... I do like people noticing me. Thank you for noticing me. Thank you. ... Because I have to have MY NEEDS MET. I have to HAVE MY NEEDS MET.[7]

This self-reflexive and ironic aside parodies Finley's perceived public image as a Political Feminist performer. It also resists the embedding of monologue into a dramatic text, as Finley's work continually draws attention to its construction as a 'performance', to the 'authentic' status of the text, and also the author/creator/persona of 'Karen Finley' who performs it.

Subsequently, Finley flops onto the lounge, reclines, and delivers the first 'formal' monologue of the performance entitled 'Thanks for Nothing'. 'Thanks for Nothing' explores a female character's relationship with her unfaithful lover, known only as 'He':

> It started as a waking dream. The four glasses and the teapot you gave me, crushed in the rusting Little Pony lunch box, with the words 'the tortured soul of a misogynist' written inside of the lid, by me. I dreamed I gave him his lunchbox back and I woke with a start. I decided to wait for the meaning later. I could not call my therapist, for it was Thanksgiving.[8]

Finley performs this text in a voice and manner entirely different from the earlier improvisational persona, her diction switches rapidly to become more formal and her delivery changes to a kind of detached storytelling mode. 'A grin came to my lips and I said out loud, "He's back in town." Of course he is in town, he always came to town on Thanksgiving, to see his first set of children at his Aunt Tilly's house.'[9] This strange and unsettling performance style is a noted technique of Finley's, as she delivers her texts in a manner that is sometimes described as 'trance-like' as she snaps between personae sometimes mid-sentence.[10] Therefore, Finley's 'trance' can be read as parodic representation, a self-conscious avoidance of a fixed dramatic character, an 'I'.

This formal performance persona also recalls earlier modernist monologues found in the work of Ibsen, Strindberg, and O'Neill, particularly their concentration on the lives of the bourgeoisie, and a preoccupation with the individual psyche and modern psychology. The chaise longue upon which Finley lies and a number of references to therapists, Freudian theory and Oedipal dynamics throughout 'Thanks for Nothing', and indeed in several other texts included in *Shut Up and Love Me*, reinforce this association.

In the context of *Shut Up and Love Me*, Finley's performance also mocks the comportment of the 'proper' lady, a Stepford wife, or the character of a melodrama, themes that Finley has addressed and subverted previously in works such as *The Theory of Total Blame* (1988). During a later monologue from *Shut Up and Love Me* entitled 'Daddy', the subject of the text Stella describes tilting her head as if 'having a case of the Katherine Hepburns', a reference to the mannered, sassy and comic persona of the 1940s star.[11] This depiction also captures much of Finley's more affected speech. Indeed, there is a marked difference between 'Katherine Hepburn Finley' and the 'Karen Finley' that frequently turns to the audience to comment casually in off-the-cuff asides. Later in 'Thanks for Nothing' there is a reflection on Thanksgiving in which Finley's acerbic persona interjects and segments the monologue:

> Now let us go out of the story for a moment, away from my own personality disorder, so I can get you up to speed on my take on

this national holiday of bird roasting and stuffing. My six-year old daughter puts the day into perspective. 'Who cares about Thanksgiving? You don't get any presents!' Exactly, it is just a holiday where we give thanks to our friends, our family, our work situation, our health, our wonderful lives, our CRUMMY LIVES. Things that are GOING WELL, NOT GOING WELL. BUT WE'RE STILL HERE ALL TOGETHER, CELEBRATING WITH A ROOM FULL OF EMOTIONAL DERELICTS THAT LOOK LIKE YOU![12]

This unexpected and rapid movement between the Katherine Hepburn performance persona and confrontational shouting undercuts the melodramatic style of the text, familiar to the cinema of the 1950s and the drama of the late eighteenth and nineteenth centuries, through parody and the comic capacity of the aside.

Further, this tactic of peppering the performance with fragments and deviations continues to develop. At one point in the Melbourne performance of *Shut Up and Love Me* she pointedly shouts, 'This is not TV. This isn't *Friends*', contrasting the popular 1990s sitcom *Friends* with her performance in a moment that at once celebrates the overt

Figure 6.1 Karen Finley, in *Shut Up and Love Me* (*Photo*: Dona Ann McAdams).

'theatricality' of *Shut Up and Love Me* and undercuts any unthinking identification with the melodramatic and predictable sitcom mode.

These asides recall the Brechtian impulse to comment upon what is being said and provoke critical consideration on the part of the audience. They also serve as a jolt to any identification with a dramatic character, as the 'real-life' persona of 'Karen Finley' unsettles and intermingles with the personae performed in the spoken texts. Additionally, as Finley lies on the chaise longue, a piece of paper denoting the 'script' rests beside her and throughout her performance she periodically reads from a number of similar leaves of paper lying about the stage.

This tactic of obviously using the script marks a simple shift towards the act of recitation, rather than remembered repetition and mimesis, and draws attention to the reflexive, performative elements in the work. Finley is not trying to inhabit a character, rather she plays with ingredients of naturalistic drama – linear script and fixed dramatic personae – to reveal its workings and bias. In the recorded version of 'Thanks for Nothing', Finley halts on the line, 'Being Thanksgiving, JFK was congested'. In response to a reaction from the audience, she laughs and says, 'It's an extraordinary line I know', before performing it a second time.[13] Again, as in her earlier comments on turning down the lights in the auditorium, the repetition of lines and the restarting of the spoken texts draw attention to the artificiality of the performance event.

In the place of the sitcom and the modernist monologue, Finley puts forward the following elements: multiple personae, non-linearity, and playful use of taboo. Indeed, later monologues see female personae propositioning their fathers or picking up crippled Vietnam veterans so as to have sex with their stumps. Such monologues are hilarious and shocking articulations of unseemly desires and the so-called pornographic elements of contemporary culture and intimate relationships that are exercised from the friendly sitcom format. In the words of Rebecca Schneider,

> White performance artist Karen Finley ... enacts and critiques the cultural dramas of disembodied bodies. ... She stands before her

audience and ushers forth an onslaught of identities like some virus run rampant – a virus she insists her spectators take seriously.[14]

Significantly, it is through use of the solo voice and by mixing 'formal' monologues and asides that Finley's performance sustains its 'virus-like' movement between different personae and the transgressive interjection of parody and irony. These features continue to develop in Finley's more recent performances that critique US culture and politics following 9/11.

Make Love

Make Love responds to the aftermath of 11 September 2001 by focusing on those residents directly affected, the city of New York as a whole and, in a larger context, the American political and cultural environment. In Finley's words, 'All of New York had become nice overnight or overday. It was terrifically inconvenient and terrifying and not good for sales.'[15] In this performance, which draws upon the cabaret tradition and that of the chanteuse, Finley and up to eleven others perform as Liza Minnelli, the iconic actress of the motion picture *Cabaret* (1972).

Along with Finley, there are two other principal Lizas, a singer Liza #1, and a pianist, Liza #2.[16] The piece combines monologue with musical interludes, songs and medleys, dialogic exchanges between the Lizas, and Finley's familiar asides. 'Could someone please suck the President's dick please, for world peace?' asks Finley near the start of the recorded version of *Make Love*. 'It takes the edge off.'[17] The monologues investigate the community reaction to the traumatic events of 9/11 in contrast to US political rhetoric, specifically that of the administration of George W. Bush, and reveals a developing climate of fear within twenty-first-century American culture.

The performance begins with Liza#2 on piano playing a medley of 'lounge-style tunes that turns into a medley of American war tunes'.[18] Liza #1 is made up in Liza Minnelli drag, consisting of a glamorous

Figure 6.2 Karen Finley as Liza Minnelli (*Photo*: Dona Ann McAdams).

sparkling gown, long false eyelashes and a black elfin wig. She/he proclaims, 'Liza's BACK.' Finley enters with a line of additional Lizas, both men and women, trailing behind her. All are dressed in Liza drag: glittery frocks; wigs; one dressed in leather bondage gear; several others wearing black trilbies. 'Oh,' begins Finley, 'There are so many different parts of me.'[19] The various representations of Minnelli introduce themselves, 'I'm leather-daddy Liza', before sitting in a line at the back of the stage from where they observe as Finley performs the first formal spoken text entitled, 'Emotional Fallout':

> You are going to die when you are going to die. When it's your time to die it's your turn to die. You could be next. You could be next in line.

> This was the reassurance I was paying for from my taxi driver. This was the sensitive nuance applied to my approach to La Guardia.
>
> Hello. Hello. Yes may I have a taxi to the airport? And yes can you please be sure to send me a driver who will predict my death on the plane?[20]

Finley performs this text in a version of the trance-like style observed earlier in *Shut Up and Love Me*. The monologue emphasizes the events of 9/11 and its subsequent associations with death, fear and terrorism, as now ubiquitous elements in the experience of the subjects of New York City. This attention to the individual and collective psyche of New Yorkers is embodied in the multiple Liza's, who stand in solidarity and act as a reflection of the city community and nation. As Finley notes in an introduction to *Make Love*, in the aftermath of the attacks she was struck 'by the fragmentation, the splitting of personalities, and the projections of a nation's fears onto New Yorkers'.[21] *Make Love* explores the climate of fear – as the taxi driver remarks 'You could be next' – and uses Liza Minnelli as a mediating image and form of collective personae as a way to avoid approaching the events of 9/11 in an expository, didactic fashion. As Finley explains, 'Liza' is a consciously employed device

> Drag, impersonation, and Liza as a known archetype, a phenomenon. Liza as an imaginary creature, a goddess, a diva to project onto and live through, to experience through her. Liza, as a parody, as an artistic device to make information less threatening.[22]

The multiple Lizas act as communicational and symbolic personae, applauding and laughing along with the audience, and occasionally engaging in cabaret-style banter with Finley. They underline the melancholy elements in the work, as when Finley rails against the reaction to 9/11 by a values obsessed, American nation:

> Because you're such a good good person. BETTER THAN ME.
> And I know you're sitting there with your values. ... We are your fear. We are everything that you have not done with your life. And

you're lookin' at me. And now you can give me your pity. And now you can give me your charity. And now you can give me your love and I just take it. I just take it ... cause I think to myself, as we all know. It was someone's mother. It was someone's brother. Someone's father. Someone's child.[23]

As the tone of the piece becomes one of frustration, even anger, the Lizas cease laughing along with the audience, their faces begin to fall and they no longer smile. They remain still until the end of the monologue, staring at Finley/Liza and out into the audience.[24] While the many Lizas are silent, they are also visibly empathetic to Finley's words, as though invested in the political intent behind them.

In *Make Love* Finley moves further away from using her 'real-life' persona in performance, after recognition that many in her audience associate the public figure of 'Karen Finley' with the image of Finley as either the victim or hero of the culture wars.[25] Significantly then, it is no longer simply 'Karen Finley' highlighting an injustice or illustrating an issue, but a stage full of figures. And when Finley intones, 'We are your fear,' it is clear that this applies to each and every Liza, including any identity at odds with what Finley calls the 'current chaos of [the] nation'.[26] In their uniformity, the Lizas are copied figures representative both of the collective identities of New York, but also of the national response to 9/11. This development aesthetically modulates the persona of 'Karen Finley' as it emphasizes both collective experience and multiple perspectives.

However the blurring of the single author/creator/performer also remains a key part of Finley's performance. The monologue entitled, 'The Discovery in the Safety of the Past', describes an email from the *Wall Street Journal* and alludes to Finley's position as a well-known artist with a public profile:

> I went to my room and there was an email from a journalist from the *Wall Street Journal* wanting to interview me about the drama – the art direction of the World Trade Centre attack compared to the art direction of the attack on the Pentagon.[27]

Therefore, while there is a self-conscious awareness that the 'style of Karen Finley' might be avoided by foregrounding the multiple Liza Minnellis, Finley continues to integrate elements which might be drawn from her 'real life' into the monologues.

> Oh, yes I did get your email about the dramatic art direction of the crash. Why don't you talk to Eric Bogosian he saw the whole thing from his window I talked to him about it or, or better Richard Serra. *(Address audience)* I felt that sculptors weren't given enough opportunity in the press.
>   I paused and for a moment I felt detachment, and that this conversation would be appreciated in the next Whitney Biennial.
>
> On the marquee of the State Theatre where I was to perform was: now playing Karen Finley and *Apocalypse NOW*.[28]

'The Discovery in the Safety of the Past' refers to the Whitney Museum of American Art, an institution of the New York art-scene, along with well-known artists Eric Bogosian and Richard Serra, and points to the problem of art after 9/11. It knowingly reflects upon the insensitivity of the press and elements of New York arts community to the attacks, more concerned with 'art direction' and the Biennial than the move towards 'apocalypse now'. The monologue also comments upon the making of *Make Love*, itself a work examining the wake of 9/11 and the incommensurability of producing art about tragedy and national trauma amidst an increasing culture of fear.

The state of Middle America

In the immediate aftermath of 9/11, as President George W. Bush proclaimed that the US was in a state of war, there was an explosion of patriotism in which American flags, for example, became ubiquitous.

According to theorist Slavoj Žižek, this proliferation signalled a shift in American politics:

> The result of September 11 is an unprecedented strengthening of American hegemony, in all its aspects. ... 'What is at stake are no longer different economical or political choices, but our very survival – in the war on terrorism, you are either with us or against us.'[29]

Make Love rejects this 'with us or against us' dogma and the increasingly dominant neoconservative rhetoric.[30] In Finley's monologues, this rejection is staged through highlighting a gulf between the insularity of cosmopolitan New York with that of 'middle America'.

'The Discovery in the Safety of the Past' contrasts Finley/Liza's own 'New York' persona with the conservatism and repetitive concerns of a small town:

> No I don't want to look at your town. No I don't want to look at it. ... You want to know where I got (this dress). You wanna know. You wanna really know where I got it. Yes this, this dress is made out of the rubble of the World Trade Centre hand sewn by Giuliani and the New York police and they gave it to me. ... You feel better now. HOW CLOSE WERE YOU! WHAT DO YOU MEAN YOU DON'T HAVE A *NEW YORK TIMES*? WHAT DO YOU MEAN YOU DON'T HAVE A *NEW YORK TIMES*? *USA TODAY* IS NOT A PAPER.[31]

This text demonstrates a response to the events of 9/11 that parodies the repetitious questions – 'how close were you?' – asked of the residents of New York after the attacks. The name of the town is scarcely remembered, 'Was it Madison? Ann Arbor?' and is ultimately unimportant. Instead, it stands for *every* town. Like Gray's toy town, Sag Harbor, Finley suggests the true space of terror at the turn of the millennium is the perceived insularity of small town thinking: 'Hello, can you please help me? I am in a state of high alert – I am in a state of Mid-America.'[32]

The description of a dress sewn from the World Trade Centre rubble parodies the collection of World Trade Centre memorabilia. This refers directly to an earlier monologue in *Make Love*, where Finley/Liza boards a plane with two women who have bought the entire Lower Manhattan stock of World Trade Centre salt and pepper shakers, wrapped chillingly in the obituary pages of the *New York Times*. It critiques the impulse in wider American culture to treat the event on the level of iconography that rapidly integrates with slick consumerism. It also parodies a culture characterized by its systemic relationship with neoliberalism, whereby the ultimate value of goods derives from market forces. As Finley/Liza points out, with irony, 'This isn't the time to ignore capital gains.'[33]

In *Make Love*, ignorance is typically hidden behind the surface display of 'good manners' and middle America is depicted as a stifling, morally self-righteous place where you cannot get a drink after nine, where you must be 'nice' and 'polite', where you are told to pray, and where the 'intellectual' *New York Times* is replaced by *USA Today* – 'NOT A PAPER'. The monologues in *Make Love* consider and juxtapose elements of cosmopolitan New York with parochial mid-America. They are undoubtedly left-wing and New York-centric, but they also reflect upon the so-called 'values' of American culture.

In monologues such as 'The Discovery in the Safety of the Past', the use of Minnelli as a type of filter for the performance is integral. In the words of Finley, 'The "divaness" of Liza, an iconic New Yorker, becomes the place to throw our pathos, hilarity, mockery and taboos about 9/11.'[34] The Liza persona, with its allusion to a shifting sexuality and a liberal, playful, New York sensibility thus reinforces the contrast between the static 'State of Mid-America' and the thriving difference of New York City. Finley's appropriation of Minnelli as a subversive figure is effective not only because of her position as a drag icon, but also because of the themes of *Cabaret* (1972), a popular film set in 1930s Berlin against a background of a growing tide of fascism. *Make Love* clearly parallels the undercurrent of paranoia depicted in the movie with an American culture suddenly characterized by a climate of fear.

Indeed, a number of monologues focus upon the propagation of terms such as 'security' and 'fear' and politicized notions of 'patriotism' and 'the flag' that pervaded American culture following the World Trade Centre attacks. In 'The Discovery in the Safety of the Past', Finley/Liza reflects,

> America was built and grows from fear ... and our projections of a nation OF LIVING WITH FEAR. Our leaders always telling us about the heightened tension. Of the fear. Of the 'national security', so we're in 'national bondage' ...
> Our country is a national S&M torture chamber. ... Keep on doing what you want to do. But it's a scary world out there. ... The heightened alerts. The heightened alerts.[35]

Furthermore, *Make Love* also highlights the vast economic and social shifts that occurred after 9/11. This encourages reflection upon global changes that takes into account not only the New York subjects directly affected by the attacks, but also those non-American subjects of both the First and Third Worlds, whose lives have been altered by the events. Indeed, while the text of *Make Love* is particularly framed by its cosmopolitan New York sensibility, the performance also considers the events of 9/11 in this larger context. This is evident in several monologues that depict subjects moving through airports, travelling on airplanes and thus moving beyond New York and mid-America into the outside world. In a monologic section simply titled 'Insert', Finley/Liza travels on an airplane and recalls a number of encounters: with a Palestinian Canadian who tells of his Jewish wife and children; a Vietnamese emigrant; two Holocaust survivors; and a music teacher from Bedford Stuyvessant High School:

> I see the Canadian passport. I think, Oh no, I will have 17 hours explaining American foreign policy. Yes he is Canadian but he is also Palestinian and I do listen to his views about American foreign policy. After a few hours I take his hand and say I am sorry, it is a long flight.[36]

In this text Finley/Liza counters any nostalgia for a blinkered view of 'America' through an acute awareness of difference in which the events of 9/11 are placed in a historical and global context. The focus on subjects from minority ethnicities with some having undergone horrific life events, such as a Vietnamese/American woman whose family lived through the My Lai massacre, a Holocaust survivor, and the Palestinian/Canadian acknowledges that the experience of tragedy brought on by 9/11 and foreign policy decisions made by the US have a global resonance. According to Žižek,

> The Shattering impact of the September 11 attacks can be accounted for only against the background of the border which today separates the digitalized First World from the Third World 'desert of the Real'. It is the awareness that we live in an insulated artificial universe which generates the notion that some ominous agent is threatening us all the time with total destruction.[37]

When considered in relation to Žižek's claims, the monologue 'Insert' reveals this 'insulated artificial universe' and the divide between the First and Third Worlds. This text, encompassing the stories of emigrants and their perspectives on America, invites a focus on these 'minority' viewpoints that call for 'difference' amidst the seeming homogeneity of the national response.

Further, the 'ominous agent' Žižek describes is also questioned through the interaction between the two salt and pepper shaker collectors, from the earlier monologue 'Security', and their encounter with a Muslim passenger on a plane:

> She is traditionally dressed in a burqua. She has two babies. One must be just over a year and the other is a newborn. Kanga and Quagga [the salt and pepper shaker collectors] are helping the Muslim woman get to her seat, a mother, another mother. ...[38]

In this monologue, Kangaroo and Quagga, despite their insensitive collecting of 9/11 memorabilia, go out of their way to help a Muslim mother, 'another mother', to her seat. Through this simple courtesy, they implicitly challenge the ominous agent threatening the First World by contradicting the 'us and them' vision articulated by President

George W. Bush at the time. 'You are', Bush stated in a speech of 2001, 'either with us or against us.'[39] Thus, Kangaroo and Quagga, while they are willing participants in neoliberal economic culture, refuse to wholly trust the rhetorical shift in politics following 9/11. Instead, they acknowledge the woman in a burqua as a mother who, like them, is confronted with a world undergoing change that cannot be limited to simplistic categories.

In contrast to Finley's work, Eve Ensler's hugely popular *The Vagina Monologues* also draws heavily upon the idea of multiple identities by staging as monologues the personal experiences of women reflecting on their relationship with their vaginas. The work premiered in 1996 as a one-woman show in which Ensler in appeared onstage, barefoot and holding note cards. The monologues were based on series of interviews, conducted by Ensler, with a range of women. Some of the material that ended up in the final script was taken verbatim from conversations while other parts were shaped by Ensler based on her own experiences or conversations with others. Each of the monologues was performed in a different voice.[40] Subsequently, *The Vagina Monologues* has evolved into a globally distributable format that commonly combines testimonies from women and the re-performance of these confessional monologues onstage (often by celebrity performers), alongside an activist agenda that attempts to celebrate women's voices and bodies, condemn violence against women, and fundraise in support of the V-Day movement.[41]

However, while the fundraising and activist agenda of the work is now a global force, scholars have frequently questioned the utopic and essentializing aspects of the performance, the monologues and their aesthetic. In the words of Shelly Scott,

> *The Vagina Monologues* paints such a utopian female unity as a goal to strive for but offers no way to attain it. The message of the performance, sandwiched between celebratory jokes, seems to begin – and end – with Vagina = (potential) Victim.[42]

Indeed, the key underpinnings of the work – the authentic voices and celebratory reflections from a variety of female subjects –

simultaneously draws on the notion of individual subjective experience and the idea of a universal and utopic collectivity (all of which may have contributed positively to the popularity and reach of the work). The risk, as Scott and others notes, is that the monologues oversimplify female diversity and fail to incorporate the idea of female difference into activism.[43] *The Vagina Monologues* then, may use the monologue form not as a way of interrupting dominant ideology but as a form of performance that diminishes notions of difference and complexity in female experience.

Conversely, *Make Love* considers the wider cultural resonances in American culture after the events of 9/11 or, as Finley puts it, that 'beautiful day for a tragedy'. Finley's well-known persona is filtered through the cultural archetype of Liza Minnelli in monologues that do not seek to provide an all-encompassing perspective of the events or their impact on American culture, but critique ideological rigidity in the political rhetoric of a stark new millennium.

The Passion of Terri Schiavo

The Passion of Terri Schiavo premiered in the exhibition 'Navigate' at the Baltic Art Centre in Newcastle Upon Tyne, England, on the 1st of July 2005. Just over two weeks later it was performed, in a workshop performance, as a part of a double bill at the Bowery Poetry Club and Cafe in New York City.[44] Subsequently, in 2007, *The Passion* formed the third section of a performance triptych *Wake Up!*, a solo show that also included *She Loved Wars* and *The Dreams of Laura Bush*.[45]

The workshop performance of *The Passion of Terri Schiavo* in New York is characterized by minimal lighting and with the stage, containing a table, lectern, microphone and projection screen, enclosed by heavy curtains separating the performance space from the café, which looks out onto the street. Finley stands on a low stage at the rear of the Bowery Club, dressed in a black shift and reading glasses, speaking to a small, seated audience. The spoken text is composed of short speech fragments or grabs, sometimes single sentences, performed in Finley's distinctive intonation. It begins:

> No one loves Terri like I do. No one loves Terri like I do. I can feel Terri. I have spoken with Terri. Terri and I communicate in a way I communicate with no one else. Terri makes me feel alive for she is so dead.[46]

The text refers to the case of Terri Schiavo, an American woman who collapsed in her home in 1990, at twenty-six years of age, and who remained comatose until her death in March 2005. In 2000, after significant consultation with specialist doctors who found her persistent vegetative state to be almost certainly irreversible, Michael Schiavo – Terri Schiavo's husband and guardian – sought permission to have her feeding tubes removed, thus allowing her to die. A protracted legal battle ensued as Terri Schiavo's parents repeatedly challenged the removal of the feeding tubes in the Florida and then the US supreme courts.

The Schiavo case soon spilled over into the national political arena after George W. Bush called an emergency sitting of the US Senate and House of Representatives in March 2005 in order to pass what came to be known as the 'Palm Sunday Compromise'. This bill transferred jurisdiction of the Schiavo case from state to federal courts and allowed Terri's parents to mount further appeals. The move by the president was widely interpreted as a means of placating the significant evangelical Christian voter base of Bush and the Republican Party.[47] In each case the challenges put forward by Terri's parents were denied. Schiavo's feeding tubes were finally removed on 18 March 2005. She passed away on 31 March 2005.[48]

On the same day, President Bush issued a national address on the passing of Terri Schiavo:

> I urge all those who honor Terri Schiavo to continue to work to build a culture of life, where all Americans are welcomed and valued and

protected, especially those at the mercy of others. The essence of civilization is that the strong have a duty to protect the weak. In cases where there are serious doubts and questions, the presumption should be in the favor of life.[49]

As this excerpt demonstrates, the subject of Terri Schiavo was and is political. It is important to note that Schiavo is approached in Finley's performance, and in the subsequent analysis, as an already mediatized, politicized subject. Marranca asserts that the Schiavo case was a 'theatre of death' where the dilemma of Terri Schiavo played out 'a public spectacle of life and death matters' in America.[50] *The Passion of Terri Schiavo* foregrounds the dissemination of the Schiavo case as a media story, in which Schiavo becomes a controversial figure in the public debate on an individual's right-to-die.

Finley explores, through monologue, the various discourses that spoke over, and for, Schiavo:

> Anyone and everyone loves Terri and we do not discriminate. We do not allow someone to not show their love to Terri even if they have no idea what they are saying and are crazy. People who love Terri do not have to be rational or reasonable. We invite people who do not have their facts right to love Terri and set their own agenda in matters of faith and state.[51]

Central to Finley's performance is her representation of Terri Schiavo not as a dramatic character, but as a conglomeration of media commentary. Finley neither performs as Schiavo's husband Michael, nor any other 'character' from the media coverage of the case. Nor does Finley perform as a persona that recognizably privileges her own 'real life' self, a noted feature of much of her earlier work. As Finley states, 'It's not "Karen Finley", it's the "Passion" which actually becomes the character.'[52] As such, *The Passion of Terri Schiavo* positions the 'Passion' as the primary performance persona.

The spoken text is a mash-up of the various opinions, voices, sentiments and media detritus. This includes voices of those committed to saving Terri Schiavo or 'supporting' her right to die. Initially, the text appears to be verbatim as Finley exclaims, 'Terri is all of us. ... We are all Terri.' Indeed, such lines are especially evocative of the public debate during which figures such as the Reverend Jesse Jackson stated, 'We are all potentially Terris.'[53] However, in *The Passion of Terri Schiavo*, these phrases are now skewed, as Finley continues, 'We are all Terri. We all want to go back to the vegetative state.'[54] It is the bringing together of the following elements: the sentiment surrounding the Schiavo case, the media grabs and their recontextualization in performance that constitutes the 'Passion' persona.

Finley employs a clear association with the stories and retellings of the Passion of Christ as the performance draws important allusions between depictions of Christ's suffering and Terri Schiavo.[55] As she suggests, the notion of the Passion brings together the 'fervor or fever' of emotion and belief that surrounded the case and recalls a similar zeal present in certain Christian rituals and beliefs.[56] *The Passion of Terri Schiavo* thus draws analogies between fanatical religious fervour and the heightened public debate and media coverage of the Schiavo case. This is underwritten by the fact that the case now occupies a symbolic significance in American culture as Schiavo was appropriated as a symbol for the 'pro-life' movement.[57]

The 'Passion as persona' resonates with devotional Christian connotations of faith, unwavering conviction, sacrifice and redemption. Similarly, in performance, Finley delivers the text in a devotional style reminiscent of a priest delivering a sermon. The result is a contrast between her authoritative performance of monologue and the text itself, which is ironic and parodic:

> I am holding a cabbage. This is Terri. This vegetable is Terri. Eat Terri. She is this head of lettuce. I love vegetables. I love Terri. Could Terri be a fruit? This watermelon is Terri. Eat your vegetables. This is the body of Christ. The body of Terri.[58]

This monologue explicitly contradicts the traditional form of the Passion Play as a means of disseminating Christian values and morals throughout the culture. Instead, Finley subverts the ceremonial communion text

'I am holding a cabbage. ... This is the body Christ' in a work that knowingly blasphemes. However, this blasphemy is strategic as it highlights what Finley may consider the larger blasphemy, the appropriation of Schiavo's life story by the (neo)conservative Christian right.

Finley also acknowledges the public reaction over the 2005 film *The Passion of the Christ*, and its concurrent media coverage, as an influence on *The Passion of Terri Schiavo*. The performance alludes to this impact particularly as the opinions of *The Passion of the Christ* director Mel Gibson figure in the text:

> Mel Gibson understands Terri. He has never met her. He understands though. Mel faxed his displeasure with Terri's right to die from a Mexican restaurant. He could not spell her name. ... If only Mel could place the wine on Terri's dry cracked lips, Jesus' blood. Terri is being crucified. Terri is being left to die. Terri needs the body of Christ. Terri is an amazing human being.[59]

This text thus responds, through mocking reference to Gibson as a priest giving over the holy sacrament, to the use of Schiavo as a politicized, mediatized product. Once again, Finley controversially blasphemes in order to reveal what she sees as hypocrisy in Gibson's self-righteous position (the performance coming prior to Gibson's own fall from grace, a decline well documented by the media). Additionally, the performance refers to Congressional disputes over the case of Terri Schiavo. Indeed, in the debate over the so-called 'Palm Sunday Compromise', several Republican speakers evoked the 'Passion of Christ' in reference to Schiavo. In the words of Tom Delay (R-Texas), 'Terri Schiavo has survived her Passion weekend, and she has not been forsaken.'[60] In response, Finley's performance explores the subject of Terri Schiavo foremost as an identity that 'speaks' meaning for others:

> I am so happy because there is a chance that Terri will stay with us. At the final hour we will have her stuffed. There will be a wax museum look alike of Terri. Terri will be in every wax museum in the world. A taxidermist is offering his services to stuff Terri.[61]

The performance contrasts the absurdity of having Schiavo 'stuffed' as if she were some kind of trophy elk, with the suggestion that Terri 'stands for something' important, namely as a symbol of the ongoing debate over right-to-die issues in America.[62] 'Don't tell me,' exclaims the Passion/Finley, 'Terri doesn't stand for something just because she can't stand for herself.'[63]

The New York performance of *The Passion of Terri Schiavo* focuses almost completely on the text and its delivery. And in the absence of Finley's overt, performative, confrontational body, the work noticeably privileges monologue. The performance particularly recalls the trajectory of monologue characterized by the work of Beckett where, in a manner similar to *Not I*, Finley reduces solitary speech to a primary action fundamentally isolated from traditional dramatic speech. This is significant considering that it is the politics of the body that particularly frames previous examinations of Finley's work. Yet, while Finley's body is not central to this workshopped performance, this can also be read as a reflection of the status of the 'body' of Terri Schiavo. Schiavo was described as being in a 'persistent vegetative state', a living body whose brain is persistently unresponsive.[64] In the debate surrounding her, Terri's body was reduced in part to a symbol of the body, an image or even icon that others imbued with meaning.

The vegetative state

The Passion of Terri Schiavo, performed during the second term of George W. Bush, foregrounds a number of elements corresponding to the influence of neoconservative ideology on American culture in the early twenty-first century. Indeed, Irving Kristol's desire was for neoconservatism to address a society that is 'spiritually impoverished', whereby traditional conservatism provides an intellectual framework that concentrates on social and cultural stability.[65] As cultural theorists Michael Hardt and Antonio Negri analyse, this (re)creation of traditional, 'stable' conceptions of the nuclear family, that are explicitly connected to opposition to abortion and homosexuality, are arguably not so much about returning to the past as they are about inventing a contemporary political social order.[66] As such, an endless attention to, even obsession with, 'values' is a noted feature of the ideology of contemporary neoconservatism and indeed the rhetoric historically associated with conservatism and the Christian Right.[67]

Finley's performance playfully considers the terms often associated with the neoconservative ideological framework, including 'faith' and 'family values' in contrast to a 'spiritually impoverished' society. As she declares, 'Terri is a nickname for Theresa. ... It is by no accident that Terri is named Theresa. Terri is a saint. And maybe if she dies that is what God wants, a saint like Terri.'[68] Indeed, Finley's canonization of Schiavo draws attention to the grounding of the debate over Schiavo's right to die in language that evokes moral certainties and fixed values:

> The normal life ceases with Terri. Terri's life is a testament to something bigger and more idealistic than our daily life of meals and chores. Terri's life is magnificent. By loving Terri I become magnificent.[69]

However, in exploring this symbolic rendering of Schiavo as saint-like and beyond everyday life, the performance also pushes the neoconservative privileging of family values to extremes:

> I love Terri like I used to love binge drinking and crystal meth. I love Terri almost as much as I love my daddy whom I never met. I love Terri as much as I love my mother who told me I couldn't do a goddamn thing. I love Terri almost as much as I love my drunk father who porked me when I was four. I love Terri almost as much as I love my mother who beat the shit out of me with a belt while telling me to pray to Jesus. I love Terri as much as I love my sister who burned me with cigarettes. I love Terri more than I love the rapist who got me pregnant. I love Terri as much as my mammogram that I can't afford. I love Terri like fast food and no carbs. I love Terri in a way that I wish I could be loved. I love Terri like I love bowling.[70]

The Passion persona is now infiltrated by a binge drinking drug user; whereby the love of Schiavo is somehow indicative of abuse in a larger social context. These juxtapositions demonstrate Finley's efforts to subvert the ideology of neoconservatism present in the rhetoric surrounding the Schiavo case, which foregrounds conservative morals and 'family values' over 'spiritually impoverished' liberalism.

Finley continually returns to the various discourses that speak over and for the subject of Terri Schiavo. The text of *The Passion* could be newspaper headlines, advertisement jingles, or the sound bite of a radio talkback segment. It is a familiar format especially evocative of mass media and disposable quotes from consumer culture brought to critical attention by artists such as Barbara Kruger. It is also reminiscent of the satiric one-liner of the stand-up comic. The performance contrasts the media frenzy surrounding the case with popular reality television programmes, making tongue-in-cheek 'pitches' for new television shows featuring Terri because, 'Terri can be a lot of fun':

> *Kill Your Idol*: This show would be a different take on *American Idol*. This show would have different catatonic idols would be wheeled around on stage with their caretakers and then each week one of the contestants would be taken off their life support, voted by America. The contestants would be in make-up. And dressed and used as puppets. They would lip-synch. Terri has a winning personality.
>
> Another show would be *Survivor*: on an island people would be left on their own with brain-dead contestants and would have to try and keep them alive.[71]

By contrasting the disposable reality TV format with the popular mediatization of Terri Schiavo, the performance emphasizes the potential for Schiavo to become a disposable product of consumer culture. Finley distorts the media coverage of the Schiavo case through equating Terri's status with the mass appeal of the *American Idol* or *Survivor* franchises. The macabre nature of Finley's *Kill your Idol* where stylists would plaster make-up on the comatose patients' faces satirizes the hyperbole of 'right-to-die' cases by placing them at the level of crass TV celebrity. Here, Finley's performance draws attention to the intersection of the 'values' of neoconservatism and free-market economics.

Indeed, the juxtaposition of the Schiavo case with a parody of reality TV and consumer culture addresses the subject of Terri Schiavo from within an American culture influenced by the ideology of neoconservatism. *The Passion of Terri Schiavo* pushes the mockery of reality TV product to malevolent ends. It points to the identity of Schiavo being one that can and will be simultaneously consumed and sanctified. It is this disjunction that Finley addresses in her work. Through the strategic use of knowing blasphemy and confronting humour – which is in bad taste or even transgressive – Finely mobilizes the monologue as a radical intervention.

The danger here is that Finley, by echoing the talkback style radio grab in the construction and delivery of the text, is oversimplifying the performance's interrogation of the influence of ideology on American culture. This easy parody of reality TV denies the undeniably moral, if flawed, roots of neoconservatism and its complex relationship with neoliberal economics. The risk is in equating the 'evils' of commercial culture with those of the conservative and neoconservative ideology as if they are somehow synonymous with one another. There is also only a small divide between Finley's parody of the disposable quote and the object of parody itself. In this way, *Kill Your Idol* fails to address the complexity of the 'right-to-die' issue by merely putting it alongside a swipe at consumer culture.

The performance does, however, highlight that Terri Schiavo's image is made as mediatized and consumable as any episode of *American Idol*. And that Schiavo's identity is simultaneously at risk of being overwritten with the 'spiritual' 'family values' upheld by neoconservative ideology. Schiavo is thus an embodiment of the conflicting public and media discourses surrounding her. In the performance of *The Passion of Terri Schiavo* and its parodies of neoconservative American culture and the Christian 'pro-life' movement, Schiavo is an unspeaking, unmoving, unthinking and finally unrepresentable body. The comatose subject is overlaid with numerous ideological narratives that infiltrate the 'Passion' of Terri Schiavo.

In employing the Passion persona Finley distances her own viewpoint and positions Schiavo as a figure situated at the intersection of the ideologies that seek to appropriate the circumstances of her life and death. Finley stated that the case was a 'narrative for the nation', within which a grim manifestation of American contemporary culture can be found.[72] Her critique of those who would speak for Schiavo also extends to the president's handling of the issue:

> Does everyone have to be smart? George Bush understands what it is like to be in a vegetative state. Terri is about the rights of dumb people. … Does everyone have to think? Can't you just exist? Isn't that what being a couch potato is about? Isn't that what consumer culture is about? Not to think? To be just a body of constant attention and the object of our desires?[73]

In emphasizing the importance of upholding a 'culture of life' it is clear that the president addressed the case of Terri Schiavo as a moral issue, albeit one influenced by political motives. This approach likewise reflects the influence of ideology that privileges 'moral certainty' and neoconservative 'values' over empirical evidence. *The Passion of Terri Schiavo* interrogates the logic of fixed 'value' systems and by doing so throws up considerable political and ethical challenges to conservative culture in the twenty-first century and ideologies such as neoconservatism that often operate on a binary level: Good versus Evil, Pro-life versus Pro-choice, the White Picket Fence versus the Urban Ghetto.

In contrast, Finley's performances undercut such certainties suggesting an alternative reading of American culture by extending the historical trajectories of US monologue, combining idiosyncratic performance personae and the actions of parody and taboo to sharpen her use of solo speech. In the tradition of anti-mainstream American performance, Finley's monologues are multifaceted constructions that provide the artist with a means to explore public debate, critically comment upon the actions of current ideology, and to reflect upon US culture and politics. Intersecting with the diverse histories of American performance cultures that privilege the alternative voice as a mode of commenting on dominant political order, Finley's work positions the radical monologue as a unique means of antagonistic engagement with contemporary culture.

7
Future Monologue

The reinvigoration of the American monologue comes about through a unique combination of aesthetic innovation and sociopolitical engagement. The solo artists examined here contemplate not only their dramatic performance or literary past, but use the form as a calculated and playful incursion into the texture of the contemporary world, its politics and the effect of that politics on lived social and cultural realities. This resurgence also links back to the rich history of American oratory as a radical response to dominant political rhetoric and ideology and the foregrounding of solo performance as a way of exploring the practices and institutions that create political orders.

In this closing chapter I trace two prominent trajectories that present themselves for the future of the genre. The first draws upon the history of monologue as a combination of comic rant, passionate address, fiery sermon and transgressive speech. The second develops the monologue as an affective and playful rendering of the minute and frequently banal everyday. Discussion of these two interrelated trajectories will suggest that the genre is capable of responding to politics through a different type of engagement: one that is increasingly removed from the twentieth-century tradition of 'political theatre' after Brecht and indicative instead of an aesthetically and formally expanded notion of agonistic solo performance. Indeed, several common features have punctuated the innovative use of monologue over the past three decades:

- an ironic, parodic perspective on the past and present
- interrogation of historical, subjective and narrative authority
- the problem of the self, a feature of the dramatic history of monologue since Shakespeare, that continues to be redefined as often fragmenting, multiple personae

- linear dramatic speech being replaced by multilayered solo texts
- finally, there is the changing influence of media and mediatization on the production and performance of monologue, and indeed the wider culture.

I contend that the combination of these elements in contemporary monologue can be seen as a response to political rhetoric and ideology because of the way in which monologue artists from the 1980s to the 2000s make visible texts, bodies and performances that open up spaces of ambiguity and disjunction within the dominant economic and social narratives that constitute contemporary Western culture. Indeed, by taking into account the influence of trends in global performance from the last thirty years, such as the privileging of monologue in postdramatic theatre, alongside the links to monologue in alternative oratory and performance histories, I argue that we might best call this form postmonologue.

Monologue and the postdramatic

The relationship between the contemporary American monologue and the notion of the postdramatic – a term introduced by Hans-Thies Lehmann in the 1990s to describe a variety of West-European examples of performance that troubled the ingredients of traditional dramatic enactment: character, story, dialogue, conflict and catharsis – is not an obvious one. However, recent theoretical re-examination of Lehmann's term suggests that the notion of the postdramatic has gained international currency and influence, and is widely translated and readily applied to contemporary performance from the United States and elsewhere. Further, the postdramatic increasingly repositions new forms and strategies of political engagement in performance.[1] Therefore, one of the ways of examining how American monologue engages with new modes of social and political reflection is to consider the notion of the monologue in relation to the postdramatic.

According to Lehmann, theatre can be divided along two axes, the *intra-scenic* axis and the *extra-scenic* (or theatron) axis. Theatrical discourse is simultaneously directed at the interlocutors in the play along the *intra-scenic* axis, and directed *extra-scenically* at the designated space of the spectators.[2] In simple terms there exists the insular world of the play, in which characters react to one another in a fictional universe, and the 'real' external world in which the spectators interact with the theatre space and the performance. The postdramatic contrasts the features of Western drama common since Aristotle (mimetic enactment within a cohesive story-world) with non-linear, non-dialogic, non-cathartic events to break down traditional distinctions between these intra and extra-scenic dimensions.

The monologue is important to postdramatic theatre because it achieves this break between real and fictional worlds. Monologue can easily address the external world and thereby connect personal experience with the experience and perception of art. In the words of Lehmann,

> All the different varieties of monologue ... including solo performance, have in common that the *intra-scenic axis recedes compared to the theatron axis*. The actor's speaking is now accentuated above all as a 'speaking to' the audience; his/her speech is marked as the speech of a real speaking person, its expressiveness more as the 'emotive' dimension of the performer's language than as the emotional expression of the fictive character represented. ... In postdramatic theatre, the theatre situation is not simply added to the autonomous reality of the dramatic fiction to animate it.[3]

Monologue then, is a genre that has the potential to disrupt the 'smooth functioning' mimetic and dialogic elements of drama that uphold the dramatic fiction. This conception recalls the notion of the monologue as a deviant discourse that breaks away from linguistic norms. As Pavis notes, the monologue has the potential to communicate 'directly with all of society'.[4] Therefore, in contemporary monologues the historic potential of the genre to fracture the unity of dramatic dialogue and the dramatic play is more prevalent than ever.

As Lehmann argues, 'In the age of media, it is precisely such forms of speaking ... namely the monologue and the chorus, that move into the centre of theatre.'[5] Increasingly, over the past thirty years, there has been a trend in Western theatre and performance in which dialogic plays are frequently translated into monologues and non-theatrical texts gain renewed currency. This trend can be readily seen in the global intensification of documentary theatre forms and the prevalence of documentary theatre in the West.[6] Performances including David Hare's *The Permanent Way* (2003) and *Stuff Happens* (2004), the 'reality trend' theatre of Rimini Protokoll, the work of Australian company Version 1.0, and Katie Pollack and Paul Daley's *The Hansard Monologues: A Matter of Public Importance* (2013) are a few examples that indicate the revival of the form as a mode of performance that is increasingly layered and playful in its use of notions of authenticity. These documentary works each address contemporary political and social questions such as the privatization of public assets indicative of neoliberal economics (*The Permanent Way*), the bureaucratization of the political (Rimini Protokoll), or the ethical bankruptcy of political and media figures who deceive the public (*Stuff Happens*, Version 1.0). Yet, in staging the 'real' and drawing on documentary texts or non-professional participants they also disturb, through their innovations to language and form, ideas of inherent authenticity and factual reportage.[7] Contemporary documentary theatre is thus a multilayered response to global issues that takes up elements of the monologue form as it was developed in the 1990s by artists like Anna Deavere Smith.

Innovations to the monologue genre not only continue in solo works for performance, but in theatrical play texts too. Contemporary American playwrights such as Suzan-Lori Parks, Wallace Shawn, Sarah Ruhl and Tony Kushner often insert astonishing monologic sections into their works. Moreover, if we widen our view to include other Western examples, the plays of British artist Sarah Kane reveal a distinctive use of monologic language. In Kane's *Crave* (1998) and *4:48 Psychosis* (2000), and her contemporary Martin Crimp's work such as *Attempts on Her Life* (1997) and *Fewer Emergencies* (2005), the 'characters' often speak in individualized monologues.[8]

Similarly, Karen Jürs-Munby suggests that a productive *agonism* – a kind of inherently political verbal struggle – is a key element in the texts of Elfriede Jelinek.

> Jelinek's figures generally are not *dramatic* protagonists and antagonists but *post*-protagonistic figures. … They are not characters entering into dialogue with one another but more like structural figures speaking in endless monologues that are traversed by several voices. … These figures are at best place-holders for individuals but more often than not 'text-bearers' where different discourses intersect.[9]

Jelinek's texts then, suggest that monologues become the means of antagonism and dissent for these postdramatic figures. Such moves away from traditional dialogic forms indicates that a broad range of twenty-first-century works use monologue to convey a deep unease about the shape of contemporary Western culture. In the context of American theatre Robinson detects, in the work of the Wooster Group, an attention to opening up spaces that confront 'cultural absence' and the notion of ruin 'without the guarantee of deliverance'.[10] Additionally, in recent works by American playwrights, Robinson also observes characters that are so 'emptied out' and 'affectless or, if forthcoming, so skeptical of their own disclosures that they revert to self-blurring ambivalence'.[11] Monologue, as used in these contemporary plays and performances, arguably re-emerges in the current century as a form that intensifies the fragmented language and isolated subjects of global capitalism.

Further, frameworks for monologue like the postdramatic also explicitly extend the genre beyond a 'text-centered approach' and take into account notions of sound, image, movement and idiosyncrasies of voice, gesture and body.[12] Indeed, as in the monologue artists examined in this book, the 'real' individual body and voice of the performer of the monologue is situated alongside the written and spoken text to provoke new readings that can enhance the solo speech. Lehmann discusses a turn to monologue through examination of Robert Wilson's *Hamlet – A Monologue* (1994) and observes Wilson's rearrangement of Shakespeare's text into solitary speech. He also points to the legacy of Brechtian techniques in the construction of a performance persona, whereby Wilson's performance is 'obviously *verfremded* (defamiliarized)' ensuring that 'at each moment one is aware of the quotation, [the "exhibition"] of the Hamlet text as a material for the persona of the performer Wilson'.[13]

Hamlet – A Monologue is part of a tradition of monological and 'monodramatic' versions of the original Shakespeare text due, in part, to the primacy of Shakespeare's soliloquies. Heiner Müller's *Hamletmachine* (1977) is a seminal example of such a work in its condensing of the dramatic text into five monologic fragments. In the original text the reflexive character of Hamlet expresses questions of identity, tradition, autonomy and interiority that, as we saw, are possibly indicative of the beginnings of the modern self. In Müller's *Hamletmachine* the eponymous character is now cut adrift. Dialogue, as the previous expression of social interaction between subjects, is replaced by radically fragmented solo speech. Yet, unlike the crisis of the inner self that finds expression through the monologues of Shakespeare, the text of *Hamletmachine* becomes a sign for the fractured and alienated social experience of contemporary subjects. These monologic interventions become stark reminders of the individualizing nature of capitalist culture and the speed of neoliberal expansion.

Wilson and Müller are not the only ones to play with the character of Hamlet as a solo monologue performance. Japanese playwright and theatre-maker Takeshi Kawamura also borrows from the original *Hamlet* in his radically fragmented play *Hamletclone* (2000) and the Wooster Group's 2005 version of *Hamlet* reconstructs Richard Burton's 1964 performance of the Shakespearian original at the Lunt-Fontanne Theatre in New York. The Wooster Group's version of *Hamlet* demonstrates a continuing interest within vanguard contemporary theatre in translating the Shakespearian text from a dialogue to a monologue.

The monologic structure of *Hamletmachine* also prefigures other contemporary examples of theatre that problematize dialogue as the fundamental means of dramatic expression. This preference for work with a 'monodramatic tendency,' such as the canonical American play-texts often refigured into monologic sections by New York's the Wooster Group, signals the end of the traditional use of dialogue.[14] Similarly, the Nature Theater of Oklahoma transfer verbatim recordings of phone calls, or improvised retellings of famous movie or theatre plots, into monologic speech in solo works such as *Rambo Solo* (2008) or collective pieces such as *Romeo and Juliet* (2009) and *Life and Times* (2010–). These works are epically banal and frequently hilarious versions of contemporary American monologue that push the depersonalized deadpan voice found in Robert Wilson, Richard Foreman, the Wooster Group, and Laurie Anderson's work to absurd extremes.

However, in the context of a Western culture that commonly privileges the individual experience and monologic voice, the blurring that frequently typifies contemporary American solo performance – between autobiography, playful confession, quotation, ambiguous personae and parody alongside material drawn from real testimony or real events – is not without its complications. Indeed, as the previous chapters have noted, one of the seductive qualities of the monologue is its apparent claim to authenticity. And while Gray, Anderson, Smith and Finley all negotiate the 'reality-status' of their texts by mobilizing distinct performance personae, the notion of 'truthfulness' in monologue remains a contested area.

As the contrasting readings of Mike Daisey and Eve Ensler's work alongside that of Gray and Finley indicates, questions of authenticity, aesthetic form, solo voice and body, efficacy and politics continue to figure as complicated elements of monologue performance. Indeed, while American monologuists of the last three decades typically engage with notions of individuality and authenticity, how they position this negotiation within exploration of contemporary politics and culture is critical. One way to enhance understandings of these negotiations is to position an interrogation of monologue alongside recent theorizations of performance and culture.

A postpolitical present

Indeed, new and future monologues may also respond to a present Western context in which power is primarily directed to the management of 'consensus' in a way that vitally restricts imagination and, simultaneously, the production of political art by limiting the possibility of alternative forms of creativity and activism.[15] As Erik Swyngedouw puts it, the postpolitical present

> is structured around the perceived inevitability of capitalism and a market economy as the basic organizational structure of the social and economic order, for which there is no alternative. The corresponding mode of governmentality is structured around dialogical forms of consensus formation, technocratic management and problem-focused governance, sustained by populist discursive regimes.[16]

In response to this organization and distribution of power, contemporary American monologues provide a mode of localized, transgressive and linguistic performance that may address consensual politics through the use of solo performance as a response to global culture and politics.

In the epilogue to *Postdramatic Theatre*, Lehmann reflects upon the relationship between politics (issues of social power) and performance. According to Lehmann, it is not through direct, moralistic means that performance can positively engage with the political, but rather through the 'implicit substance and critical value of its *mode of representation*'.[17] Performance can make visible the 'broken thread' between personal experience and the experience of the world – what he calls an *aesthetic of responsibility* – in a way that answers the tedium of a 'daily flood of artificial formulas of intensification' or, in other words, the numbing effect brought about by endless flows of media images and capital in contemporary Western culture. For Lehmann, it does so not by representing the 'fictive figure' (Hamlet) or a fictive tragedy, but by upholding the banal and trivial, the simple everyday encounter, look or gesture.[18]

This 'banalization' can be readily seen in the work of American monologuists in a manner that is both witty and representative of the everyday. Gray recalls the details of his daily life throughout all of his monologues, while Anderson too offers a detached view of everyday experience. Similarly, though more overtly, Anna Deavere Smith approaches the politicized and mediatized events of the Los Angeles riots through the recording of everyday viewpoints from a variety of subject positions/local perspectives. These performances gain power when juxtaposed against the imposing ideological foundations that surround them: a homeless woman's bleeding feet encourages reflection on the disjunction between the perpetual growth of the neoliberal economic vision and the lived experience of human subjects; or as the perspective of gang member Twilight Bey becomes a document of social experience in the context of contemporary class and race politics in America.

Further, as Mouffe argues, contemporary artistic and cultural practices that bring about the cultivation and release of *affects* 'constitute a crucial site of intervention for counter-hegemonic practices', because of the ways they can help to imagine and enhance the antagonistic dimensions of everyday life.[19] Affect, as discussed by Brian Massumi (after Spinoza) refers to a 'gap between *content* and *effect*'.[20] Affect is a felt intensity that accompanies a change, or transition, in the body. It is neither emotion, nor does it contain subjective content.[21] According to Lehmann, one means of provoking affect is through the breaking of taboo. As he puts it:

> In the age of rationalization, of the ideal of calculation and of the generalized rationality of the market, it falls to the theatre to deal with extremes of affect by means of an *aesthetics of risk*, extremes which always also contain the possibility of offending or breaking taboos.[22]

This conception of an *aesthetics of risk* is a fruitful notion for the analysis of US monologue, particularly when applied to the performances of

Karen Finley. Finley uses monologue, in conjunction with techniques drawn from performance art and body art, as a method of unsettling taboo. Taboo, as Lehmann discusses it, can be defined as 'a socially anchored form of affective reaction that rejects ("abjects") certain realities, forms of behaviour or images as "untouchable", disgusting or unacceptable prior to any rational judgement'.[23] The performances of *Shut Up and Love Me, Make Love,* and *The Passion of Terri Schiavo* each contain elements that, through monologue, question accepted realities. Finley uses erotic, transgressive language and parody to approach taboo subjects such as sexual desire, the events of 9/11, and the case of Terri Schiavo.

Finley's uncovering of taboo subjects should not be seen as an isolated or neutral act, but as a starting point for analysis of current culture and politics. Through reflection on the events of 9/11, *Make Love* critiques the dominant ideological reaction to the attacks and the impact this blinkered political rhetoric had on the wider American culture. Similarly, *The Passion of Terri Schiavo* uses the media debate on an American subject's right-to-die and, through a satiric and blasphemous appropriation of Christian narratives, challenges the exploitation of Terri Schiavo in the service of conservative and neoconservative ideology.

The ability of monologue to break down the distance between the spectator and their reaction to what is happening in the present – their capacity to be affected by it – may partly enable the form's effective ability to engage with politics. Moreover, the content and aesthetic of the performances of Gray, Anderson, Smith and Finley is largely non-dramatic and draws attention to the world outside the performance space. Indeed, their monologues do not privilege literary and dramatic traditions, rather, their performances are produced through the use of historical material and documents, from the 'autobiographic' self, from the traditions of American solo performance and oratory and from the contemporary social, cultural or political world around them.

As noted earlier, Lehmann contends that postdramatic theatre is political not by the message or theses it contains, but by the means in which its mode of representation provokes 'acts and actions' that confront 'the spectators with abysmal fear, shame and even mounting aggression'.[24] For Lehmann, theatre is political not due to either its overt political statements or engagement, but due to its 'basic disrespect for tenability'.[25] With this statement in mind, the political potential of contemporary monologues are articulated, once again, in the poetic interruptions of Karen Finley. Finley's *The Passion of Terri Schiavo* is knowingly offensive, blackly comic and blasphemous. In this work the holy body of Christ becomes a combination of the comatose body of Terri Schiavo and a mixture of garden fruits and vegetables: '[Terri] is this head of lettuce. ... This watermelon is Terri. Eat your vegetables. This is the body of Christ. The body of Terri.'[26] This monologue is constructed in a manner that is likely to produce the shock, disorientation, not to mention the mixture of humour, pain and fun, that typifies Finley's recent monologues.

The affective potential of Karen Finley's monologues works in conjunction with the powerful production of monologue as a textual and linguistic form. *The Passion of Terri Schiavo* privileges solitary speech over all other elements of performance. Further, the solo body and solo voice come together to create works that are transgressive and political. In contrast to monologues that remain based in images or abstraction, this performance examines the case of Terri Schiavo through the *explicit* engagement with politics and positions the contemporary monologue as both a mode of aesthetic innovation *and* a linguistic, textual form capable of critique through its content. Finley's performances can be read as textual responses to power or countercultural sermons.

As the critical reception of Finley's more recent work *The Jackie Look* (2010) demonstrates, her work continues to critique the factors underpinning the uneven historical and political distributions of American power, often in unsettling and disturbing ways.[27] Finley's renderings of three iconic American women – Liza Minnelli, Terri Schiavo and Jacqueline Kennedy-Onassis – reveals underlying tensions between features of the neoliberal American

Dream, optimism, patriotism, individual wealth and celebrity, and the lives of contemporary women in the United States.

Significantly, Hardt and Negri suggest that the 'return to the traditional family' should not be misconstrued as a mere return to fixed 'Modern' values. Instead, they argue that the 'traditional family' is an ideological formation that is 'constructed retrospectively through the lens of contemporary anxieties and fears' and should therefore be considered as 'part of a political project against contemporary social order'.[28] The monologue work of Finley uses both affective and linguistic means to highlight, therefore, the contradictions of a world vision that attempts to reconcile both economic individualism and expansion with 'traditional moral values'. Finley's performance reveals neoconservative claims for the 'return to the traditional family' and 'moral, religious values' as the welding of an ideological project onto twenty-first-century American society and culture.

Conversely, Spalding Gray uses intellectual, communicational and linguistic techniques to examine aspects of the mythological narratives of American history. Gray's confessional mode, in its use of a self-reflexive persona and historical material, invites reflection on historic American cultural and military/political actions. Further, just as current reconsideration of *Swimming to Cambodia* can provoke parallels to American foreign policy in the post-9/11 era, at the time of its first performance the monologue was positioned within the context of the Cold War. Gray's work intervenes into politics by contrasting his wry observations with aspects of American mythology that makes known the primacy of a powerful 'global' American identity that is white, male, capitalist and insensitive to cultural difference. This identity is shown, in keeping with neoliberalism, to uphold the values of individualized choice whereby one is free to 'buy into' culture either through the search for a perfect moment on a Thai beach or through an interaction with a prostitute named Joy. Yet, against this backdrop, Gray also lays out the tragedy of Cambodia's past in grim, ultimately affective, terms.

In writing the final chapter of this book I revisited the audio recording of *Life Interrupted* (2006), Gray's last and unfinished monologue. The work is read by Gray's long-time friend Sam Shepard and details the serious car crash in Ireland in which Gray sustained the injuries that ultimately led to his subsequent period of severe depression. Listening to Gray's words read in Shepard's laconic Illinois drawl draws immediate attention to all the numerous, often barely noticeable, aspects of Gray's voice and delivery that made his work so compelling. The aura of the individual artist and the 'grain' of Gray's voice is missing. Yet, Gray's final monologue – much of which takes place in a gruesome Irish hospital – also recalls Gray's parody of himself as the privileged American traveller thrust into an unsettling relationship with a new experience of culture, geography and historical specificity. As Francine Prose suggests in the Foreword to the work, 'It always seemed as if he were just going on, or returning from a trip, even when the journey had taken him no farther than a walk through the neighborhood he so loved: downtown Manhattan.'[29] Gray's work continues to be contemporary because of his use of the confessional monologue as a way of drawing attention to individual subjectivity while simultaneously disturbing ideas of authentic self and exploring the complexity of historical experience.

In contrast, Anna Deavere Smith's work relies on a specific community, rather than autofiction, for its content. *Twilight: Los Angeles, 1992* draws upon, in particular, communication with multiple subjects. Hardt and Negri theorize that one method of alternative politics available to contemporary subjects is gained through the collaboration and social interaction between subjectivities. This alternative politics emerges, not through a hierarchic central point or harmony between individuals, but 'in the space *between*, in the social space of communication ... created in collaborative social interactions'.[30] In Hardt and Negri's terms, Smith's integration of documentary techniques within the performance of monologue draws upon the very collaborative communication they proclaim.

Yet, Smith's work not only reveals differences and collaborative interactions, but also extends and animates productive sites of tension and disruption in the processes of counterposing diverse narratives of contemporary experience. Smith's work responds to issues of race and class politics within a specific community in a manner that ultimately addresses these very same issues in the context of wider American culture. Her work belongs to the long tradition of groundbreaking American orators that address the legacy of inequality in the history of US culture and politics and the use of solo speech as a mode of civil rights action. Smith's work, including her exploration of illness, death and the American health system in *Let Me Down Easy*,[31] places side by side the economically, socially and politically diverse testimonies of American citizens and, in their juxtapositioning, reveals the divisions between, and disenfranchisement of, large segments of the community. Smith's work shows that for the radically disenfranchised, such as Twilight Bey, Rodney King or the New Orleans physicians working in the aftermath of Hurricane Katrina, American society is underpinned by systemic inequality in economics, race and class.

Conversely, the monologues of Laurie Anderson intervene into politics through engagement with media and information culture, rather than community collaboration. Anderson integrates monologue within a hybridized performance environment. She uses linguistic and communicational features to invite contemplation on the means of communication under current globalized conditions. She employs a cool persona where the monologues, as a mode of representation and as texts, are depersonalized and draw upon traditions of quotation and the deadpan voice that are found in American music and performance from the 1970s and post-punk culture of the 1980s.

Anderson's persona also begins to encourage reflection, primarily through the performance of solo speech, on the political reality of US culture, in particular on the reality for Mexican immigrants who join the ranks of voluntary and involuntary migrants, and the reality for a Playboy Bunny aware of the exploitative economic situation of women working for fourteen cents an hour in the garment district.

Consequently, Anderson's recent works such as *Homeland* (2007) continue to consider the by-products of American, and indeed Western culture through their monologic content as well as their mediatized images and voice.

The legacy of these contemporary American monologue artists provides various techniques with which to intervene in and disrupt consensual thinking about our political present: Gray, through obsessive and parodic confession, Anderson, through cool irony, Smith, through documentary and collaboration, and Finley, through transgressive distortion. Yet, whether the features they use in the performance of monologue are affective and corporeal or more overtly linguistic and textual, the sociopolitical American context they address is a material one. Importantly, each of the monologists examined in this book reflects on US culture, challenges American mythologies and historical conceptions of individuality, economic freedom, freedom of speech, race and class in American culture.

In the diverse traditions of solo speech and oratory throughout US history, combined with influences drawn from the innovative use of monologue in Western theatre, these artists reveal fundamental and difficult contradictions at the core of American society. US monologue performances enable this critique through the use of parody, mediatization and personae, everyday material and affective performance, non-dramatic material, and finally through their position as monologues – a historically solitary, linguistic and political form.

Future forms

Future monologists will continue to intervene into culture and politics in myriad ways. However, more recent trends can also be traced back to the ways in which seminal artists such as Gray, Anderson, Smith and Finley engaged with and contested their world. Future innovations can therefore draw in new combinations of *ironic-autobiography* into a *radical* critique of civil rights, or a *documentary* form that synthesizes with the *cool everyday* self.

While the monologues of Gray, Anderson, Smith and Finley exist principally as linguistic performances, their innovations also occur at the level of language, body, images, voice, intensity and aesthetic. These artists mix elements of Western monologue performance but also remain part of the American tradition of using virtuoso solo performance as an antagonistic response to current events. They belong to the varied traditions of countercultural performance in the United States, and the intersection between civil, religious and political discourse with alternative aesthetic and political intervention. Contemporary American monologues are innovative jeremiads for the twenty-first century – they are a form of political sermon, confession or rant that explores the realities of the everyday life and the legacy of the American Dream. Contemporary monologues reanimate a mode of aesthetics and engagement with politics, through language and performance.

Future monologues are also likely to integrate new technologies and employ non-dramatic elements (images, light, sound and so on) in ways that question the centrality of the linguistic text. The further integration and internalization of mediatized culture into contemporary monologue suggests building on cool works like those of Anderson, in particular for its use of monologue as one element within a hybridized performance environment. Elements of this approach can be seen in performances disseminated as podcasts, such as the recent trend towards audio tours and interactive performances. These monologues can be seen in British company Rotozaza's 'autotheatro' series, including the monologic and instructional performance *Wondermart* (2009) – a tour through the branded space of the twenty-first-century supermarket – and in the collaborations between Ant Hampton and Tim Etchells in *The Quiet Volume* (2010) and *Lest We See Where We Are* (2014).

Future potentials for monologue also suggests an increasing mediatization of the documentary theatre techniques used by Anna Deavere Smith to include more multimedia elements. This trend is already beginning to be observed in recent documentary theatre wherein sophisticated understandings of media culture and forms of non-textual theatre are enhancing documentary forms and playfully re-examining notions of authenticity. A trace of Smith's approach can be found in the voiceprint scripts of Roslyn Oades and in the new innovations made to the documentary form and other recent monologues that privilege innovative language, speech and commentary.

The frequently monologic and deceptively simple texts of companies such as the United Kingdom' Forced Entertainment and the United States' Nature Theater of Oklahoma employ aspects of banal speech, as do the pop-cabaret texts of Young Jean Lee. These works emphasize a kind of 'slow dramaturgy', theorized elsewhere by Peter Eckersall and myself, as a kind of interruption of neoliberal culture through an attention to slowness and the everyday.[32] Such approaches provide a model of political and ecological performance in that they offer an aesthetic alternative to the apparent smoothness and speed of capatalist development, that is a key part of contemporary social, political and economic flows.

Future monologues have the capacity to privilege dramaturgical slowness in relation to swiftly changing mediatized, globalized culture and to contest political realities through emphasizing language, speech and commentary. Future monologuists can likewise draw upon notions of transgressive speech, everyday minutiae, cool personae and the ironic intervention of self and autobiography. They may also mobilize media as an affective and hybrid response to global culture or monologue as a radical performance of civil rights and protest. The legacy of works by Gray, Anderson, Smith and Finley are evident in these potentials, potentials that signal that the monologue genre remains innovative, critical and joyful.

The innovations made by artists such as Gray, Anderson, Smith and Finley underpin the resurgence of the monologue as a contemporary genre of solo performance and a particularly American phenomenon. These artists use solo speech as a means through which to respond to their specific social environment. They have each helped to reinvent the monologue genre as a sophisticated means of critically engaging with US culture. Their characteristic combination of politics and aesthetics suggests an enriched form of solo performance that paves the way for monologic responses to our present. In closing, these performances and their future inheritors may be better titled postmonologue works.

Postmonologues point towards further developments in global monologue performance and new forms arising from the traditions of oratory and storytelling and the solo speech-act in Western drama. They are likely to have continued relevance as a mode of political critique because postmonologues are creative and critically effective reflections that situate the personal in relation to world events. The notion of the postmonologue looks forward to the next generation of monologue artists that privilege new linguistic and performative acts, and new political potentials for performance.

Notes

Introduction

1 Georgio Agamben, *What Is An Apparatus? And Other Essays*, trans. David Kishik and Stefan Pedatella (Stanford: Stanford University Press, 2009), 39–54.
2 Ibid., 44, 51–3.
3 Ibid., 53.
4 Deborah R. Geis, *Postmodern Theatric[k]s: Monologue in Contemporary American* (Drama, Ann Arbor: University of Michigan Press, 1995).
5 Shannon Jackson, *Social Works: Performing Art, Supporting Publics* (New York and London: Routledge, 2011), 147.
6 Chantal Mouffe, *On the Political* (London and New York: Routledge, 2005), 9.
7 Baz Kershaw, *The Radical in Performance: Between Brecht and Baudrillard* (London and New York: Routledge, 1999), 60–1. See also David Román, *Performance in America: Contemporary U.S. Culture and the Performing Arts* (Durham and London: Duke University Press, 2005).
8 For further discussion of consensus and contemporary political order, see Mouffe, *On the Political*, 2005. See also Chantal Mouffe, *Agonistics: Thinking the World Politically* (London: Verso, 2013); Slavoj Žižek, *The Ticklish Subject: The Absent Centre of Political Ontology* (London and New York: Verso, 1999), and Jacques Rancière, *The Emancipated Spectator* (London and New York: Verso, 2009).
9 Alan Read, *Theatre in the Expanded Field: Seven Approaches to Performance* (London: Bloomsbury Methuen, 2013), xv.
10 Kershaw, *The Radical in Performance*, 15.
11 Marvin Carlson, *Performance: An Introduction* (London and New York: Routledge, 1996), 79–101; See also Bonnie Marranca, 'Performance, a Personal History', *Performing Arts Journal* 28, no. 1 (PAJ82) (2006): 3–19.
12 Michael Kirby, 'On Acting and Not-Acting', in *Acting (Re)Considered*, ed. Phillip B. Zarrilli (London and New York: Routledge, 1995), 43–58.

13 Kirby, 'On Acting and Not-Acting', 47, 56–8.
14 Carlson, *Performance*, 114–17; Roselee Goldberg, *Performance: Live Art since 1960* (New York and London: Harry N. Abrams Inc., 1998), 28; Richard Schechner, *Performance Studies: An Introduction* (Abingdon, London and New York: Routledge, 2006).
15 Geis, *Postmodern Theatric[k]s*, 152. See also Michael Peterson, *Straight White Male: Performance Art Monologues* (Jackson: University Press of Mississippi, 1997), 12.
16 Carlson, *Performance*, 79; Goldberg, *Performance*, 12.
17 Carlson, *Performance*, 82–6.
18 Deirdre Heddon, *Autobiography and Performance* (Houndmills and New York: Palgrave Macmillan, 2008).
19 Carlson, *Performance*, 117.
20 Heddon, *Autobiography and Performance*, 2.
21 Theodore Shank, *Beyond the Boundaries: American Alternative Theatre* (Ann Arbor: University of Michigan Press, 2002), 195. See also: Jo Bonney, 'Preface', in *Extreme Exposure: An Anthology of Solo Performance Texts from the Twentieth Century*, ed. Jo Bonney (New York: Theatre Communications Group, 2000), xi–xvi.
22 Sherrill Grace, 'Theatre and the AutoBiographical Pact: An Introduction', in *Theatre and AutoBiography: Writing and Performing Lives in Theory and Practice*, ed. Sherrill Grace and Jerry Wasserman (Vancouver: Talonbooks, 2006), 15. See also Shannon Jackson, *Professing Performance: Theatre in the Academy from Philology to Performativity* (Cambridge: Cambridge University Press, 2004) and Román, *Performance in America*.
23 Published in English as Hans-Thies Lehmann, *Postdramatic Theatre*, trans. Karen Jürs-Munby (Abingdon and London: Routledge, 2006).

Chapter 1

1 Paul C. Castagno, *New Playwriting Strategies* (London and New York: Routledge, 2012), 197; Dmitri Nikulin, *On Dialogue* (Lanham, MD: Lexington Books, 2006), 193–4.

2 Ken Frieden, *Genius and Monologue* (Ithaca: Cornell University Press, 1985), 18.
3 Clare Wallace, 'Monologue Theatre, Solo Performance and Self as Spectacle', in *Monologues: Theatre, Performance, Subjectivity*, ed. Clare Wallace (Prague: Litteraria Pragensia, 2006), 4.
4 Patrice Pavis, *Dictionary of the Theatre: Terms, Concepts, and Analysis* (Toronto and Buffalo: University of Toronto Press, 1998), 219.
5 Ibid.
6 Frieden, *Genius and Monologue*, 20.
7 Pavis, *Dictionary of the Theatre*, 218.
8 Geis, *Postmodern Theatric[k]s*, 15–16.
9 Euripides, *Medea and Other Plays*, trans. Philip Vellacott (London: Penguin Books, 1963), 53–4.
10 Geis, *Postmodern Theatric[k]s*, 16.
11 Ibid., 15.
12 Sophocles, *Electra and Other Plays*, trans. E. F. Watling (London: Penguin Books, 1953), 40.
13 Wolfgang Clemen, *Shakespeare's Soliloquies*, trans. Charity Scott Stokes (London and New York: Methuen, 1987), 3; C. H. MacKay, *Soliloquy in Nineteenth-century Fiction* (Basingstoke, Hampshire: Macmillan, 1987), 1; Lloyd A. Skiffington, *The History of English Soliloquy: Aeschylus to Shakespeare* (Lanham, MD: University Press of America, 1985), ix.
14 Geis, *Postmodern Theatric[k]s*, 8–9.
15 Clemen, *Shakespeare's Soliloquies*, 3.
16 Skiffington, *The History of English Soliloquy*, 74.
17 Ibid., 76–7.
18 Ibid., 87.
19 The aside is another key category of monologue. Frieden defines it as a 'staged self-address' (1985, 19), and it is a device that is particularly important to comedy as it can be used to set up irony and build comic effect.
20 *Othello*, Act 2: Scene 1, from William Shakespeare, *The Complete Works of William Shakespeare: Comprising his Plays and Poems* (London: Spring Books, 1963).

21 Clemen, *Shakespeare's Soliloquies*, 4–5.
22 Frieden, *Genius and Monologue*, 133.
23 Skiffington, *The History of English Soliloquy*, 87, 96–7.
24 *Hamlet*, dir. by Laurence Olivier, The Criterion Collection, (1948) 2000, DVD Rec.
25 *Hamlet*, Act 1: Scene 2, from Shakespeare, *The Complete Works of William Shakespeare*.
26 Geis, *Postmodern Theatric[k]s*, 16–17.
27 See Frieden, *Genius and Monologue*.
28 See Charles Taylor, *Sources of the Self: The Making of the Modern Identity* (Cambridge, MA: Harvard University Press, 1989), 175, 503; Steve Pile and Nigel Thrift, 'Introduction', in *Mapping the Subject: Geographies of Cultural Transformation*, ed. Steve Pile and Nigel Thrift (London and New York: Routledge, 1995), 8–9.
29 Terry Eagleton, *William Shakespeare* (Oxford and New York: Blackwell, 1987), 72, 74–5.
30 Ibid., 75.
31 See Eagleton, *William Shakespeare*, 72–5; John Lee, *Shakespeare's Hamlet and the Controversies of Self* (Oxford: Clarendon Press, 2000), 150, 203, 228; Christopher Pye, *The Vanishing: Shakespeare, the Subject, and Early Modern Culture* (Durham: Duke University Press, 2000), 109, 125.
32 See Clemen, *Shakespeare's Soliloquies*.
33 Brian Richardson, 'Drama and Narrative', in *Cambridge Companion to Narrative Theory*, ed. David Herman (Cambridge: Cambridge University Press, 2007), 151; Brian Richardson, 'Point of View in Drama: Diegetic Monologue, Unreliable Narrators, and the Author's Voice on Stage', *Comparative Drama* 22, no. 3 (1988): 202.
34 Wallace, 'Monologue Theatre, Solo Performance and Self as Spectacle', 10.
35 Glennis Byron, *Dramatic Monologue* (London and New York: Routledge, 2003), 45.
36 Wallace, 'Monologue Theatre, Solo Performance and Self as Spectacle', 11.
37 Andrew Kennedy, *Dramatic Dialogue: The Duologue of Personal Encounter* (Cambridge and New York: Cambridge University Press, 1983), 199; Geis, *Postmodern Theatric[k]s*, 29.

38 Henrik Ibsen, *Plays*, trans. Michael Leverson Meyer (London: Eyre Methuen, 1980), 178.
39 Anton Chekhov, *Uncle Vanya*, trans. Elisaveta Fen (London: Penguin Books, 1954), 103–4.
40 Ibid., 104.
41 Jovan Hristić, 'Time in Chekhov: the Inexorable and the Ironic', *New Theatre Quarterly* 1, no. 3 (August 1985): 271–82.
42 Chekhov, *Uncle Vanya*, 150–1.
43 Peta Tait, 'Performative Acts of Gendered Emotions and Bodies in Chekhov's "The Cherry Orchard"', *Modern Drama* 43, no. 1 (Spring 2000): 87–99.
44 Geis, *Postmodern Theatric[k]s*, 21.
45 Eugene O'Neill, *Nine Plays* (New York: The Modern Library, 1954), 487.
46 Mark Maufort, 'Exorcisms of the past: Avatars of the O'Neillian Monologue in Modern American Drama', *The Eugene O'Neill Review* 22, no. 1/2 (1998): 123.
47 O'Neill, *Nine Plays*, 495–6.
48 Marc Robinson, *The American Play 1787-2000* (New Haven and London: Yale University Press, 2009), 168–9.
49 Annette J. Saddik, *Contemporary American Drama* (Edinburgh: Edinburgh University Press, 2007), 40–71.
50 Tennessee Williams, *A Streetcar Named Desire and Other Plays* (London: Penguin Books, 1962), 234.
51 Robinson, *The American Play*, 272.
52 Marc Robinson, *The Other American Drama* (Cambridge: Cambridge University Press, 1994), 34.
53 Geis, *Postmodern Theatric[k]s*, 22; Robinson, *The American Play*, 271.
54 Arthur Miller, *'A View from the Bridge' and 'All My Sons'* (London: Penguin Books, 1961), 157.
55 Arthur Miller, *Death of a Salesman* (London: Penguin Books, 1961), 63.
56 David Savran, *Breaking the Rules: The Wooster Group* (New York: Theatre Communications Group, 1988), 191.
57 Bertolt Brecht, 'New Technique of Acting', in *Brecht on Theatre: 1918-1932*, ed. John Willett (McGraw Hill: Ryerson, 1964), 136–47, 139.

58 Variously, and often mistakenly, translated as the 'Alienation effect' or 'estrangement effect'.
59 Brecht, *Brecht on Theatre*, 37, 44, 56, 136–7.
60 Darko Suvin, *To Brecht & Beyond: Soundings in Modern Dramaturgy* (Sussex and New Jersey: The Harvester Press; Barnes & Noble Books, 1984), 69.
61 Geis, *Postmodern Theatric[k]s*, 24–5.
62 Ibid.
63 Brecht, *Brecht on Theatre*, 139.
64 Bertolt Brecht, *Parables for the Theatre*, trans. Eric Bentley (London: Penguin Books, 1966), 30.
65 Geis, *Postmodern Theatric[k]s*, 25; Brecht, *Brecht on Theatre*, 136–40.
66 Viewed 2 July 2014, notes and documentation by the author. See also, Sarah French and Georgie Boucher, 'Viewing the Burlesque Hour: The Pleasures of the masochistic gaze', *Australasian Drama Studies* no. 63 (December 2013): 6–23.
67 Mark Berninger, '"I am walking slowly in a dense jungle": Monologue in Harold Pinter's *Moonlight* and *Ashes to Ashes*', in *Monologues*, ed. Clare Wallace (Prague: Litteraria Pragensia, 2006), 90–109.
68 See Mark Taylor-Batty, *The Theatre of Harold Pinter* (London and New York: Methuen, Bloomsbury, 2014), 184.
69 Berninger, '"I am walking slowly in a dense jungle"', 92–3.
70 Enoch Brater, *Beyond Minimalism: Beckett's Late Style in the Theatre* (New York and Oxford: Oxford University Press, 1987), 3.
71 Samuel Beckett, *The Complete Dramatic Works* (London and Boston: Faber and Faber, 1990), 376.
72 Geis, *Postmodern Theatric[k]s*, 27.
73 Brater, *Beyond Minimalism*, 18–23.
74 Ibid., 8–11; See also Enoch Brater, *10 Ways of Thinking About Samuel Beckett: The Falsetto of Reason* (London: Methuen Drama, 2011), 111–12.
75 Samuel Beckett, *Krapp's Last Tape and Embers* (London and Boston: Faber and Faber, 1965), 20.
76 Laurens De Vos, '"Little is left to tell": Samuel Beckett's and Sarah Kane's Subverted Monologues', in *Monologues*, ed. Clare Wallace (Prague: Litteraria Pragensia, 2006), 114.

77　Geis, *Postmodern Theatric[k]s*, 26–7; Kennedy, *Dramatic Dialogue*, 30.
78　De Vos, '"Little is left to tell"', 119.
79　Geis, *Postmodern Theatric[k]s*, 25.

Chapter 2

1　Brecht, *Brecht on Theatre*, 277.
2　Thomas Habinek, *Ancient Rhetoric and Oratory* (London: Blackwell, 2005), 47.
3　Sandra M. Gustafson, *Eloquence is Power: Oratory Performance in Early America* (Chapel Hill and London: University of North Carolina Press, 2000).
4　Sacvan Bercovitch, *The American Jeremiad* (Madison and London: University of Wisconsin Press, (1978) 2012), 7.
5　Nell Irvin Painter, *Sojourner Truth: A Life, A Symbol* (New York and London: W. W. Norton and Company, 1996), 125, 167.
6　Sarah Jane Cervenak, 'Gender, Class, and the Performance of a Black (Anti) Enlightenment: Resistances of David Walker and Sojourner Truth', *Palimpsest: A Journal on Women, Gender, and the Black International* 1, no. 1 (2012): 68–86.
7　Painter, *Sojourner Truth*, 3–4.
8　Peter C. Myers, *Frederick Douglass: Race and the Rebirth of American Liberalism* (Lawrence: University Press of Kansas, 2008), 189; David B. Chesebrough, *Frederick Douglass: Oratory from Slavery* (Westport and London: Greenwood Press, 1998), 107–8.
9　John Stauffer, 'Frederick Douglass and the Aesthetics of Freedom', *Raritan* 25, no. 1 (2005), 115.
10　Myers, *Frederick Douglass*, 2.
11　See Jeffrey C. Alexander, *The Performance of Politics: Obama's Victory and the Democratic Struggle for Power* (New York: Oxford University Press, 2010) and Jeffrey C. Alexander, *Performance and Power* (Cambridge: Polity Press, 2011).
12　Michael Heale, *The Presidential Quest* (London and New York: Longman, 1982), 225.

13 Colleen J. Shogan and Thomas H. Neale, 'The President's State of the Union Address: Tradition, Function, and Policy Implications', Congressional Research Service. Available online: http://www.crs.gov (accessed 10 December 2014).

14 Alexander, *Performance and Power*, 2011.

15 See Timothy Raphael, *The President Electric: Ronald Reagan and the Politics of Performance* (Ann Arbor: University of Michigan Press, 2009); Brian Massumi, *Parables for the Virtual: Movement, Affect, Sensation* (Durham, NC: Duke University Press, 2002), 39–42.

16 Wallace, 'Monologue Theatre, Solo Performance and Self as Spectacle', 4.

17 Richard Schechner, *The End of Humanism: Writings on Performance* (New York: Performing Arts Journal Publications, 1982), 44, 158; Rebecca Schneider, 'Solo Solo Solo', in *After Criticism: New Responses to Art and Performance*, ed. Gavin Butt (London: Blackwell, 2005), 32; Shank, *Beyond the Boundaries*, 155.

18 Wallace, 'Monologue Theatre, Solo Performance and Self as Spectacle', 13.

19 Gustafson, *Eloquence is Power*, xv.

20 Bonney, 'Preface', xiv.

21 Ibid.

22 Carlson, *Performance*, 86. See also John Limon, *Stand-up Comedy in Theory, or, Abjection in America* (Durham and London: Duke University Press, 2000).

23 Lenny Bruce, 'How to Talk Dirty and Influence People: An Autobiography of Lenny Bruce', in *Extreme Exposure*, ed. Jo Bonney (Cambridge, MA and London, 2000), 44.

24 Allen Ginsberg, 'Howl', in *The Portable Beat Reader*, ed. Ann Charters (New York: Viking, 1992), 62.

25 Imani Perry, *Prophets of the Hood: Politics and Poetics in Hip Hop* (Durham and London: Duke University Press, 2004), 26.

26 Adam Bradley, *Book of Rhymes: The Poetics of Hip Hop* (New York: Basic Civitas, 2009), 164–5; Perry, *Prophets of the Hood*, 78.

27 Miles White, *From Jim Crow to Jay-Z: Race, Rap and the Performance of Masculinity* (Urbana, Chicago and Springfield: University of Illinois Press, 2011).

28 Jay-Z, *Know What I Mean? Reflections on Hip Hop*, ed. Michael Eric Dyson (New York: Basic Civitas, 2007), x.
29 Jay-Z, *The Blueprint*, U.S.A.: Roc-A-Fella Records, 2001.
30 White, *From Jim Crow to Jay-Z*, 53–4.
31 For further recent discussion of the intersections between performance, autobiography and critiques of neoliberalism, see Jen Harvie, *Fair Play: Art, Performance and Neoliberalism* (Houndsmills and New York: Palgrave Macmillan, 2013); Heddon, *Autobiography and Performance*; Maurya Wickstrom, *Performance in the Blockades of Neoliberalism: Thinking the Political Anew* (Houndsmills and New York: Palgrave Macmillan, 2012).
32 Mouffe, *Agonistics*, 88–90.
33 See Román, *Performance in America*.

Chapter 3

1 Spalding Gray, *A Spalding Gray Retrospective, Seven Monologues Performed by Spalding Gray*, presented by the Wooster Group at the Performing Garage: including *Booze, Cars, and College Girls*; *Forty-Seven Beds*; *In Search of the Monkey Girl*; *India and After (America)*; *Nobody Wanted to Sit Behind a Desk*; *A Personal History of the American Theatre*; and *Sex and Death to Age 14*. Viewed 7 July 2005 at the Theatre on Film and Tape Archive, The New York Public Library for the Performing Arts. The monologue is also published in Gray, *Swimming to Cambodia: The Collected Works of Spalding Gray*, 1987.
2 Spalding Gray, 'The Seventies', in *The Journals of Spalding Gray*, ed. Nell Casey (New York: Alfred A. Knopf, 2011), 62.
3 Ibid., ix.
4 Savran, *Breaking the Rules*, 110.
5 Philip Auslander, *Presence and Resistance: Postmodernism and Cultural Politics in Contemporary American Performance* (Ann Arbor: University of Michigan Press, 1992), 65.
6 William Demastes, *Spalding Gray's America* (New York: Limelight, 2008), 88.

7 Vincent Canby, 'Soloists on the Big Screen', *The New York Times*, 22 March 1987, 19. See also, Auslander, *Presence and Resistance*, 60. *Swimming to Cambodia* – directed by Jonathan Demme, produced by Shafransky and with music by Laurie Anderson – was a highly regarded, unexpected success that grossed over US $ 1 million.
8 Henry M. Sayre, 'True Stories: Spalding Gray and the authenticities of performance', in *Performance and Authenticity in the Arts*, ed. Ivan Gaskell and Salim Kemal (Cambridge: Cambridge University Press, 1999), 254.
9 *Swimming to Cambodia*, dir. Jonathan Demme, written and performed by Spalding Gray, Los Angeles, CA: Evergreen Entertainment, 1996, DVD Rec.
10 Gray, *Swimming to Cambodia*, 19.
11 Frieden, *Genius and Monologue*, 104; Sayre, 'True Stories: Spalding Gray and the authenticities of performance', 263.
12 Gray, *Swimming to Cambodia*, 20.
13 Ibid., 20–1.
14 Auslander, *Presence and Resistance*, 77–8, 80–1.
15 Spalding Gray, *It's a Slippery Slope* (New York: The Noonday Press, 1997), 6.
16 Philip Auslander, 'Performance and Therapy: Spalding Gray's Autopathographic Monologues', in *Bodies in Commotion: Disability and Performance*, ed. Carrie Stendahl and Philip Auslander (Ann Arbor: University of Michigan Press, 2005), 163–74.
17 *Swimming to Cambodia*, DVD Rec.
18 Gray, *Swimming to Cambodia*, 91–2.
19 Auslander, *Presence and Resistance*, 77–8.
20 The Wooster Group. Available online: http://www.thewoostergroup.org/twg/wooster.html (accessed 20 July 2002).
21 Sayre, 'True Stories: Spalding Gray and the authenticities of performance', 259.
22 See Heddon, *Autobiography and Performance*.
23 Gray, *Swimming to Cambodia*, 28.
24 Ibid., 31.
25 Gray, *The Journals of Spalding Gray*, 137.

26 Gray, *Swimming to Cambodia*, 15, 26–31.
27 Ibid., 50.
28 John D. Dorst, '"Sidebar Excursions to Nowhere": The Vernacular Storytelling of Errol Morris and Spalding Gray', in *Folklore, Literature, and Cultural Theory: Collected Essays*, ed. Cathy Preston (New York: Garland Publishing, 1995), 133.
29 Gray, *Swimming to Cambodia*, 20, 86, 87.
30 Michael Peterson, *Straight White Male: Performance Art Monologues* (Jackson: University Press of Mississippi, 1997), 57–60.
31 Peggy Phelan, 'Spalding Gray's *Swimming to Cambodia*: The Article', *Critical Texts* 5, no. 1 (1988): 29.
32 Auslander, *Presence and Resistance*, 63.
33 See D. Soyini Madison, 'The Mike Daisey Affair: Labor and Performance', *Communication and Critical/Cultural Studies* 9, no. 2 (June 2012): 234–40.
34 Ira Glass, 'Retraction', *This American Life*, Episode 460, 16 March 2012, Radio podcast, accessed 8 July 2014.
35 Shannon Steen, 'Neoliberal Scandals: Foxconn, Mike Daisey, and the Turn Toward Nonfiction Drama', *Theatre Journal* 66, no. 1 (March 2014): 1–18.
36 See Linda Hutcheon, *A Poetics of Postmodernism: History, Theory, Fiction* (New York and London: Routledge, 1988).
37 William Demastes, 'Spalding Gray's "Swimming to Cambodia" and the Evolution of an Ironic Presence', *Theatre Journal* 41, no. 1 (1989): 86.
38 Gray, *Swimming to Cambodia*, 87.
39 Demastes, *Spalding Gray's America*, 8.
40 Gray, *Swimming to Cambodia*, 53.
41 Spalding Gray, *Morning, Noon and Night* (New York: Farrar; Straus and Giroux, 1999), 3.
42 Demastes, *Spalding Gray's America*, 186.
43 Gray, *Morning, Noon and Night*, 6–7.
44 Alisa Solomon, 'Soloing Through the Gray Zone', *Village Voice*, 17–23 November 1999. Available online: http://www.villagevoice.com/issues/9946/solomon.php (accessed 3 December 2007).

45 Gray, *Morning, Noon and Night*, 57.
46 Ibid., 27.
47 Ibid., 66.
48 Ibid., 8.
49 Ibid., 75–6.
50 Ibid., 147–8.
51 Ibid., 146.
52 Spalding Gray, *Monster in a Box* (London: Picador; Pan Books, 1991), 34.
53 Gray, *Morning, Noon and Night*, 71.
54 Ibid., 36.
55 See Francis Fukuyama, *The End of History and the Last Man* (New York: Avon Books, (1992) 2006).
56 In the context of the 1980s' political scene, neoconservative politics may be observed in the administrations of Margaret Thatcher and Ronald Reagan. Under these two leaders, ideologically loaded approaches to concepts such as patriotism, family values, personal responsibility and social community began to be hinged onto policies (both domestic and foreign) that privileged neoliberal (free-market) economics. During the 1990s and 2000s, the influence of neoconservatism can be further observed in the administration of George W. Bush. For detailed discussion, see: Irving Kristol, *Neoconservatism: The Autobiography of an Idea* (Chicago: Elephant Paperbacks, 1999); Francis Fukuyama, *After the Neocons: America at the Crossroads* (London: Profile Books, 2006); Irwin Stelzer (ed.), *Neo-conservatism* (London: Atlantic Books, 2004).
57 Kristol, 'A Conservative Welfare State', 147–8.
58 Ibid., 34–6.
59 Gray, *Morning, Noon and Night*, 70.
60 Ibid., 75.
61 Ibid., 79–80.
62 Fredric Jameson, *Postmodernism or, The Cultural Logic of Late Capitalism* (Durham: Duke University Press, 1991), 19.
63 Ibid.
64 Ibid., 21.
65 Solomon, 'Soloing Through the Gray Zone', np.

66 Gray, *Morning, Noon and Night*, 132.
67 Gray, *The Journals of Spalding Gray*, 270.
68 Gray, *Morning, Noon and Night*, 143.
69 Gray, *The Journals of Spalding Gray*, 179.

Chapter 4

1 Kathleen Hall Jameson, *Eloquence in an Electronic Age: The Transformation of Political Speechmaking* (New York and Oxford: Oxford University Press, 1988), 119, 242–3.
2 Mike Deaver, in conversation, 'Television and the Presidency: The Office of the President, 1992', in *Paley Centre Seminars* (New York: The Paley Centre of Media), accessed 20 January 2013.
3 For further discussion, see Auslander, *Presence and Resistance*, 59; Lenora Champagne (ed.), *Out From Under: Texts by Women Performance Artists* (New York: Theatre Communications Group Inc., 1990), 47–8; Goldberg, *Performance*, 13–14; Marranca, 'Performance, a Personal History'. An entire album of 'O Superman' remixes was also released in 2003 by Independent Dutch label, Staalplaat.
4 Carlson, *Performance*, 115.
5 Auslander, *Presence and Resistance*, 72; Gunter Berghaus, *Avant-garde Performance: Live Events and Electronic Technologies* (New York: Palgrave Macmillan, 2005), 219–20; Sean Cubitt, 'Laurie Anderson: Myth, Management and Platitude', in *Art Has No History!: The Making and Unmaking of Modern Art*, ed. John Roberts (London: Verso, 1994), 282, 295.
6 Berghaus, *Avant-garde Performance*, 222.
7 Cubitt, 'Laurie Anderson', 292–3.
8 Laurie Anderson, *Home of the Brave*, USA: Warner Bros., 1986, Video Rec.
9 Amelia Jones, *Body Art: Performing the Subject* (London and Minneapolis: University of Minnesota Press, 1998), 210–12.
10 Will Hermes, 'Electronic Expressions in the Service of the Soul', *The New York Times*, 25 June 2010. Available online: http://www.nytimes.com (accessed 22 July 2014).

11 See Rosi Braidotti, *The Posthuman* (London: Polity Press, 2013).
12 See Rosemary Klich and Edward Scheer, *Multimedia Performance* (London and New York: Palgrave Macmillan, 2012), 44–6.
13 See Johannes Birringer, *Media and Performance: Along the Border* (Baltimore: Johns Hopkins University Press, 1998), 65.
14 Cubitt, 'Laurie Anderson', 286.
15 Shank, *Beyond the Boundaries*, 131.
16 Lehmann, *Postdramatic Theatre*, 118.
17 Simon Reynolds, *Rip It Up and Start Again: Postpunk 1978-1984* (New York: Penguin Books, 2005), 2, 162.
18 Brian Eno and David Bryne, *Once In A Lifetime lyrics*, Universal Music Publishing Group, Warner/Chappell Music, Inc., 1981.
19 *Home of the Brave*, Video Rec.
20 Auslander, *Presence and Resistance*, 74–5.
21 The Nature Theater of Oklahoma, video excerpt from *Life and Times: Episode 1*, performing for WNYC Radio's 'Spinning on Air' with David Garland, 3 March 2013. Available online: https://www.youtube.com/watch?v=-RgS35slSxs (accessed 10 January 2014).
22 Berghaus, *Avant-garde Performance*, 223.
23 Ibid., 222.
24 Cubitt, 'Laurie Anderson', 284.
25 Auslander, *Presence and Resistance*, 75.
26 *Home of the Brave*, Video Rec.
27 See Lev Manovich, *The Language of New Media* (Cambridge, MA and London: The MIT Press, 2001) and *Software Takes Command* (New York and London: Bloomsbury, 2013).
28 See Jay David Bolter and Richard A. Grusin, *Remediation: Understanding New Media* (Cambridge, MA and London: The MIT Press, 1999).
29 Laurie Anderson, *Empty Places: A Performance* (New York: Harper Perennial, 1991), 113.
30 Ibid., 117.
31 Goldberg, *Performance*, 150.
32 Milton Friedman, *Capitalism and Freedom* (Chicago: University of Chicago Press, 2002), 4.

33 Margaret Thatcher, interview with Douglas Keay, *Women's Own*, 23 September 1987, found at *The Margaret Thatcher Foundation*. Available online: http://www.margaretthatcher.org/essential/biography.asp (accessed 3 December 2007). See also Harvie, *Fair Play*, 2013.
34 Anderson in Goldberg, *Performance*, 153.
35 Ibid.
36 Ibid.
37 Lehmann, *Postdramatic Theatre*, 118, 121.
38 Ibid., 118.
39 Anderson, *Empty Places*, 113.
40 Ibid., 58.
41 Steffen Mau, Heike Brabandt, Lena Laube and Christof Roos, *Liberal States and the Freedom of Movement: Selective Borders, Unequal Mobility* (London and New York: Palgrave Macmillan, 2012), 162.
42 Anderson, *Empty Places*, 58.
43 Ibid., 72.
44 Ibid., 73.
45 Ibid., 78.

Chapter 5

1 Anna Deavere Smith, *Fires in the Mirror: Crown Heights, Brooklyn and Other Identities* (New York: Anchor Books, 1993), xxvii.
2 See Alison Forsyth, 'Performing Trauma: Race Riots and Beyond in the Work of Anna Deavere Smith', in *Get Real: Documentary Theatre Past and Present*, ed. Alison Forsyth and Chris Megson (London and New York: Palgrave Macmillan, 2009); Dorinne Kondo, '(Re)visions of Race: Contemporary Race Theory and the Cultural Politics of Racial Crossover in Documentary Theatre', *Theatre Journal* 52, no. 1 (2000): 81–107; Carol Martin (ed.), *A Sourcebook of Feminist Theatre and Performance: On and Beyond the Stage* (New York: Routledge, 1996); Sandra L. Richards, 'Caught in the Act of Social Definition On the Rood with Anna Deavere Smith', in *Acting Out: Feminist Performances*, ed. Lynda Hart and Peggy

Phelan (Ann Arbor: University of Michigan Press, 1993), 35–54; Cherise Smith, *Enacting Others* (Durham and London: Duke University Press, 2011); Debby Thompson, '"Is Race a Trope?": Anna Deavere Smith and the Question of Racial Performativity', *African American Review* 37, no. 1 (2003): 127–38.

3 See Forsyth and Megson (eds), *Get Real*; and Carol Martin (ed.), *Dramaturgy of the Real on the World Stage* (New York and London: Palgrave Macmillan, 2012).

4 See Venise T. Berry and Carmen L. Manning-Miller (eds), *Mediated Messages and African-American Culture: Contemporary Issues* (Thousand Oaks: Sage Publications, 1996); Lou Cannon, *Official Negligence: How Rodney King and the Riots Changed Los Angeles and the LAPD* (New York: Times Books, 1997); Gary Dawson, *Documentary Theatre in the United States* (Westport, CT and London: Greenwood Press, 1999).

5 The work was commissioned by the Mark Taper Forum in Los Angeles and later performed at the New York Shakespeare Festival in 1993. The recorded version of *Twilight: Los Angeles, 1992* includes approximately twenty-five monologues. These monologues are divided into approximately forty-seven segments, several of which are pieces of a single monologue broken up into two or three parts.

6 *Twilight: Los Angeles, 1992*, dir. by Marc Levin, conceived, written and performed by Anna Deavere Smith, 2001, Alexandria, Va.: PBS Home Video, Video Rec. Viewed 8 July 2005 at the Theatre on Film and Tape Archive, The New York Public Library for the Performing Arts.

7 Anna Deavere Smith, *Twilight: Los Angeles, 1992* (New York: Anchor Books, 1994), 1.

8 Ibid., 2.

9 Martin, *A Sourcebook of Feminist Theatre and Performance*, 1996, 92.

10 Elin Diamond, *Unmaking Mimesis* (London: Routledge, 1997), v.

11 Carol Martin, 'Bearing Witness: Anna Deavere Smith from Community to Theatre to Mass Media', in *A Sourcebook of Feminist Theatre and Performance: On and Beyond the Stage*, ed. Carol Martin (New York: Routledge, 1996), 83; Thompson, '"Is Race a Trope?"', 134–5.

12 Smith, *Twilight*, 6.
13 Peterson, *Straight White Male*, 14, 193.
14 Alan Filewod, *Collective Encounters* (Toronto, Buffalo and London: University of Toronto Press, 1987), viii.
15 Ibid., 14, 16; See also Thomas Irmer, 'A Search for New Realities: Documentary Theatre in Germany', *TDR: The Drama Review* 50, no. 3 (2006): 17–20; Michael Anderson and Linden Wilkinson, 'A Resurgence of Verbatim Theatre: Authenticity, Empathy and Transformation', *ADS: Australasian Drama Studies* 50 (April 2007): 153–69.
16 Smith, *Twilight*, 15.
17 Forsyth and Megson, *Get Real*, 3.
18 See Claire Bishop, *Artificial Hells: Participatory Art and the Politics of Spectatorship* (London and New York: Verso, 2012); Jackson, *Social Works*. It is also interesting to note that an echo of Deavere Smith's process might be found in a typically postcolonial approach to history where identity, race and history are shown to be contingent and performative.
19 Forsyth, 'Performing Trauma', 144.
20 The diverse team consisted of: Dorinne Kondo (Japanese American anthropologist & feminist scholar); Hector Tobar (Guatemalan-American reporter who cover the riots); Elizabeth Alexander (African American poet & University of Chicago professor) and Oskar Eustis (resident director at the Mark Taper Forum in Los Angeles where *Twilight* premiered) – Smith, *Twilight: Los Angeles, 1992*, xxiii.
21 Timothy Brennan, *At Home in the World: Cosmopolitanism Now* (Cambridge, MA: Harvard University Press, 1997), 111–13; Jill Dolan, 'Introductory Essay: Fathom Languages: Feminist Performance Theory, Pedagogy, and Practice', in *A Sourcebook of Feminist Theatre and Performance*, ed. Carol Martin (New York: Routledge, 1996), 12.
22 Ibid., Brennan, 112.
23 Ibid.
24 Smith, *Twilight*, 232–4.
25 Ibid., 112.

26 Ibid., 172.
27 Martin, 'Bearing Witness', 86.
28 Ibid., 185.
29 Judith Butler, *Gender Trouble: Feminism and the Subversion of Identity* (New York: Routledge, 1990). In researching the relationship between the press and the presidency, as part of the American character project, Smith details a number of conversations with Butler. A section from one of these interviews/conversations is later included in the play *House Arrest* (2004).
30 Cherise Smith, *Enacting Others*, 12–13.
31 Thompson, '"Is Race a Trope?"', 132, 137.
32 Smith, *Twilight*, 140.
33 Thompson, '"Is Race a Trope?"', 134–5.
34 Schechner, *Performance Studies*, 206.
35 See Eddie Paterson, 'Paperless and Penless: headphone performance, audio-scripting and new approaches to writing for performance', in *Strange Bedfellows*, Australasian Association of Writing Programs, 2010. Available online: http://d3n8a8pro7vhmx.cloudfront.net/theaawp/pages/85/attachments/original/1385080487/Paterson.pdf?1385080487 (accessed 10 January 2013); Caroline Wake, 'Headphone Verbatim Theatre: Methods, Histories, Genres, Theories', *New Theatre Quarterly* 29, no. 4 (2013): 321–35.
36 Paterson, 'Paperless and Penless'; Caroline Wake, 'The Politics and Poetics of Listening: Attending Headphone Verbatim Theatre in Post-Cronulla Australia', *Theatre Research International* 39, no. 2 (2013): 82–100.
37 Smith, *Twilight*, 70, 73.
38 Ibid., 100–1.
39 Ibid., 101–2.
40 Peggy Phelan, 'Reciting the Citation of Others; or, A Second Introduction', in *Acting Out*, ed. Lynda Hart and Peggy Phelan (Ann Arbor: University of Michigan Press, 1993), 28.
41 Smith, *Twilight*, 254–5.
42 Ibid.
43 Ibid., 199.

Chapter 6

1 C. Carr, '"Telling the Awfullest Truth": An Interview with Karen Finley', in *Acting Out: Feminist Performances*, ed. Lynda Hart and Peggy Phelan (Ann Arbor: University of Michigan Press, 1993), 153–60.
2 British conservatives threatened to prosecute her for breaking a law that prohibited 'indecent acts' committed in 'proximity to the Queen' – Karen Finley, *A Different Kind of Intimacy: The Collected Writings of Karen Finley, a Memoir* (New York: Thunder's Mouth Press, 2000), 40.
3 Jill Dolan, 'Introductory Essay: Fathom Languages', 14. The NEA 4 won their case in 1993 and were rewarded their grants. However, the Clinton Administration later challenged the decision, taking the case to the Supreme Court. In 1998, the NEA 4 lost their case, with the government confirming their own right to place restrictions on funding due to value judgements – Finley, *A Different Kind of Intimacy*, 100–5.
4 See John Freeman, *New Performance/New Writing* (London and New York: Palgrave Macmillan, 2006), 89–90; Geis, *Postmodern Theatric(k)s*, 160–6; Lynda Hart and Peggy Phelan (eds), *Acting Out: Feminist Performances* (Ann Arbor: University of Michigan Press, 1993); Martin, *A Sourcebook of Feminist Theatre and Performance*; Rebecca Schneider, *The Explicit Body in Performance* (London and New York: Routledge, 1997), 100–4.
5 This performance took place on 22 March 2001. All notes and documentation of this performance are by the author.
6 See Auslander, *Presence and Resistance*, 126–7; Limon, *Stand-up Comedy in Theory, or, Abjection in America*, 2000; Marranca, 'Performance, a Personal History', 7.
7 Author's notes.
8 Finley, *A Different Kind of Intimacy*, 287.
9 Ibid., 287.
10 Finley describes this as being 'different from acting. ... I put myself into a state, for some reason it's important, so that things come in and out of me. I'm almost like a vehicle' in Richard Schechner, 'Karen Finley: A Constant State of Becoming, an interview by Richard Schechner', in

A Sourcebook of Feminist Theatre and Performance, ed. Carol Martin (New York: Routledge, 1996), 258.
11 Finley, *A Different Kind of Intimacy*, 302.
12 *Karen Finley: Live* (*Shut Up and Love Me* (2001), *Make Love* (2003)), directed by Timothy Greenfield-Sanders, devised, written and performed by Karen Finley, USA: Perfect Day Films Inc., 2004, DVD Rec.
13 Ibid.
14 Schneider, *The Explicit Body in Performance*, 100.
15 Karen Finley, 'Make Love', *The Drama Review* 47, no. 4 (Winter 2003): 61.
16 Ibid.
17 *Karen Finley: Live*, DVD Rec.
18 Finley, 'Make Love', 54.
19 *Karen Finley: Live*, DVD Rec. Each performance may contain a number of different versions of Liza. On any given night, 'Kidney-dialysis Liza' and/or 'Fucked-up Liza' might make an appearance. Finley's daughter also performs as a rendering of the iconic figure – Finley 'Make Love', 53; Karen Finley, personal communication with the author, New York, 2005.
20 Finley, 'Make Love', 54.
21 Ibid., 51–3.
22 Ibid., 53.
23 *Karen Finley: Live*, DVD Rec.
24 Ibid.
25 Finley, pers. comm., 2005.
26 Finley, 'Make Love', 53.
27 Ibid. 62.
28 Ibid.
29 Slavoj Žižek, *Welcome to the Desert of the Real* (London and New York: Verso, 2002), 144.
30 Remembering Irving Kristol, neoconservatism advances 'patriotism as natural and healthy sentiment' and privileges the 'conservative ideal of the normal household' that embodies 'family values', see 'A Conservative Welfare State', 143–8.
31 *Karen Finley: Live*, DVD Rec.
32 Finley, 'Make Love', 61.

33 *Karen Finley: Live*, DVD Rec.
34 Finley, 'Make Love', 53.
35 Ibid., 60.
36 Ibid., 66.
37 Žižek, *Welcome to the Desert of the Real*, 33.
38 Finley, 'Make Love', 58.
39 George W. Bush, *President Welcomes President Chirac to White House*, November 2001. Available online: http://www.whitehouse.gov/news/releases/2001/11/20011106-4.html (accessed 4 December 2007).
40 Shelly Scott, 'Been There, Done That: Paving the Way for *The Vagina Monologues*', Modern Drama 46, no. 3 (2003): 405.
41 Eve Ensler, *The Vagina Monologues* (New York: Villard, 2008).
42 Scott, 'Been There, Done That', 418.
43 Ibid., see also, Christine M. Cooper, 'Worrying about Vaginas: Feminism and Eve Ensler's *The Vagina Monologues*', Sings: Journal of Women in Culture and Society 32, no. 3 (2007): 727–58.
44 Performances of *The Dreams of Laura Bush* and *The Passion of Terri Schiavo*, took place on 18 July 2005. All notes and documentation of these performances are by the author.
45 Karen Finley, *The Reality Shows* (New York: The Feminist Press, 2011).
46 Ibid., 89.
47 Joseph A. Pika and John A. Maltese, *The Politics of the Presidency* (Washington, DC: CQ Press, 2005), 261. Pika and Maltese note that a memo reading 'This is an important moral issue and the pro-life base will be excited' and claiming that the issue could garner support from Christian conservatives in the 2006 midterm elections was 'circulated among Senate Republicans and leaked to the press' – Ibid., See also Jon Eisenberg, *Using Terri: The Religious Right's Conspiracy to Take Away our Rights* (New York: Harper, San Francisco, 2005), 157.
48 Pika and Maltese, *The Politics of the Presidency*, 261–2.
49 George W. Bush, *President Discusses Schiavo, WMD Commission Report*, 31 March 2005. Available online: http://www.whitehouse.gov/news/releases/2005/03/20050331.html (accessed 4 December 2007).
50 Bonnie Marranca, 'Performance, a Personal History', 10.

51 Finley, *The Reality Shows*, 100.
52 Finley, pers. comm., 2005.
53 Eisenberg, *Using Terri*, 191.
54 Karen Finley, 'Participating in Artistic Citizenship: Constructing a National Narrative – Considering the Passion of Terri Schiavo', in *Artistic Citizenship: A Public Voice for the Arts*, ed. Mary Campbell and Randy Martin (New York and London: Routledge, 2006), 186.
55 Expressions of The Passion of Christ reside in many interrelated texts from noncanonical gospels, liturgy, homilies, sermons, poems and hymns, meditations, prayers, in visionary literature and indeed in much visual art, theology and literature. The dramatic representation of Christ's suffering and death through Crucifixion, commonly called the 'Passion Play', is thought to have its origins in the twelfth and thirteenth centuries, though versions continue to be performed to this day. See Thomas H. Bestul, *Texts of the Passion: Latin Devotional Literature and Medieval Society* (Philadelphia: University of Pennsylvania Press, 1996); Ellen M. Ross, *The Grief of God* (New York and Oxford: Oxford University Press, 1997), vii; Glynne Wickham, *The Medieval Theatre* (Cambridge and New York: Cambridge University Press, 1987), 62–5.
56 Finley, pers. comm., 2005.
57 Pika and Maltese, *The Politics of the Presidency*, 261.
58 Finley, 'Participating in Artistic Citizenship', 186.
59 Ibid.
60 Eisenberg, *Using Terri*, 169.
61 Finley, 'Participating in Artistic Citizenship', 186.
62 Martin Durham, 'The Christian Right', in *New Political Thought: An Introduction*, ed. Adam Lent (London: Lawrence and Wishart, 1998), 72–88.
63 Finley, 'Participating in Artistic Citizenship', 186.
64 Pika and Maltese, *The Politics of the Presidency*, 261.
65 Kristol, *Neoconservatism*, 37, 134–5.
66 Michael Hardt and Antonio Negri, *Empire* (Cambridge, MA and London: Harvard University Press 2000), 148.
67 Durham, 'The Christian Right', 75–6.

68 Finley, 'Participating in Artistic Citizenship', 190.
69 Ibid., 189.
70 Ibid., 191.
71 Finley, *The Reality Shows*, 103.
72 Finley, pers. comm., 2005.
73 Finley, *The Reality Shows*, 91–2.

Chapter 7

1 Karen Jürs-Munby, Jerome Carroll and Steve Giles, 'Introduction', in *Postdramatic Theatre and the Political: International Perspectives on Contemporary Performance*, ed. Karen Jürs-Munby, Jerome Carroll and Steve Giles (London: Bloomsbury, Methuen, 2013), 1–2.
2 Lehmann, *Postdramatic Theatre*, 127.
3 Ibid., 127–8.
4 Pavis, *Dictionary of Theatre Terms*, 219; Frieden, *Genius and Monologue*, 20.
5 Lehmann, *Postdramatic Theatre*, 130.
6 Forsyth and Megson, *Get Real*; Martin, *Dramaturgy of the Real*.
7 Jürs-Munby et al., 'Introduction', 26.
8 Lehmann, *Postdramatic Theatre*, 18.
9 Karen Jürs-Munby, 'Agon, Conflict and Dissent: Elfriede Jelinek's *Ein Sportstück* and its Stagings by Einar Schleef and Just a Must Theatre', *Austrian Studies* 22 (2014): 17.
10 Robinson, *The American Play*, 326.
11 Ibid., 327.
12 Lehmann, *Postdramatic Theatre*, 127.
13 Ibid., 126.
14 Ibid.
15 See Žižek, *The Ticklish Subject*, 236–7; Mouffe, *On the Political*; and Rancière, *The Emancipated Spectator*.
16 Erik Swyngedouw, 'Apocalypse Forever? Post-Political Populism and the Spectre of Climate Change', *Theory, Culture, Society* 27, no. 2–3 (2010): 215.

17 Lehmann, *Postdramatic Theatre*, 178.
18 Ibid., 181.
19 Mouffe, *Agonistics*, 2013, xvii.
20 Massumi, *Parables for the Virtual*, 24.
21 Ibid., 27–8. Similarly, Hardt and Negri note: 'Unlike emotions, which are mental phenomena, affects refer equally to body and mind. In fact, affects such as joy and sadness, reveal the present state of life in the entire organism, expressing a certain state of the body along with a certain mode of thinking.' – Michael Hardt and Antonio Negri, *Multitude* (New York: The Penguin Press, 2004), 108.
22 Lehmann, *Postdramatic Theatre*, 186–7.
23 Ibid., 186.
24 Ibid., 187.
25 Ibid., 186.
26 Finley, 'Participating in Artistic Citizenship', 186.
27 See Hilton Als, 'The Way of Her Flesh: Laura Linney and Karen Finley show the public lives of women', *The New Yorker*, 15 February 2010. Available online: http://www.newyorker.com/magazine/2010/02/15/the-way-of-her-flesh (accessed 6 March 2014); Ben Brantley, 'Karen Finley Wears Pearls, Not Chocolate', *The New York Times*, 12 February 2010. Available online: http://www.nytimes.com/2010/02/12/theater/reviews/12jackie.html?_r=0 (accessed 6 March 2014).
28 Hardt and Negri, *Empire*, 148.
29 Francine Prose, 'Foreword', *Life Interrupted: The Unfinished Monologue* (New York: Audio Renaissance, 2006), CD Rec.
30 Hardt and Negri, *Multitude*, 222.
31 Charles Isherwood, 'Woman of 1,000 Faces Considers the Body', *The New York Times*, 8 October 2009. Available online: http://www.nytimes.com/2009/10/08/theater/reviews/08easy.html (accessed 14 June 2013).
32 See Peter Eckersall and Eddie Paterson, 'Slow Dramaturgy: Renegotiating Politics and Staging the Everyday', *Australasian Drama Studies*, no. 58 (April 2011): 178–92.

Bibliography

Agamben, Georgio, *What Is An Apparatus? And Other Essays*, translated by David Kishik and Stefan Pedatella, Stanford: Stanford University Press, 2009.

Als, Hilton, 'The Way of Her Flesh: Laura Linney and Karen Finley show the public lives of women', *The New Yorker*, 15 February 2010. http://www.newyorker.com/magazine/2010/02/15/the-way-of-her-flesh (accessed 6 March 2014).

Alexander, Jeffrey C., *The Performance of Politics: Obama's Victory and the Democratic Struggle for Power*, New York: Oxford University Press, 2010.

Alexander, Jeffrey C., *Performance and Power*, Cambridge: Polity Press, 2011.

Anderson, Laurie, *Empty Places: A Performance*, New York: Harper Perennial, 1991.

Anderson, Laurie, *United States*, New York: Harper & Row, 1984.

Anderson, Michael and Wilkinson, Linden, 'A Resurgence of Verbatim Theatre: Authenticity, Empathy and Transformation', *ADS: Australasian Drama Studies* 50 (April 2007): 153–69.

Auslander, Philip, 'Performance and Therapy: Spalding Gray's Autopathographic Monologues', in *Bodies in Commotion: Disability and Performance*, edited by Carrie Stendahl and Philip Auslander, 163–74. Ann Arbor: University of Michigan Press, 2005.

Auslander, Philip, *Presence and Resistance: Postmodernism and Cultural Politics in Contemporary American Performance*, Ann Arbor: University of Michigan Press, 1992.

Beckett, Samuel, *The Complete Dramatic Works*, London and Boston: Faber and Faber, 1990.

Beckett, Samuel, *Krapp's Last Tape and Embers*, London and Boston: Faber and Faber, 1965.

Bercovitch, Sacvan, *The American Jeremiad*, Madison and London: University of Wisconsin Press, (1978) 2012.

Berghaus, Gunter, *Avant-garde Performance: Live Events and Electronic Technologies*, New York: Palgrave Macmillan, 2005.

Berninger, Mark, '"I am walking slowly in a dense jungle": Monologue in Harold Pinter's *Moonlight* and *Ashes to Ashes*', in *Monologues*, edited by Clare Wallace, 90–109. Prague: Litteraria Pragensia, 2006.

Berry, Venise T. and Manning-Miller, Carmen L. (eds), *Mediated Messages and African-American Culture: Contemporary Issues*, Thousand Oaks: Sage Publications, 1996.

Bestul, Thomas H., *Texts of the Passion: Latin Devotional Literature and Medieval Society*, Philadelphia: University of Pennsylvania Press, 1996.

Birringer, Johannes, *Media and Performance: Along the Border*, Baltimore: Johns Hopkins University Press, 1998.
Bishop, Claire, *Artificial Hells: Participatory Art and the Politics of Spectatorship*, London and New York: Verso, 2012.
Bolter, Jay David and Grusin, Richard A., *Remediation: Understanding New Media*, Cambridge, MA and London: The MIT Press, 1999.
Bonney, Jo, 'Preface', in Jo Bonney (ed.), *Extreme Exposure: An Anthology of Solo Performance Texts from the Twentieth Century*, edited by Jo Bonney, xi–xvi. New York: Theatre Communications Group, 2000.
Bradley, Adam, *Book of Rhymes: The Poetics of Hip Hop*, New York: Basic Civitas, 2009.
Braidotti, Rosi, *The Posthuman*, London: Polity Press, 2013.
Brantley, Ben, 'Karen Finley Wears Pearls, Not Chocolate', *The New York Times*, 12 February 2010. http://www.nytimes.com/2010/02/12/theater/reviews/12jackie.html?_r=0 (accessed 6 March 2014).
Brater, Enoch, *Beyond Minimalism: Beckett's Late Style in the Theatre*, New York and Oxford: Oxford University Press, 1987.
Brecht, Bertolt and Willett John (ed.), *Brecht on Theatre: 1918-1932*, McGraw Hill: Ryerson, 1964.
Brecht, Bertolt and Willett John (ed.), *Parables for the Theatre*, translated by Eric Bentley, London: Penguin Books, 1966.
Brennan, Timothy, *At Home in the World: Cosmopolitanism Now*, Cambridge, MA: Harvard University Press, 1997.
Bruce, Lenny, 'How to Talk Dirty and Influence People: An Autobiography of Lenny Bruce', in Jo Bonney (ed.), *Extreme Exposure*, edited by Jo Bonney, 44–54. Cambridge, MA and London, 2000.
Bush, George W., *President Discusses Schiavo, WMD Commission Report*, 31 March 2005. http://www.whitehouse.gov/news/releases/2005/03/20050331.html (accessed 4 December 2007).
Bush, George W., *President Welcomes President Chirac to White House*, November 2001. http://www.whitehouse.gov/news/releases/2001/11/20011106-4.html (accessed 4 December 2007).
Butler, Judith, *Gender Trouble: Feminism and the Subversion of Identity*, New York: Routledge, 1990.
Byron, Glennis, *Dramatic Monologue*, London and New York: Routledge, 2003.
Canby, Vincent, 'Soloists on the Big Screen', *The New York Times*, 22 March 1987, 19.
Cannon, Lou, *Official Negligence: How Rodney King and the Riots Changed Los Angeles and the LAPD*, New York: Times Books, 1997.
Carlson, Marvin, *Performance: An Introduction*, London and New York: Routledge, 1996.
Carr, C., '"Telling the Awfullest Truth": An Interview with Karen Finley', in *Acting Out: Feminist Performances*, edited by Lynda Hart and Peggy Phelan, 153–60. Ann Arbor: University of Michigan Press, 1993.

Casey, Nell, 'Introduction', in *The Journals of Spalding Gray*, edited by Nell Casey, ix–xvi. New York: Alfred A. Knopf, 2011.

Castagno, Paul C., *New Playwriting Strategies*, London and New York: Routledge, 2012.

Cervenak, Sarah Jane, 'Gender, Class, and the Performance of a Black (Anti) Enlightenment: Resistances of David Walker and Sojourner Truth', *Palimpsest: A Journal on Women, Gender, and the Black International* 1, no. 1 (2012): 68–86.

Champagne, Lenora (ed.), *Out From Under: Texts by Women Performance Artists*, New York: Theatre Communications Group Inc., 1990.

Chekhov, Anton, *Uncle Vanya*, translated by Elisaveta Fen, London: Penguin Books, 1954.

Chesebrough, David B., *Frederick Douglass: Oratory from Slavery*, Westport and London: Greenwood Press, 1998.

Clemen, Wolfgang, *Shakespeare's Soliloquies*, translated by Charity Scott Stokes, London and New York: Methuen, 1987.

Cooper, Christine M., 'Worrying about Vaginas: Feminism and Eve Ensler's *The Vagina Monologues*', *Sings: Journal of Women in Culture and Society* 32, no. 3 (2007): 727–58.

Cubitt, Sean, 'Laurie Anderson: Myth, Management and Platitude', in *Art Has No History!: The Making and Unmaking of Modern Art*, edited by John Roberts, 278–95. London: Verso, 1994.

Dawson, Gary, *Documentary Theatre in the United States*, Westport, CT and London: Greenwood Press, 1999.

Deaver, Mike in conversation, 'Television and the Presidency: The Office of the President, 1992', in *Paley Centre Seminars*, New York: The Paley Centre of Media, accessed 20 January 2013.

Demastes, William, *Spalding Gray's America*, New York: Limelight, 2008.

Demastes, William, 'Spalding Gray's "Swimming to Cambodia" and the Evolution of an Ironic Presence', *Theatre Journal* 41, no. 1 (1989): 75–94.

De Vos, Laurens, '"Little is left to tell": Samuel Beckett's and Sarah Kane's Subverted Monologues', in *Monologues*, edited by Clare Wallace, 110–24. Prague: Litteraria Pragensia, 2006.

Diamond, Elin, *Unmaking Mimesis*, London: Routledge, 1997.

Dolan, Jill, 'Introductory Essay: Fathom Languages: Feminist Performance Theory, Pedagogy, and Practice', in *A Sourcebook of Feminist Theatre and Performance*, edited by Carol Martin, 1–22. New York: Routledge, 1996.

Dorst, John D., '"Sidebar Excursions to Nowhere": The Vernacular Storytelling of Errol Morris and Spalding Gray', in *Folklore, Literature, and Cultural Theory: Collected Essays*, edited by Cathy Preston, 119–34. New York: Garland Publishing, 1995.

Durham, Martin, 'The Christian Right', in *New Political Thought: An Introduction*, edited by Adam Lent, 72–88. London: Lawrence and Wishart, 1998.

Eagleton, Terry, *William Shakespeare*, Oxford and New York: Blackwell, 1987.
Eckersall, Peter and Paterson, Eddie, 'Slow Dramaturgy: Renegotiating Politics and Staging the Everyday', *Australasian Drama Studies* no. 58 (April 2011): 178–92.
Eisenberg, Jon, *Using Terri: The Religious Right's Conspiracy to Take Away our Rights*, New York: Harper, San Francisco, 2005.
Eno, Brian and Bryne, David, *Once In A Lifetime Lyrics*, Universal Music Publishing Group, Warner/Chappell Music, Inc., 1981.
Ensler, Eve, *The Vagina Monologues*, New York: Villard, 2008.
Euripides, *Medea and Other Plays*, translated by Philip Vellacott, London: Penguin Books, 1963.
Filewod, Alan, *Collective Encounters*, Toronto, Buffalo and London: University of Toronto Press, 1987.
Finley, Karen, *A Different Kind of Intimacy: The Collected Writings of Karen Finley, a Memoir*, New York: Thunder's Mouth Press, 2000.
Finley, Karen, *George and Martha*, London and New York: Verso, 2006.
Finley, Karen, 'Make Love', *TDR: The Drama Review* 47, no. 4 (Winter 2003): 51–69.
Finley, Karen, 'Participating in Artistic Citizenship: Constructing a National Narrative – Considering the Passion of Terri Schiavo', in *Artistic Citizenship: A Public Voice for the Arts*, edited by Mary Campbell and Randy Martin, 181–95. New York and London: Routledge, 2006.
Finley, Karen, *The Reality Shows*, New York: The Feminist Press, 2011.
Finley, Karen, *Shock Treatment*, San Francisco: City Lights Books, 1990.
Forsyth, Alison, 'Performing Trauma: Race Riots and Beyond in the Work of Anna Deavere Smith', in *Get Real: Documentary Theatre Past and Present*, edited by Alison Forsyth and Chris Megson, 140–50. London and New York: Palgrave Macmillan, 2009.
Forsyth, Alison and Megson, Chris, 'Preface' and 'Introduction', in *Get Real: Documentary Theatre Past and Present*, Alison Forsyth and Chris Megson, ix–5. London and New York: Palgrave Macmillan, 2009.
Freeman, John, *New Performance/New Writing*, London and New York: Palgrave Macmillan, 2006.
French, Sarah and Boucher, Georgie, 'Viewing the Burlesque Hour: The Pleasures of the masochistic gaze', *Australasian Drama Studies* no. 63 (December 2013): 6–23.
Frieden, Ken, *Genius and Monologue*, Ithaca: Cornell University Press, 1985.
Friedman, Milton, *Capitalism and Freedom*, Chicago: University of Chicago Press, 2002.
Fukuyama, Francis, *After the Neocons: America at the Crossroads*, London: Profile Books, 2006.
Fukuyama, Francis, *The End of History and the Last Man*, New York: Avon Books, (1992) 2006.

Geis, Deborah R., *Postmodern Theatric[k]s: Monologue in Contemporary American* Drama, Ann Arbor: University of Michigan Press, 1995.
Ginsberg, Allen, 'Howl', in *The Portable Beat Reader*, edited by Ann Charters. New York: Viking, 1992, 62.
Goldberg, Roselee, *Performance: Live Art since 1960*, New York and London: Harry N. Abrams Inc., 1998.
Grace, Sherrill, 'Theatre and the AutoBiographical Pact: An Introduction', in *Theatre and AutoBiography: Writing and Performing Lives in Theory and Practice*, edited by Sherrill Grace and Jerry Wasserman, 13–32. Vancouver: Talonbooks, 2006.
Gray, Spalding, *Gray's Anatomy*, New York and Toronto: Vintage Books, 1994.
Gray, Spalding, *Impossible vacation*, New York: Knopf, 1992.
Gray, Spalding, *It's a Slippery Slope*, New York: The Noonday Press, 1997.
Gray, Spalding, *Monster in a Box*, London: Picador; Pan Books, 1991.
Gray, Spalding, *Morning, Noon and Night*, New York: Farrar; Straus and Giroux, 1999.Gray, Spalding, *Swimming to Cambodia: The Collected Works of Spalding Gray*, London: Picador; Pan Books, 1987.
Gray, Spalding, *The Journals of Spalding Gray*, edited by Nell Casey. New York: Alfred A. Knopf, 2011.
Gustafson, Sandra M., *Eloquence is Power: Oratory Performance in Early America*, Chapel Hill and London: University of North Carolina Press, 2000.
Habinek, Thomas, *Ancient Rhetoric and Oratory*, London: Blackwell, 2005.
Hardt, Michael and Negri, Antonio, *Empire*, Cambridge, MA and London: Harvard University Press 2000.
Hardt, Michael and Negri, Antonio, *Multitude*, New York: The Penguin Press, 2004.
Hart, Lynda and Phelan, Peggy (eds), *Acting Out: Feminist Performances*, Ann Arbor: University of Michigan Press, 1993.
Harvie, Jen, *Fair Play: Art, Performance and Neoliberalism*, Houndsmills and New York: Palgrave Macmillan, 2013.
Heale, Michael, *The Presidential Quest*, London and New York: Longman, 1982.
Heddon, Deirdre, *Autobiography and Performance*, Houndsmills and New York: Palgrave Macmillan, 2008.
Hermes, Will, 'Electronic Expressions in the Service of the Soul', *The New York Times*, 25 June 2010. http://www.nytimes.com (accessed 22 July 2014).
Hristić, Jovan, 'Time in Chekhov: The Inexorable and the Ironic', *New Theatre Quarterly* 1, no. 3 (August 1985): 271–82.
Hutcheon, Linda, *A Poetics of Postmodernism: History, Theory, Fiction*, New York and London: Routledge, 1988.
Ibsen, Henrik, *Plays*, translated by Michael Leverson Meyer, London: Eyre Methuen, 1980.
Irmer, Thomas, 'A Search for New Realities: Documentary Theatre in Germany', *TDR: The Drama Review* 50, no. 3 (2006): 16–28.

Isherwood, Charles, 'Woman of 1,000 Faces Considers the Body', *The New York Times*, 8 October 2009. http://www.nytimes.com/2009/10/08/theater/reviews/08easy.html (accessed 14 June 2013).

Jackson, Shannon, *Professing Performance: Theatre in the Academy from Philology to Performativity*, Cambridge: Cambridge University Press, 2004.

Jackson, Shannon, *Social Works: Performing Art, Supporting Publics*, New York and London: Routledge, 2011.

Jameson, Fredric, *Postmodernism or, the Cultural Logic of Late Capitalism*, Durham: Duke University Press, 1991.

Jameson, Kathleen Hall, *Eloquence in an Electronic Age: The Transformation of Political Speechmaking*, New York and Oxford: Oxford University Press, 1988.

Jay-Z, 'Intro', in *Know What I Mean? Reflections on Hip Hop*, edited by Michael Eric Dyson, ix–xii. New York: Basic Civitas, 2007.

Jones, Amelia, *Body Art: Performing the Subject*, London and Minneapolis: University of Minnesota Press, 1998.

Jürs-Munby, Karen, 'Agon, Conflict and Dissent: Elfriede Jelinek's *Ein Sportstück* and its Stagings by Einar Schleef and Just a Must Theatre', *Austrian Studies* 22 (2014): 9–25.

Jürs-Munby, Karen, Carroll, Jerome and Giles, Steve, 'Introduction', in *Postdramatic Theatre and the Political: International Perspectives on Contemporary Performance*, edited by Karen Jürs-Munby, Jerome Carroll and Steve Giles, 1–30. London: Bloomsbury, Methuen, 2013.

Kennedy, Andrew, *Dramatic Dialogue: The Duologue of Personal Encounter*, Cambridge and New York: Cambridge University Press, 1983.

Kershaw, Baz, *The Radical in Performance: Between Brecht and Baudrillard*, London and New York: Routledge, 1999.

Kirby, Michael, 'On Acting and Not-Acting', in *Acting (Re)Considered*, edited by Phillip B. Zarrilli. London and New York: Routledge, 1995, 47–58.

Klich, Rosemary and Scheer, Edward, *Multimedia Performance*, London and New York: Palgrave Macmillan, 2012.

Kondo, Dorinne, '(Re)visions of Race: Contemporary Race Theory and the Cultural Politics of Racial Crossover in Documentary Theatre', *Theatre Journal* 52, no. 1 (2000): 81–107.

Kristol, Irving, *Neo-conservatism: The Autobiography of an Idea*, Chicago: Elephant Paperbacks, 1999.

Kristol, Irving, 'A Conservative Welfare State', in *Neo-conservatism*, edited by Irwin Stelzer, 143–8. London: Atlantic Books, 2004.

Lee, John, *Shakespeare's Hamlet and the Controversies of Self*, Oxford: Clarendon Press, 2000.

Lehmann, Hans-Thies, *Postdramatic Theatre*, translated by Karen Jürs-Munby, Abingdon and London: Routledge, 2006.

Limon, John, *Stand-up Comedy in Theory, or, Abjection in America*, Durham and London: Duke University Press, 2000.

MacKay, C. H., *Soliloquy in Nineteenth-century Fiction*, Basingstoke, Hampshire: Macmillan, 1987.
Madison, D. Soyini, 'The Mike Daisey Affair: Labor and Performance', *Communication and Critical/Cultural Studies* 9, no. 2 (June 2012): 234–40.
Manovich, Lev, *The Language of New Media*, Cambridge, MA and London: The MIT Press, 2001.
Manovich, Lev, *Software Takes Command*, New York and London: Bloomsbury, 2013.
Marranca, Bonnie, 'Performance, a Personal History', *Performing Arts Journal* 28, no. 1 (PAJ82) (2006): 3–19.
Martin, Carol, 'Bearing Witness: Anna Deavere Smith from Community to Theatre to Mass Media' and 'Anna Deavere Smith: The Word Becomes You, an interview by Carol Martin', in *A Sourcebook of Feminist Theatre and Performance: On and Beyond the Stage*, edited by Carol Martin, 81–93, 185–204. New York: Routledge, 1996.
Martin, Carol, (ed.), *Dramaturgy of the Real on the World Stage*, New York and London: Palgrave Macmillan, 2012.
Massumi, Brian, *Parables for the Virtual: Movement, Affect, Sensation*, Durham, NC: Duke University Press, 2002.
Mau, Steffen, Brabandt, Heike, Laube, Lena and Roos, Christof, *Liberal States and the Freedom of Movement: Selective Borders, Unequal Mobility*, London and New York: Palgrave Macmillan, 2012.
Maufort, Mark, 'Exorcisms of the past: Avatars of the O'Neillian Monologue in Modern American Drama', *The Eugene O'Neill Review* 22, no. 1/2 (1998): 123–36.
Miller, Arthur, '*A View from the Bridge*' *and* '*All My Sons*', London: Penguin Books, 1961.
Miller, Arthur, *Death of a Salesman*, London: Penguin Books, 1961.
Mouffe, Chantal, *Agonistics: Thinking the World Politically*, London: Verso, 2013.
Mouffe, Chantal, *On the Political*, London and New York: Routledge, 2005.
Myers, Peter C., *Frederick Douglass: Race and the Rebirth of American Liberalism*, Lawrence: University Press of Kansas, 2008.
Nikulin, Dmitri, *On Dialogue*, Lanham, MD: Lexington Books, 2006.
O'Neill, Eugene, *Nine Plays*, New York: The Modern Library, 1954.
Painter, Nell Irvin, *Sojourner Truth: A Life, A Symbol*, New York and London: W. W. Norton and Company, 1996.
Paterson, Eddie, *Interview with Karen Finley*, New York, 18 July 2005.
Paterson, Eddie, 'Paperless and Penless: headphone performance, audio-scripting and new approaches to writing for performance', in *Strange Bedfellows*, Australasian Association of Writing Programs, 2010. http://d3n8a8pro7vhmx.cloudfront.net/theaawp/pages/85/attachments/original/1385080487/Paterson.pdf?1385080487 (accessed 10 January 2013).
Pavis, Patrice, *Dictionary of the Theatre: Terms, Concepts, and Analysis*, Toronto and Buffalo: University of Toronto Press, 1998.

Perry, Imani, *Prophets of the Hood: Politics and Poetics in Hip Hop*, Durham and London: Duke University Press, 2004.
Peterson, Michael, *Straight White Male: Performance Art Monologues*, Jackson: University Press of Mississippi, 1997.
Phelan, Peggy, 'Reciting the Citation of Others; or, A Second Introduction', in *Acting Out*, edited by Lynda Hart and Peggy Phelan, 13–30. Ann Arbor: University of Michigan Press, 1993.
Phelan, Peggy, 'Spalding Gray's *Swimming to Cambodia*: *The Article*', *Critical Texts* 5, no. 1 (1988): 27–30.
Pika, Joseph A. and Maltese, John A., *The Politics of the Presidency*, Washington, DC: CQ Press, 2005.
Pile, Steve and Thrift, Nigel, 'Introduction', in *Mapping the Subject: Geographies of Cultural Transformation*, edited by Steve Pile and Nigel Thrift, 1–11. London and New York: Routledge, 1995.
Pye, Christopher, *The Vanishing: Shakespeare, the Subject, and Early Modern Culture*, Durham: Duke University Press, 2000.
Rancière, Jacques, *The Emancipated Spectator*, London and New York: Verso, 2009.
Raphael, Timothy, *The President Electric: Ronald Reagan and the Politics of Performance*, Ann Arbor: University of Michigan Press, 2009.
Read, Alan, *Theatre in the Expanded Field: Seven Approaches to Performance*, London: Bloomsbury Methuen, 2013.
Reynolds, Simon, *Rip It Up and Start Again: Postpunk 1978-1984*, New York: Penguin Books, 2005.
Richards, Sandra L., 'Caught in the Act of Social Definition On the Rood with Anna Deavere Smith', in *Acting Out: Feminist Performances*, edited by Lynda Hart and Peggy Phelan, 35–54. Ann Arbor: University of Michigan Press, 1993.
Richardson, Brian, 'Drama and Narrative', in *Cambridge Companion to Narrative Theory*, edited by David Herman, 142–155. Cambridge: Cambridge University Press, 2007.
Richardson, Brian, 'Point of View in Drama: Diegetic Monologue, Unreliable Narrators, and the Author's Voice on Stage', *Comparative Drama* 22, no. 3 (1988): 193–214.
Robinson, Marc, *The American Play 1787-2000*, New Haven and London: Yale University Press, 2009.
Robinson, Marc, *The Other American Drama*, Cambridge: Cambridge University Press, 1994.
Román, David, *Performance in America: Contemporary U.S. Culture and the Performing Arts*, Durham and London: Duke University Press, 2005.
Ross, Ellen M., *The Grief of God*, New York and Oxford: Oxford University Press, 1997.
Saddik, Annette J., *Contemporary American Drama*, Edinburgh: Edinburgh University Press, 2007, pp. 40–71.
Savran, David, *Breaking the Rules: The Wooster Group*, New York: Theatre Communications Group, 1988.

Sayre, Henry M., 'True Stories: Spalding Gray and the authenticities of performance', in *Performance and Authenticity in the Arts*, edited by Ivan Gaskell and Salim Kemal, 254–71. Cambridge: Cambridge University Press, 1999.
Schechner, Richard, *The End of Humanism: Writings on Performance*, New York: Performing Arts Journal Publications, 1982.
Schechner, Richard, 'Karen Finley: A Constant State of Becoming, an interview by Richard Schechner', in *A Sourcebook of Feminist Theatre and Performance*, edited by Carol Martin, 254–66. New York: Routledge, 1996.
Schechner, Richard, *Performance Studies: An Introduction*, Abingdon, London and New York: Routledge, 2006.
Schneider, Rebecca, *The Explicit Body in Performance*, London and New York: Routledge, 1997.
Schneider, Rebecca, 'Solo Solo Solo', in *After Criticism: New Responses to Art and Performance*, edited by Gavin Butt, 23–47. London: Blackwell, 2005.
Scott, Shelly, 'Been There, Done That: Paving the Way for *The Vagina Monologues*', *Modern Drama* 46, no. 3 (2003): 404–23.
Shakespeare, William, *The Complete Works of William Shakespeare: Comprising his Plays and Poems*, London: Spring Books, 1963.
Shank, Theodore, *Beyond the Boundaries: American Alternative Theatre*, Ann Arbor: University of Michigan Press, 2002.
Shogan, Colleen J. and Neale, Thomas H., 'The President's State of the Union Address: Tradition, Function, and Policy Implications', Congressional Research Service. http://www.crs.gov (accessed 10 December 2014).
Skiffington, Lloyd A., *The History of English Soliloquy: Aeschylus to Shakespeare*, Lanham, MD: University Press of America, 1985.
Smith, Anna Deavere, *Fires in the Mirror: Crown Heights, Brooklyn and Other Identities*, New York: Anchor Books, 1993.
Smith, Anna Deavere, '*House Arrest*' and '*Piano*': *Two Plays*, New York and Toronto: Anchor Books, 2004.
Smith, Anna Deavere, *Talk to Me: Travels in Media and Politics*, New York: Anchor Books, 2001.
Smith, Anna Deavere, *Twilight: Los Angeles, 1992, On the Road: A Search for American Character*, New York: Anchor Books, 1994.
Smith, Cherise, *Enacting Others*, Durham and London: Duke University Press, 2011.
Solomon, Alisa, 'Soloing Through the Gray Zone', *Village Voice*, November 17–23, 1999. http://www.villagevoice.com/issues/9946/solomon.php (accessed 3 December 2007).
Sophocles, *Electra and Other Plays*, translated by E. F. Watling, London: Penguin Books, 1953.
Stauffer, John, 'Frederick Douglass and the Aesthetics of Freedom', *Raritan* 25, no. 1 (2005): 114–36.
Steen, Shannon, 'Neoliberal Scandals: Foxconn, Mike Daisey, and the Turn Toward Nonfiction Drama', *Theatre Journal* 66, no. 1 (March 2014): 1–18.

Stelzer, Irwin (ed.), *Neo-conservatism*, London: Atlantic Books, 2004.
Suvin, Darko, *To Brecht & Beyond: Soundings in Modern Dramaturgy*, Sussex and New Jersey: The Harvester Press; Barnes & Noble Books, 1984.
Swyngedouw, Erik, 'Apocalypse Forever? Post-Political Populism and the Spectre of Climate Change', *Theory, Culture, Society* 27, no. 2–3 (2010): 213–32.
Tait, Peta, 'Performative Acts of Gendered Emotions and Bodies in Chekhov's "The Cherry Orchard"', *Modern Drama* 43, no. 1 (Spring 2000): 87–99.
Taylor, Charles, *Sources of the Self: The Making of the Modern Identity*, Cambridge, MA: Harvard University Press, 1989.
Taylor-Batty, Mark, *The Theatre of Harold Pinter*, London and New York: Methuen, Bloomsbury, 2014.
Thatcher, Margaret, interview with Douglas Keay, *Women's Own*, 23 September 1987, found at *The Margaret Thatcher Foundation*. http://www.margaretthatcher.org/essential/biography.asp (accessed 3 December 2007).
Thompson, Debby, '"Is Race a Trope?": Anna Deavere Smith and the Question of Racial Performativity', *African American Review* 37, no. 1 (2003): 127–38.
Wake, Caroline, 'Headphone Verbatim Theatre: Methods, Histories, Genres, Theories', *New Theatre Quarterly* 29, no. 4 (2013): 321–35.
Wake, Caroline, 'The Politics and Poetics of Listening: Attending Headphone Verbatim Theatre in Post-Cronulla Australia', *Theatre Research International* 39, no. 2 (2013): 82–100.
Wallace, Clare, 'Monologue Theatre, Solo Performance and Self as Spectacle', in *Monologues: Theatre, Performance, Subjectivity*, edited by Clare Wallace, 1–16. Prague: Litteraria Pragensia, 2006.
White, Miles, *From Jim Crow to Jay-Z: Race, Rap and the Performance of Masculinity*, Urbana, Chicago and Springfield: University of Illinois Press, 2011.
Wickham, Glynne, *The Medieval Theatre*, Cambridge and New York: Cambridge University Press, 1987.
Wickstrom, Maurya, *Performance in the Blockades of Neoliberalism: Thinking the Political Anew*, Houndsmills and New York: Palgrave Macmillan, 2012.
Williams, Tennessee, *A Streetcar Named Desire and Other Plays*, London: Penguin Books, 1962.
Žižek, Slavoj, *The Ticklish Subject: The Absent Centre of Political Ontology*, London and New York: Verso, 1999.
Žižek, Slavoj, *Welcome to the Desert of the Real*, London and New York: Verso, 2002.

Production sources

Spalding Gray

A *Spalding Gray Retrospective, Seven Monologues Performed by Spalding Gray*, written and performed by Spalding Gray, presented by the Wooster Group at the Performing Garage, 1982, Video Rec. Viewed 7 July 2005 at the Theatre on Film and Tape Archive, The New York Public Library for the Performing Arts.

Monster in a Box, dir. Nick Broomfield, written and performed by Spalding Gray, US: New Line, 1992, DVD Rec.

It's a Slippery Slope, written and performed by Spalding Gray, New York: Mercury Records, 1998, CD.

Swimming to Cambodia, dir. Jonathan Demme, written and performed by Spalding Gray, Los Angeles, CA: Evergreen Entertainment, 1996, DVD Rec.

And Everything Is Going Fine, dir. Steven Soderbergh, written and performed by Spalding Gray, New York: Sundance Selects, 2010, DVD Rec.

Life Interrupted: The Unfinished Monologue, written by Spalding Gray, read by Sam Shepard, New York: Audio Renaissance, 2006, CD.

Gray, Spalding, in The Wooster Group website. http://www.thewoostergroup.org/twg/wooster.html (accessed 20 July 2002).

Laurie Anderson

Home of the Brave, dir., Laurie Anderson, music composed and performed by Laurie Anderson, USA: Warner Bros., 1986, Video Rec.

Anderson, Laurie, *Strange Angels*, Burbank, CA: Warner Bros. Records, 1989, CD.

Anderson, Laurie, *O Superman* (remix), Amsterdam: Staalplaat, 2003, CD.

Homeland, written and performed by Laurie Anderson, Melbourne International Festival, viewed 17 October 2007, notes & documentation by Eddie Paterson.

Anna Deavere Smith

Twilight: Los Angeles, 1992, dir. by Marc Levin, conceived, written and performed by Anna Deavere Smith, 2001, Alexandria, Va.: PBS Home Video, Video Rec. Viewed 8 July 2005 at the Theatre on Film and Tape Archive, The New York Public Library for the Performing Arts.

Fires in the Mirror, dir. George C. Wolfe, conceived, written and performed by Anna Deavere Smith, USA: PBS TV Series: American Playhouse: Season 11, Episode 1, 1993, Video Rec. Viewed 8 July 2005 Theatre on Film and Tape Archive, The New York Public Library for the Performing Arts.

Karen Finley

We Keep Our Victims Ready, written and performed by Karen Finley, New York: Electronic Arts Intermix, 1990, Video Rec.

Karen Finley #1-3. Excerpts from The American Chestnut, written and performed by Karen Finley, New York: Loisaida Arts Inc, 1997, Video Rec.

Shut Up and Love Me, written and performed by Karen Finley, Melbourne Performance, viewed 22 March 2001, notes & documentation by Eddie Paterson.

Karen Finley: Live (*Shut Up and Love Me* (2001), *Make Love* (2003)), directed by Timothy Greenfield-Sanders, devised, written and performed by Karen Finley, USA: Perfect Day Films Inc., 2004, DVD Rec.

The Dreams of Laura Bush & The Passion of Terri Schiavo (2005), written and performed by Karen Finley, New York Performance, viewed 18 July 2007, notes & documentation by Eddie Paterson.

Other

Glass, Ira, 'Retraction', *This American Life*, Episode 460, 16 March 2012, Radio podcast, accessed 8 July 2014.

Jay-Z, *The Blueprint*, U.S.A.: Roc-A-Fella Records, 2001, CD.

Hamlet, dir. by Laurence Olivier, The Criterion Collection, (1948) 2000, DVD Rec.

Prose, Francine, 'Foreword', *Life Interrupted: The Unfinished Monologue*, New York: Audio Renaissance, 2006, CD.

The Good Person of Szechuan, dir. Meng Jinghui, trans. Tom Wright, Malthouse Theatre, Melbourne. Viewed 2 July 2014, notes & documentation by Eddie Paterson.

The Nature Theater of Oklahoma, video excerpt from *Life and Times: Episode 1*, performing for WNYC Radio's 'Spinning on Air' with David Garland, 3 March 2013. https://www.youtube.com/watch?v=-RgS35slSxs (accessed 10 January 2014).

About the Author

Eddie Paterson is a lecturer in the School of Culture and Communication, University of Melbourne, Australia, where he teaches writing for contemporary performance, theatre, monologue and new media. His research explores the intersections between performance, politics and everyday life. His current collaborations include analysing new writing practices in disability arts and exploring bioscience laboratory spaces as sites of performance.

Index

Adams, John   42
Aeschylus
  Agamemnon   16
aesthetics
  of responsibility   162
  of risk   163–4
affect   5, 12, 35, 44–5, 51, 155, 159, 163, 164, 165, 166, 169, 171
Agamben, Giorgio   2–3
agon   17
agonism   5, 159
Albee, Edward   29
American Dream   27, 29, 39, 41, 43, 45, 51, 74, 76, 100, 128, 166, 170
American Jeremiad   41, 45, 51, 54, 75, 78
American performance, monologue in   39–52
Anderson, Laurie   2, 3, 8, 47, 49, 79–101, 108, 117, 129, 161, 163, 164, 167–9, 170, 171
  Americans on the Move   80
    (*see also* Anderson, Laurie; United States)
  Dirtday!   80
  Empty Places   11, 80, 82, 91–101
  End of the Moon, The   80
  Happiness   80
  Homeland   169
  Home of the Brave   11, 82–91, 93
  Mister Heartbreak   82 (*see also* Home of the Brave)
  persona   84, 85, 87, 88–9, 90, 91, 95, 99, 109, 117, 161, 168
  Songs and Stories from Moby Dick   80
  Strange Angels   91
  technology and performance   11, 80, 84–5, 89, 91, 100

United States   80, 91 (*see also* Anderson, Laurie; *Americans on the Move*)
anti-mainstream
  monologue   45–52, 153
Aristotle   157
'Ar'n't I a Woman?'   42, 122
authenticity   11, 33, 34, 44, 60–2, 64, 66, 69, 84, 89, 110–12, 113, 115, 117, 130, 143, 158, 161, 171
autobiography   7, 8, 9, 10, 46–7, 49, 53, 54–5, 59–61, 62, 64, 65, 66, 68, 78, 80, 87–8, 89, 93, 101, 110, 161, 164, 171
  ironic   65, 101, 169, 171

Beat writers   39, 49, 82, 90, 129, *see also* individual writers
Beckett, Samuel   10, 15, 22, 30, 33, 34–7, 52, 86, 149
  Breath   35
  Endgame   36
  Krapp's Last Tape   34, 35–6
  Not I   34, 149
  Piece of Monologue, A   34
  Waiting for Godot   36
Bernhard, Sarah   48, 129
Bhabha, Homi   113–14, 115, 122
blasphemy   148, 152, 164, 165
Bogosian, Eric   8, 109, 138
Brecht, Bertolt   10, 15, 30–3, 34, 36, 37, 39, 46, 52, 59, 90, 188, 119, 133, 155, 160
  Good Person of Szechuan, The   31–2, 33
Broomfield, Nick   55
Browning, Robert
  My Last Duchess   23

Bruce, Lenny   48–9, 54, 129
   How to Talk Dirty and Influence People   48–9
Buckley, Lord   48
Burroughs, William S.   49, 82
Burton, Richard   20, 160
Bush, George   104
Bush, George W.   44, 75, 127, 134, 138, 143, 145, 149, 153, 184
Buyer and Cellar   46
Byrne, David   79
   deadpan voice   86, 87, 88
Bythe, Alecky   119

Cabaret   134, 140
Cage, John   81
Callaghan, Sheila   45
capitalism   11, 41, 92, 96, 101, 159, 162
   commodity   128
Capote, Truman   47
censorship   75, 127–8
character revelation   19
Chekhov, Anton   15, 24–6, 34
   Anniversary, The   24
   Three Sisters, The   24
   Uncle Vanya   24, 25
Cicero   40
civil rights   41–2, 47, 49, 52, 104, 121, 122, 125
Clinton, Bill   44, 55, 70, 77, 103, 127, 191,
comedy, stand-up   48–9, 54, 129
confessional monologue   53–78, 143, 161, 166, 167, 169, 170,
confessional prose   49
confessional speech   26, 27, 48
Coppola, Francis Ford   67, 68
   Apocalypse Now   67
Crimp, Martin   45, 158–9
   Attempts on Her Life   159
   Fewer Emergencies   159

cultural commentary   2, 8, 12, 28, 29, 47, 48, 50, 51, 62, 66, 67–8, 69, 76–7, 78, 80, 90, 93, 95, 97, 100, 101, 105, 111, 118, 128, 140, 141, 144, 152–4, 164, 168, 169, 171–2

Daisey, Mike   65–6, 161
   Agony and the Ecstasy of Steve Jobs, The   11, 65
   American Utopias   65
   Invincible Summer   65
deadpan voice   80, 86, 88, 89, 90, 161, 168
Delany, Martin   47
De La Soul   50
Demme, Jonathan   55, 182
   Swimming to Cambodia   54, 55, 56–69, 71, 72, 73, 79, 80, 166, 182
Devo   79, 81, 86
Dickens, Charles   6, 47
didactic function of monologues   18, 19, 31
documentary monologue   110–25, 167, 169, 170
Douglass, Frederick   42, 43, 104
Draper, Ruth   6, 47, 48
Dyson, Michael Eric   50

Ensler, Eve   12, 143, 161
   Vagina Monologues, The   12, 46, 143–4
Epic theatre   30–1
Etchells, Tim   170
   Lest We See Where We Are   170
   Quiet Volume, The   170
Euripides   16, 17
   Medea   16
exposition   14, 16, 18, 23, 28, 63

feminist politics   128, 130
Finley, Karen   2, 3, 8, 47, 49, 79, 127–54, 161, 164, 165–6, 169, 170, 171

Index

American Chestnut   128
Constant State of Desire, A   128
Dreams of Laura Bush, The   144
I'm an Ass Man   127, 128
Jackie Look, The   128, 165
Make Love   12, 128, 134–44, 164
Passion of Terri Schiavo, The
    12, 128, 144–58, 164, 165
  persona   128, 129–58, 161, 165
She Loved Wars   144
Shut Up and Love Me
    128, 129–34, 164
  and taboo   129, 133, 140, 153, 164
We Keep Our Victims Ready   128
Finucane, Moira   33
Fleck, John   8, 127
Forced Entertainment   171
Foreman, Richard   2, 185, 61
forerunner monologues   15, 16–17
Fornes, Marie Irene   45
fragmented persona   129–34
Freudian psychiatry   24, 131
Friends   132

Garvey, Marcus   47
Geis, Deborah   3, 7, 10, 16, 35
Gettysburg address   41–2
Gibson, Mel
  Passion of the Christ, The   148
Ginsberg, Alan   49, 54
  Howl   49
Glass, Philip   81
  Einstein on the Beach   81, 85
Goethe, Johann Wolfgang von
  Proserpina   22
Goldberg, Whoopi   48
Gomez, Marga   8
Gray, Spalding   1, 2, 3, 8, 47, 53–78,
    79, 108, 117, 129, 139, 161, 163,
    164, 166–7, 169, 170, 171
  And Everything is Going Fine
    54, 55
  Gray's Anatomy   55
  It's a Slippery Slope   1, 54, 55

Journals of Spalding Gray, The   54
Leftover Stories to Tell   54
Life Interrupted: The Unfinished
    Monologue   54, 167
Monster in a Box   54, 55, 73, 80
Morning, Noon and Night   10, 54,
    56, 70–8
persona   53, 55, 56, 58, 59–61,
    62–9, 72, 73, 74, 76–7, 78, 109,
    161, 166
Sex and Death to the Age 14
    53, 54, 55, 72
Swimming to Cambodia   54, 55,
    56–69, 71, 72, 73, 79, 80, 166, 182

Hampton, Ant   170
  Lest We See Where We Are   170
  Quiet Volume, The   170
Hardt, Michael   12, 149–50, 166,
    167, 196
Hare, David   46, 158
  Permanent Way, The   158
  Stuff Happens   158
Herford, Beatrice   47, 48, 109
hip hop   39, 49–52, 82, 90, 101
Hoch, Danny   8
Hughes, Holly   8, 127

Ibsen, Henrik   15, 24, 131
  John Gabriel Borkman   24
interior monologue, prose   23
internal debate   20–1, 22
ironic-autobiography   65, 101,
    169, 171

Jackson, Jesse   105, 147
Jay Z   50, 51
jazz   48, 49, 51
Jelinek, Elfriede   46, 159
jeremiad   41, 69, 170, *see also*
    American Jeremiad
Joffe, Roland   55, 63
  Killing Fields, The   55, 56, 58, 60,
    63, 64, 66, 68

Jones, Sarah 48, 109
  Bridge and Tunnel 109

Kane, Sarah 36, 158
  Crave 158
  4:48 Psychosis 36, 158
Kaufman, Andy 48
Kawamura, Takeshi
  Hamletclone 160
Keillor, Garrison 47
Kennedy, John F. 44
Kennedy-Onassis, Jacqueline 165
Kerouac, Jack
  On the Road 49, 103
King, Martin Luther
  'I Have a Dream' 43
King, Rodney 105, 106, 115, 120, 121, 124, 168
  riots 4, 11 (*see also* Los Angeles riots)
Knowles, Christopher 86
Kristol, Irving 75, 149
Kron, Lisa 8
Kruger, Barbara 151
Kushner, Tony 46, 158
Kweli, Talib 50
Kwong, Dan 8

LeCompte, Elizabeth 29–30, 54, *see also* Wooster Group
Lee, Young Jean 88
Leguizamo, John 8, 110
  Freak 110
Lehmann, Hans-Thies 12, 86, 95, 156–7, 158, 159–60, 162–3, 164, 165
Lincoln, Abraham 42
Los Angeles riots 105, 111, 114, 115, 117, 121, 122, 163, *see also* King, Rodney riots

Mabley, Jackie 'Moms' 47, 48
McCauley, Robbie 8
Malle, Louis
  My Dinner with Andre 46

Mamet, David 29, 45
Margolin, Deb 8
Martin, Carol 108, 116
Mason, Jackie 49
mediatization 5, 9, 43, 55, 56, 151, 156, 169, 170
Miller, Arthur 15, 27, 28–30, 52
  All My Sons 28, 29
  Crucible, The 28, 29
  Death of a Salesman 28, 29
Miller, Tim 8, 127
mimetic performance 108–10, 113, 116, 118–19, 133
modern identity, and monologue 22–30
Moffet, Marjorie 47
monologue
  in American performance 39–52
  anti-mainstream 45–52
  confessional 53–78
  cultural commentary 2, 8, 12, 28, 29, 47, 48, 50, 51, 62, 66, 67–8, 69, 76–7, 78, 80, 90, 93, 95, 97, 100, 101, 105, 111, 118, 128, 140, 141, 144, 152–4, 164, 168, 169, 171–2
  defined 14
  documentary 110–25, 167, 169, 170
  dramaturgical function 14
  expository function 14, 16, 18, 23, 28, 63
  formal characteristics 5
  future of 155–72
  influence of
    performance on 6–10
  internal 20–1
  modern identity and 22–30
  origins 16–17
  political dimension 3
  postdramatic 156–62
  post-punk 79–101
  prologue 16, 19, 129

radical   127–54
rights   103–25
Shakespearean   17–22, 160
in Western drama   13–37
monologue drama   45–6
monopolylogue   109
Mos Def   50
Mouffe, Chantal   4, 51, 163
Müller, Heiner   160
   Hamletmachine   160, 161
Murphy, Eddie   48

Nas   50
Nature Theatre of Oklahoma   11, 88, 161, 171
   Life and Times   11, 88, 89, 161
   Rambo Solo   11, 161
   Romeo and Juliet   11, 161
NEA 4 artists   127, 191
Negri, Antonio   12, 149–50, 166, 167, 196
neoliberal economics   5, 12, 51, 69, 92, 93, 100, 143, 152, 158, 163, 184
neoliberalism   11, 92, 93, 96, 98, 123, 124, 125, 140, 144, 160, 166, 169, 170
9/11   4, 6, 12, 55, 73, 127, 128, 134, 136, 137, 138, 139, 140, 141, 142, 143, 144, 164, 166
'not-acting'   7

Oades, Roslyn   119, 171
   Hello, Goodbye.
      Happy Birthday   119
   I'm Your Man   119
   Stories of Love and Hate   119
Obama, Barack   43, 44, 122
Olivier, Laurence   20
O'Neill, Eugene   15, 24, 26–7, 52, 131
   Strange Interlude   26–7
one-person show   9, 10, 48, 109, 110
oratory   4, 5, 10, 13, 17, 39, 47, 51, 52, 104, 122, 155, 156, 164, 169, 172, *see also* rhetoric

and performance   40–5
political   41–5, 54, 155, 170
religious   6, 10, 41, 43, 69, 170

'Palm Sunday Compromise' bill   145, 148
Parks, Suzan-Lori   29, 158
parody   5, 10, 12, 32, 33, 37, 56, 60, 66, 67, 77, 132, 134, 136, 152, 153, 161, 164, 167, 169
Passion Play   148–9, 194
performance
   influence on monologue   6–10
   mimetic   108, 113, 118
   and oratory   40–5
   solo   1, 3, 4, 5, 8, 9, 14, 23, 37, 39, 40, 41, 44, 46–8, 50, 51, 52, 101, 103, 104, 115, 118, 125, 155, 157, 161, 162, 164, 170, 171, 172
   and technology   5, 7, 9, 35–6, 86, 170
Performance Studies   9
Performing Garage theatre   53, 56
persona   5, 7, 8, 15, 18, 19, 21, 23, 42, 44, 54, 73, 86, 87, 161, 169, 171
   Anderson, Laurie   84, 85, 87, 88–9, 90, 91, 95, 99, 109, 117, 161, 168
   in Brecht   32–3
   Douglass, Frederick   43
   Finley, Karen   128, 129–58, 161, 165
   Finucane, Moira   33
   fragmented   129–34
   Gray, Spalding   53, 55, 56, 58, 59–61, 62–9, 72, 73, 74, 76–7, 78, 109, 161, 166
   in hip hop   50
   Shawn, Wallace   46–7
   Smith, Anna Deavere   105, 107–9, 111, 13, 115, 116, 117, 122, 124, 161
   Truth, Sojourner   43
   Wilson, Robert   160

Peterson, Michael   64
Pinter, Harold   15, 30, 33–4, 35, 36, 37
  Celebration   33
  Family Voices   33
  Landscape   33
  Monologue   33
  Moonlight   33
  Old Times   33
plot exposition   18
political oratory   41–5, 54, 155, 170
political sermon   41, 43, 170
politics, feminist   128, 130
postdramatic monologue   156–62
postmonologue   4, 12, 17, 156, 172
post-politics   162
post-punk monologue   79–101
'pro-life' movement   147, 152, 193
prologue monologue   16, 19, 129
prose interior monologue   23, 24, 26
Pryor, Richard   48
Public Enemy   50
Puritanism   41–2, 51

radical monologue   127–54
Raphael, Timothy   44–5
Reagan, Ronald   44–5, 69, 79, 98, 104, 184
Reaganomics   69, 92, *see also* neoliberal economics
Reed, Lou   81
religious oratory   6, 10, 41, 43, 69, 170
Reno   8
rhetoric   5, 18, 39, 40, 41, 43, 44, 45, 71, 150, 151, *see also* oratory
  political   134, 139, 143, 144, 155, 156, 164
Rhode Island Trilogy   54, 72, *see also* Nayatt School; Rumstick Road; Sakonnet Point
rights monologue   103–25
right to die   144–9, 150, 151, 164
Rock, Chris   48

Roosevelt, Franklin D.   44
Rosenthal, Rachel   8
Rotozaza   170
  Wondermart   170
Rousseau, Jean-Jacques   22, 60, 63
  Confessions, The   60
  Pygmalion   22
Ruhl, Sarah   45, 158

St Augustine   18, 60
  Confession   60
Scott, Ridley
  Blade Runner   84
Sedaris, David   47
selfhood, and soliloquy   15, 17–22
Sellars, Peter   124
September 11, *see* 9/11
Shakespeare, William   17, 18, 19, 20, 21, 22, 26, 155, 160
  Hamlet   20–2, 160
  Othello   19
Shange, Ntozake   45
Shaw, Peggy   8
Shawcross, William
  Sideshow   63
Shawn, Wallace   46, 158
  Designated Mourner, The   46
  Fever, The   46
Shepard, Sam   29, 45, 167
Silverman, Sarah   48
Smith, Anna Deavere   2, 3, 8, 47, 103–25, 161, 163, 164, 167–8, 169, 170, 171
  Fires in the Mirror: Crown Heights, Brooklyn, and Other Identities   103, 104, 113
  House Arrest   119
  Let Me Down Easy   104, 107, 122, 167
  'My Enemy'   107
  persona   105, 107–9, 111, 113, 115, 116, 117, 122, 124, 161
  On the Road: A Search for American Character   103

Twilight: Los Angeles, 1992
    104, 105–10, 111, 113, 114,
    118, 120, 122, 124, 125, 167
Smith, Patti   81
Soderbergh, Stephen
    And Everything is Going Fine
    54, 55
soliloquy   23, 26, 27, 30, 160
    selfhood and   15, 17–22
    Shakespearean   17–22, 160
solo performance   1, 3, 4, 5, 8, 9, 14,
    23, 37, 39, 40, 41, 44, 46–8, 50,
    51, 52, 101, 103, 104, 115, 118,
    125, 155, 157, 161, 162, 164,
    170, 171, 172
Sophocles   17
Sprinkle, Annie   8
stand-up comedy   48–9
State of the Union address   44, 45
Strindberg, August   15, 24, 131

taboo   49, 129, 133, 140, 153, 163, 164
'talking cure'   24, 60
Talking Heads   79, 81, 86, 87, 89
technology and performance   5, 7, 9,
    35–6, 86, 170
    in the works of Laurie
        Anderson   11, 80, 84–5, 89,
        91, 100
    in the works of Roslyn Oades   119
Tennyson, Alfred Lord   23
Thatcher, Margaret   92–3, 184
Theodore, Brother   47, 129
'thought asides'   26, 27
'To be or not to be'   20
Tomlin, Lily   48, 109, 110
    Search for Signs of Intelligent Life in
        the Universe, The   110
Truth, Sojourner   42, 43, 104, 122
Twain, Mark   6, 47

Verfremdungseffekt   31, 118
Version 1.0   158
Vidal, Gore   47
vocal processing   84

Wallace, Clare   23, 45, 46–7
Washington, George   42, 74
Weaver, Lois   8
Western drama   13–37, 157, 172
'What to the Slave is the Fourth of
    July?'   43
Whitman, Walt   54
Wilder, Thornton
    Our Town   55
Williams, Robin   48
Williams, Tennessee   15, 24,
    27–8, 52
    The Glass Menagerie   27–8
Wilson, Robert   2, 79, 81, 85, 86, 88,
    160, 161
    CIVIL warS, the   79, 85
    Einstein on the Beach   81, 85
    Hamlet – A Monologue   160
Wing-Davey, Mark   119
Wondermart   170
Wooster Group   1, 2, 29, 54, 79, 85,
    86, 159, 160, 161
    L.S.D. (… Just the High
        Points…)   29, 30
    Nayatt School   54, 55
    Point Judith   54
    Rumstick Road   54, 55
    Sakonnet Point   54
Worrall, Kristin   88

X, Malcolm   47, 104

Young Jean Lee   88, 171

Žižek, Slavoj   12, 139, 142